THE
CHURCH IN FRANCE
1789—1848 :

THE
CHURCH IN FRANCE
1789—1848 :
A Study in Revival

BY

C. S. PHILLIPS, M.A., D.D.

Liberty is the most precious gift that man can have. . . .
It rests upon the recognition of God's divers ways of dealing
with His children.—*Bishop Creighton.*

NEW YORK / RUSSELL & RUSSELL
1966

FIRST PUBLISHED IN 1929
REISSUED, 1966, BY RUSSELL & RUSSELL
A DIVISION OF ATHENEUM HOUSE, INC.
L.C. CATALOG CARD NO: 66—24748

REPRINTED FROM A COPY IN THE COLLECTIONS OF
THE BROOKLYN PUBLIC LIBRARY

PRINTED IN THE UNITED STATES OF AMERICA

HVNC LIBRVM
WALTERO
EPŌ : TRVRONENSI
GRATI ANIMI TESTIMONIVM
NEC NON REVERENTIAE ATQVE AMORIS
PIGNVS
D. D. D.
C. S. P.

I DESIRE to express my deep gratitude to Mr. R. E. Balfour, Fellow of King's College, Cambridge, who has given me much help with the proofs and, in addition, made many valuable suggestions.

C. S. P.

CONTENTS

FOREWORD

ON November 17, 1790, the National Assembly was debating the question of administering the Constitutional Oath to the clergy. In the course of a passionate speech the protagonist of the opposition, the Abbé Maury, uttered the warning : *' Prenez garde : il n'est pas bon de faire des martyrs.'* It would have been well for France and the Revolution if the Assembly had heeded. But passion had darkened counsel and the oath was imposed. From that moment the Church became the foe of the Revolution, in the interest of its own spiritual autonomy. Previously, its opposition had been in great measure confined to the aristocratic and wealthy *haut clergé*, whose interests were bound up with the *ancien régime*. But now a divorce was effected between organized Catholicism and the cause of liberal institutions, the effects of which remain to this day.

The French clergy became the focus of opposition to the Revolution and stirred up infinite trouble. The revolutionary leaders retorted by a persecution which grew ever fiercer as time went on. Just as in the case of the Roman Catholic propaganda in England under Elizabeth, it is hard to say how far the opposition was inspired by religious, how far by political motives. Undoubtedly both kinds of motives were present. But the result in any case was persecution—the persecution of the Catholic religion as such. And persecution had its usual effect. *Sanguis martyrum semen ecclesiae.* The

Church of France, which had entered the revolutionary period rich, powerful, but spiritually languid and in many ways corrupt, emerged from it poor indeed, but filled with a moral and religious fervour long unknown. This new spirit Napoleon did his best to compromise and destroy by a policy that favoured the Church in order to enslave it. Yet behind the mean complaisances of a worldly episcopate it lived on : nor did the Church's too ready reliance on the interested support of the civil power under the Restoration avail to extinguish it, though this unquestionably perverted its activity. Set free at length by the revolution of 1830 to do its work in the strength of its own innate resources, the Church in France entered on one of the most brilliant periods of its history.

THE CHURCH IN FRANCE

CHAPTER I

THE CHURCH BEFORE THE REVOLUTION

IT is a common failing of ecclesiastical historians to make the Church's good periods better, and its bad periods worse, than they actually were. We shall do well, then, to be on our guard lest, in the desire to make the Church of Lacordaire and Montalembert shine with a more brilliant light, we darken more than is just the Church of the *ancien régime*. There has certainly been small disposition to exaggerate the merits of the latter. And indeed it was not a period of which the French Church has cause to be particularly proud. The eighteenth century was an unwholesome atmosphere for man's spiritual instinct : moreover, the Church in France was much too rich and important for its own good. As the immediate heir of the great Church of the *Grand Siècle*—the Church of Pascal and Bossuet and Fénelon—it was content to live on its traditions and the merits of its forebears.

On the other hand, it was not the mass of corruption that it has sometimes been represented as being. It is the misfortune of the French Church of the later eighteenth century to be judged almost exclusively by a comparatively small minority of prelates and abbés who hung about the Court and shared generously in the frivolity, wantonness, and irreligion of the fashionable society of the time. For men of this sort no censure can be too severe. They owed their position entirely to their birth and influence. It was an unwritten law that bishop-rics—with the exception of five sees, called *évêchés de laquais*—should be exclusively confined to mem-bers of noble families. ' To be a bishop nowadays,' says one of them, ' a man must be a *gentilhomme.*' Even the great Bossuet himself was deemed ineligi-ble for the archbishopric of Paris because he sprang from the mere *noblesse de robe.* On the other hand, the young Talleyrand was made Bishop of Autun when barely thirty. His entering into the ecclesias-tical state at all was quite avowedly a *pis-aller.* To do him justice, he had no sort of inclination or desire for the priesthood : but he was a younger son and, as his lameness disqualified him for the army, the Church and a bishopric at the first opportunity seemed the only resource. The fact that he was a gambler and a roué and did not believe in the Christian religion was not regarded as a serious objection. According to Louis XVI, Loménie de Brienne, Archbishop of Sens and Cardinal, did not believe even in God. This, however, did not pre-vent him from demanding eloquently the persecu-tion of heretics. At the coronation of Louis XVI in 1775 he thus addressed the new monarch : ' You will disapprove of culpable systems of toleration. . . To you is reserved the privilege of giving the final blow to Calvinism in your dominions.' Another specimen of the same class was also a cardinal, Louis de Rohan, Prince Bishop of Stras-bourg, the sorry hero of the *affaire du collier.* It is hard to say whether he was more fool or knave : but beyond doubt he was both.

Such men were in receipt of enormous incomes :

for besides their bishoprics they held several rich abbeys *in commendam*. This system of *abbés commendataires* was one of the worst abuses of the time, enabling a high-born ecclesiastic to enjoy all the emoluments and privileges belonging to the abbot of a great monastery without the annoyance of keeping religious vows or even of visiting the house of which he was the nominal head. Even if bishoprics and abbacies *in commendam* were not forthcoming, there were plenty of stalls and dignities in cathedral and capitular churches awaiting the noble young ecclesiastic as a second-best. Thirty-four *chapitres nobles*—nineteen for men, fifteen for women—were exclusively reserved for the high-born.

But even the higher clergy (to say nothing of the lower) was not exclusively composed of atheist bishops and *abbés galants*. The faults of many of the bishops lay rather in a disposition to be indolent and inefficient than in anything worse. In the case of the lower clergy—the rank and file of the ecclesiastical profession, curés, *vicaires*, etc.—a decent level of character and effort seems to have been fairly generally attained. No doubt there were many black sheep among them : but diligent parish priests were by no means uncommon. De Tocqueville indeed goes so far as to say : ' I do not know whether, all things considered and in spite of the scandalous vices of some of its members, there was ever a body of clergy in the world more remarkable than the Catholic clergy of France at the moment when they were surprised by the Revolution.' This certainly appears an exaggeration. But the history of the revolutionary period was to prove that the tie between priest and people was often close and affectionate : and if the temptations inseparable from a religious monopoly were unfavourable to heroic virtue, the coming of persecution was to prove that the capacity even for this was latent in many after all.

We have dwelt on the fairer side of the picture because it is one which has been too much ignored. But indubitably there was a darker side too. It is useless to pretend that the eighteenth century was a particularly creditable period in the history of the French, or of any other, Church. There is a complete absence of great and distinguished names. The bishops were mostly aristocratic nonentities when they were not infidels and debauchees. Nor did the lower clergy make good the lack of distinction in the higher. Their intellectual standard was low : their theology and their preaching alike were jejune, conventional, and undistinguished. In the immense mental travail of the time the clergy played no part, unless it were such a man as the Abbé Raynal, whose writings clearly proclaim him an atheist. The attitude towards the Church of the great majority of the educated classes was one of contemptuous hostility. The lower classes were less averse from religious practice : but no doubt ignorance and superstition had something to do with this. Nearly one half of the personnel of the clerical order and the major part of its wealth belonged to monastic foundations, the inmates of which were usually idle and self-indulgent and not infrequently immoral.

The Church was rent by controversy of a peculiarly unprofitable and exasperating kind. The Jansenism of the middle of the eighteenth century was a very different thing from the Jansenism of Pascal and Port Royal, having got itself mixed up in the meanwhile with a variety of alien ingredients. As for the Jesuits, who formed the main-spring of the anti-Jansenist crusade, their methods were not unworthy of their reputation. Twenty-seven years before the Revolution (in 1762) their order was suppressed in France : but up to the moment when their hour of doom sounded they had been supreme at the French court and had wielded all the resources of absolutism in the interests of obscurantism and reaction.

The clergy generally had no sympathy for religious freedom of any kind. The Protestants still groaned under the most monstrous disabilities. They were forbidden to worship together : every form of official career was closed to them. Indeed they were without any legal existence at all, owing to the Church's exclusive custody of the *état civil* (i.e. registers of marriage, etc.). When, in 1788, Louis XVI proposed to restore the *état civil* to the Protestants, the Assembly of the Clergy protested loudly, one orator asking, ' Will you crucify Christ afresh ? ' As late as 1762 Jean Calas was broken on the wheel at Toulouse, a victim of Catholic fanaticism. Four years later a youth called de la Barre was beheaded at Arras on an ill-substantiated charge of having mutilated a crucifix.

The Church was entrusted with the monopoly of national education. But its failure to educate is sufficiently indicated by the fact that in 1789 the majority of the nation were unable to read.

Altogether the Church might fairly be considered an expensive luxury in view of the enormous privileges and wealth it enjoyed. This wealth contributed but little to the needs of the State. As a privileged order, the clergy, like the nobles, were exempt from ordinary taxation. Their share in the State's burdens was confined to a payment (carefully designated *don gratuit*), voted and raised by themselves, which seems to have averaged no more than three million livres per

annum.   Further, the riches of the Church were
most inequitably distributed.   The higher clergy
(or at least the most fortunate among them) rolled
in princely opulence. Loménie de Brienne's annual
income from ecclesiastical sources amounted to
680,000 livres per annum—i.e. £27,000.   On the
other hand, the village curés frequently lived on
the verge of starvation.   The bulk of the tithe was
impropriated by wealthy *gros décimateurs*, a beggarly stipend called *portion congrue* being given to
the parish priest who did the work.   Under Louis
XIV this was fixed at three hundred livres per
annum : under Louis XV it was raised to five
hundred livres.   He had not even the consolation
of knowing that ability might raise him to
authority and wealth, for it has been seen that
bishoprics and other rich preferments were almost
exclusively confined to ecclesiastics of noble birth.
It is not surprising, then, that the result of this
financial and social inequality, coupled with the
natural disposition of high-born prelates to lord it
over God's heritage, was to arouse a bitter feeling
of jealousy and resentment in the lower against the
higher clergy.   This feeling was to play an important part in the working out of the revolutionary
movement in its early stages.

CHAPTER II

THE CIVIL CONSTITUTION OF THE CLERGY, 1789-91

THE attitude of the Church in 1789 has been
frequently represented as one of blind, uncompromising hostility to every kind of change.
As a matter of fact, it was nothing of the sort. The
close connection of the upper clergy with the
noblesse tended naturally to engage them in the
ways of reaction. But the representatives of the
clerical order in the States General were far from
being confined to the prelates—in fact the latter
were quite a minority. Of the clerical deputies
actually elected only forty-four were bishops, while
the members of the lower clergy numbered two
hundred and eight. And the curés, coming as they
did from the ranks of the *bourgeoisie*, were naturally sympathetic to the ideas and aspirations
of the Tiers État. On all points which did not
concern their own privileges the clergy showed
themselves prepared to go a long way on the path
of reform. Nor were the lower clergy in the least
inclined to submit tamely to the lead of their
ecclesiastical superiors. More and more a *parti
des curés* began to make itself felt in opposition to
the aristocratic conservatism of the bishops. It was
this party which was chiefly instrumental in winning for the Tiers État its first great victory—the
' reunion of orders.' The nobles were determined
on the three orders sitting separately : the great

7

majority of the prelates were of the same opinion. But when a deadlock seemed to have been reached, individual members of the clerical order took their seats with the Tiers Etat in numbers that daily increased. The opposition, finding its hand forced, had to yield. On June 27, 1789, the King decreed the union of the three orders.

The triumph of the more advanced elements in the Assembly was thus assured. The vast structure of class-privilege and immunity was doomed. Especially there was now to be a revolution in the whole system of taxation. Under the old régime those best able to pay had been exempt. This was to be the case no longer. And not income only, but capital was to be tapped. It was the financial necessities of the State which had compelled the convening of the States General. France was bankrupt : and money had to be found somehow. The temptation presented by the enormous endowments of the Church was specially irresistible. Besides the tithes, amounting to eighty or ninety million livres per annum, it possessed landed property yielding a similar amount. The Assembly laid hands on both.

The tithes were the first to go. On the night of August 4, 1789—Carlyle's ' new Night of Pentecost '—when the two privileged orders made their famous renunciation, it was proposed that tithes should be *redeemed*. The clergy, carried away by the enthusiasm of the hour, accepted this, together with the abolition of sundry other financial privileges. The morrow brought regrets, and they tried to wriggle out of their concession. But the Assembly not merely refused to permit this, but, on August 11th, decreed the total abolition of tithes with the proviso that ' the needs of divine worship should be supplied in another manner.'

The ecclesiastical lands soon followed. On October 10th, Talleyrand, in the name of the committee of finances, introduced a report recommending the appropriation of the Church's property by the nation. Two days later (October 12th) Mirabeau proposed (1) that ' the possessions of the clergy are the property of the nation subject to the duty of providing for the members of that order ' ; (2) that ' the disposal of these possessions should be such that no curé shall have less than twelve hundred livres a year with lodging.' This proposal met with considerable opposition. But Mirabeau's genius and influence carried all before it : and, on November 2nd, his motion was carried with the substitution of the words ' at the disposal of the nation ' for ' the property of the nation.' On December 19th it was decreed that four hundred million francs' worth of Church property should be alienated immediately to provide a security for the issue of paper money. This was the beginning of the notorious *assignats*.

The Church was thus effectually ' disendowed ' —at least in the sense that it ceased to possess and administer property of its own. But the Assembly had more than its money in view. Already, on August 20, 1789, the famous *Comité Ecclésiastique* had been set up. This proposed, on December 17th, that the State should withdraw the civil sanction hitherto given to religious vows, and that in consequence those who wished to withdraw from the monastic profession should be at liberty to do so. Those, on the other hand, who had no such desire might remain as they were. If this proposal had been carried out, the civil power would in no way have exceeded its competence. But the Assembly went further and decreed the suppression of religious vows and religious orders altogether (February

13, 1790). Those who quitted, or were extruded from, the cloister were to receive a pension. This decision applied to houses for men only. For the moment, women's convents were not affected.

Such an entrenchment on the Church's spiritual autonomy and the religious liberty of the individual was serious enough. But the Ecclesiastical Committee designed something infinitely more sweeping still. As a preliminary, it was proposed, on April 9, 1790, that all ecclesiastical property should be handed over immediately and a money salary substituted. This proposal was accepted, and, on April 14th, the complete expropriation of the clergy was voted by the Assembly. The ground being thus prepared and the clergy reduced to the position of ' salaried functionaries of the State,' the Committee, on May 29, 1790, produced its masterpiece—the ' Civil Constitution of the Clergy.'

It is necessary here to indicate the various strands of opinion and motive that combined to produce this fatal project—' the capital error of the Revolution,' as even a strongly anti-clerical historian admits. From one point of view, it was a final and extreme expression of that ' Gallican ' spirit which had so often made the Church of France a thorn in the side of the Holy See.

Between the theory and the historical practice of Gallicanism there is a wide difference. Theoretically, it stands for the setting up of the authority of the collective mind of the Church, represented by a General Council, as against an autocratic and infallible Papacy, and for the claim of National Churches to at least a measure of autonomy. Practically, it has too often become the mere pretext for a tyranny of the State over the Church. The legal mind is, in the nature of things, inclined to Erastian views of Church polity : and it is not surprising to find that the focus of Gallican opposition to Roman claims was the Parlement, the supreme judicial authority in France. The Gallican spirit of the Parlement was transmitted to the *Comité Ecclésiastique* through the strong legal element the latter included. This element had also (like the Parlement) a decided Jansenist flavour. Circumstances indeed had contributed to a close connection between Gallicanism and Jansenism. The Jansenists had been the object of bitter and incessant persecution by the Jesuits, who were the great champions of ecclesiastical centralization and (previously to their temporary extinction in 1772) had reigned supreme at Rome. The hour of revenge had now sounded. Rome was to be made to pay the penalty of a policy of repression and calumny that had lasted for over a century. Revenge is never disposed to be nice in its choice of means. In the fabrication of the Constitution Civile Jansenism made common cause with those who were less the enemies of Rome than of Christianity itself.

The unbelief which had made such ravages among the upper classes in France during the eighteenth century had two major prophets—Voltaire and Rousseau. Of these Voltaire's influence made for a complete denial of God : Rousseau's for a vague theism. But the disciples of both combined under the Revolution to attack the Church. Mirabeau was deeply impregnated with the teaching of Voltaire and the Encyclopaedists. He made no pretence of belief in Christianity. And his fanatical hatred of religion was shared by many in the National Assembly. For such the Catholic faith was a ' superstition ' to be destroyed with as little delay as possible, that an age of Reason and Enlightenment might succeed. The disciples of

Rousseau (of whom Robespierre was the chief)
pursued the same object in the interest of their
Être Suprême. For both shades of opinion the
Constitution Civile was merely a means to an end.
That end was the extinction of the Christian
religion in general and of Catholicism in particular.
For in the eyes of the great majority of Frenchmen
Christianity meant, and still means, Catholicism.

The Constitution Civile, indeed, made no claim
to alter the dogmas of the Church, but only to
regulate its discipline. In this respect it was little
to the taste of the *philosophes*. But it had the
advantage of realizing Mirabeau's pet ideal of *un
clergé fonctionnaire, officier de morale et d'instruction:*
and with this once achieved, all things were possible.
At least the Church and the clergy would be
thoroughly under the thumb of the civil authorities : and the elements of ' superstition ' could be
gradually eliminated.

Political animus reinforced the religious. Mirabeau and his followers regarded the Church as hope-
lessly bound up with the *ancien régime* and its
abuses : both must be swept away together. ' If
you wish for a revolution,' they declared, ' you
must begin by decatholicizing France.' This was
at least explicit : and should have warned the
Jansenist authors of the Constitution Civile. But
they took no heed, and went on cheerfully with
their project of reforming the Church with the
assistance of those who only desired to lay it in the
dust.

The chief provisions of the Constitution Civile
may be briefly summarized thus. An entirely new
delimitation of ecclesiastical divisions was effected
on the basis of the civil divisions recently set up.
Each department was to form a single diocese.
The title of ' archbishop ' was abolished : but the

eighty-three dioceses were to be grouped into ten metropolitanates. The cathedrals were to become parish churches, with the bishop as curé assisted by a number of *vicaires*. Places with less than six thousand inhabitants were to form a single parish, other existing parishes being suppressed and merged. All cathedral dignities were abolished. Further, the method of appointment to ecclesiastical offices was to be by popular election. Bishops were to be chosen by the electoral assembly of the department, curés by the electoral assembly of the district. A bishop-elect was to apply for confirmation to the metropolitan. He was forbidden to seek confirmation from the Pope, though he was directed to write to the Holy Father ' as Head of the Universal Church in witness of the unity of faith and communion that he must maintain with him.' Before consecration he must take an oath ' to watch with care over the faithful of the diocese committed to him, to be faithful to the nation, the law, and the King, and to maintain with all his power the constitution decreed by the National Assembly and accepted by the King.' In a similar way curés must apply to the bishop for canonical institution : and must take the same oath as the bishops. Finally a scale of payment was fixed for the clergy, though this was subsequently modified : and it was laid down that in order to be absent from his charge for more than fifteen days a bishop must secure the leave of the directory of the department, a curé that of his bishop and of the directory of the district.

Such was the *Constitution Civile du Clergé*. It was called Constitution Civile as having no concern with the doctrines or the essential structure of the Church, but only regulating its position in regard to the State. This at least was what its authors and defenders continually affirmed. But, as a matter of fact, its provisions obviously went far beyond this. So long, of course, as the Church is a powerful and organized body possessed of property and claiming the allegiance of many of the State's subjects, it is impossible for the State to treat it as if it did not exist. Relations of some kind between the Church and the State are inevitable, and the State cannot leave it to the Church to decide by itself what those relations are to be. There is, however, a world of difference between this and a claim by the State to refashion the internal organization of the Church from top to bottom according to its own desires and on the lines of its own secular organization.

The question is not whether the changes in the constitution of the Church of France made by the Constitution Civile were excellent and desirable in themselves. Good or bad, it was not the business of the National Assembly to make them. At least, the moment such a power is conceded to the secular legislature, the Church ceases to be an autonomous and independent body. It becomes what the Erastian would make it—a mere department of the State organization. It was as such that Mirabeau regarded it. He was fond of comparing it to the Army and the Judicature. But the Church itself can never accept such a view.

It is the abiding strength of Ultramontanism that with all its faults and errors it stands for the right of the Church to govern itself, to make its own rules of doctrine and discipline. And this right existing, the Church must insist on the line of distinction being kept clear between those who are its members and those who are not. By the terms of the Constitution Civile even Protestants and Jews were to take part in the election of bishops

and parochial clergy. Such confusion between
' Catholic ' or ' Christian ' and ' citizen ' is inad-
missible.

Even the claim that the Constitution did not
interfere with the doctrines of the Church does not
seem to correspond with the facts. By it the
authority which the Pope had hitherto exercised
in regard to the Church was virtually abrogated.
Now that authority may be part of the divine
ordering of the Church or it may not : but even in
the latter alternative its rejection (so far at least
as *spiritual* jurisdiction is concerned) is not the
business of the national legislature, but of the
national Church.

The Constitution was accepted by the Assembly
on July 12, 1790. Before becoming law it required
the royal sanction. Louis XVI was in a quandary.
Himself a loyal Catholic, he could not help seeing
how displeasing such a measure must be to the
Pope. On the other hand, his timid nature shrank
from a possible breach with the Assembly. The
Pope had already warned him that if he accepted
the Constitution he would precipitate his kingdom
into schism. But he continued to hope that Rome
might be led to take a different view. He determined to give the sanction and ask the Pope to give
at least a provisional approval till such time as the
royal difficulties were tided over. The Pope was
willing to appoint a commission of cardinals to
report on the matter : but he was not encouraging
as to the prospects of the report being favourable.
On August 24th the King gave his sanction, and
the Pope immediately expressed his grief at the
step. Meanwhile the French bishops, both individually in a shower of pastorals and in a joint
pronouncement, condemned the new measure.

Under these circumstances the putting of the

Constitution Civile into execution was not un-
attended with difficulties. The bishops entirely
ignored the changes it made, and went on as
though nothing had happened. The clergy generally took up an attitude of passive resistance. The
death of the Bishop of Quimper creating the first
vacancy in the episcopate under the new conditions, Expilly, curé of Morlaix and a member of
the Assembly, was elected to fill it. But he was to
discover that it was one thing to be elected, another
to secure consecration.

The Assembly now determined to bring pressure
to bear on the recalcitrant clergy. Hitherto the
oath had been exacted only from those who should
be elected to ecclesiastical offices in the future.
But now it was to be imposed on the secular clergy
generally. On November 24th, a decree was introduced ordering all bishops, curés, and *vicaires*,
together with superiors and directors of seminaries,
to take within eight days ' the oath required by
articles 21 and 38 of the Constitution Civile,' i.e.
the oath (mentioned above) to ' be faithful to the
nation, the law, and the King, and to maintain
with all their power the constitution decreed by
the National Assembly and accepted by the King.'
Failing this, they were to be deprived. Any ecclesiastic who, having refused the oath, should exercise his functions, was to be proceeded against as a
disturber of the public order.

This decree was passed on November 27th.
Again the question arose, ' Would the King sanction it or not ? ' Louis was most unwilling to do
do. He felt bitterly his helplessness in the grip of
the Revolution : and already he was meditating
flight and recourse to foreign arms as the only
escape from an intolerable situation. But the
Assembly was insistent : and in December the

sanction was given. At once the Assembly took steps to put the oath into operation.

But here an important question arose. Did the oath ' to maintain the constitution ' involve the acceptance of the Constitution Civile ? There can be little doubt that all through the history of this most unhappy measure its champions maintained a studied ambiguity on the point. And for obvious reasons. It was hoped that ignorance, or fear of appearing to repudiate the cause of reform altogether, would lead the clergy—especially the country clergy—to swallow the Constitution Civile as part of the totality of the Assembly's work. On the other hand, to refuse the oath would be to play into their enemies' hands. As a matter of fact, so far as the political changes of the time went, the attitude of the great majority of the clergy was probably one of indifference, where it was not actually approval. But the Assembly was determined to have its political and its ecclesiastical reforms taken in a single dose, and it was here that the trouble arose.

In a certain number of cases the trap laid by the partisans of the Constitution Civile operated successfully. The oath was taken in the honest belief that acceptance of the Constitution Civile was not involved in it or that the Constitution Civile would not be condemned by the Pope. A certain number of priests no doubt took the oath because they regarded the Constitution Civile as unobjectionable—a larger number because they hoped to be gainers by it. But the great majority of the clergy stood firm. If they could not swear to maintain the constitution ' without pledging themselves to the Constitution Civile they would refuse the oath altogether and take the consequences. Of the one hundred and thirty diocesan bishops

of France only four took the oath, these four including Loménie de Brienne and Talleyrand, the
latter at this time still, as Bishop of Autun, in the
first and ecclesiastical stage of his amazing career.
The rank and file of the clergy were less unanimous: yet, although in many cases all the resources of intimidation were employed, the great
bulk of them, especially in the towns, persisted
in refusing the oath.

The deprivation of the *insermentés* following.
automatically in accordance with the Assembly's
decree, it became necessary to fill their places.
On January 27, 1791, the Assembly decided that
this should be done at once.   A crowd of elections
followed.   It is to be feared that the candidates
chosen were in many cases far from representing
the most shining type of clerical character.   Yet
not a few, especially among the bishops, were men
of ability and virtue.   One of them, Grégoire,
Bishop of Loire-et-Cher (Blois), destined to be the
leading figure in the Constitutional Church through
the ten chequered years of its existence, might in
certain ways even be described as great.

The first two Constitutional bishops were consecrated on February 24, 1791, Talleyrand kindly
consenting to act as a channel for the Apostolic
succession with the help of two other bishops, one
of them the future apostate Gobel.

Hitherto the Pope had refrained from making
any public pronouncement on the question of the
Constitution Civile. This silence, however, did
not argue any likelihood of his accepting it, as was
too readily surmised in some quarters. From the
early part of 1790 onwards his hostility, not merely
to the ecclesiastical policy of the National Assembly but to the whole movement for which it stood,
was unmistakably displayed both to those around

him and (in a letter) to the French episcopate. This essentially reactionary attitude of the Holy See must always be borne in view in considering subsequent happenings. It undoubtedly hardened the hearts of the revolutionary leaders in their dealings with the non-juring clergy, and provided a useful pretext for persecution. We have already seen the pressure put upon the King to induce him to refuse his sanction to the Constitution Civile. At the same time the bishops were insistently urged to resist to the utmost of their power. Still all these were but words in the ear : judgement had not been proclaimed on the house-tops. The partisans of the Constitution Civile were eager to interpret the Pope's silence as implying consent, in the hope of overcoming the scruples of the clergy in regard to the oath. But the recent events forced the Holy See into the open, and all doubts on the subject were now to be removed. On April 13, 1791, the Pope issued a solemn brief addressed to the entire Church of France. In this he formally condemned the Constitution Civile as 'heretical and schismatical,' annulled the ecclesiastical elections, and enjoined those who had taken the oath to retract within forty days on pain of suspension. A considerable number of retractations followed immediately.

Henceforth a schism was definitely constituted. In place of the old Church of France there were now two rival bodies, each claiming to be its representative—the Constitutional Church and the Church of the Non-Jurors : the former repudiated by, the latter in communion with, the Holy See. What was to be the attitude of the National Assembly towards the refractory clergy ?

Its intent to persecute was clearly indicated by the decree of November 27th. But it was not enough to threaten the clergy. The laity had also to be considered ; and the laity, especially in Paris and the large towns, showed much shyness of availing themselves of the ministrations of the constitutional clergy. The congregations in the parish churches were miserably small : while the convent chapels, which were the only places where the non-jurors could officiate, were crowded. The violence to which the waiting mob subjected the worshippers as they entered or left failed to act as a deterrent.

But these outrages disgusted the Directory of the Department of the Seine, in which Paris was situated. As moderate men averse from persecution, they sought to find a *modus vivendi* which should allow those whose consciences forbade them to attend the services of the Constitutional Church to worship after their own manner in private. Accordingly in April, 1791, they issued a decree in general terms providing that non-parochial churches might be hired by ' private persons ' for the free exercise of ' any cult whatever,' provided that the purpose for which they were intended was indicated by an inscription on the principal door. This decree seemed no more than a guarantee of that religious freedom which the Assembly itself had declared to be one of the ' Rights of Man.' On the other hand, it was not easy to square it with the decree of November 27th.

The champions of the Constitution Civile in the Assembly were naturally very angry. Unless the civil authorities bolstered it up, their pet scheme was likely to fare ill at the hands of the public. The Directors' decree was vigorously denounced ; but the Assembly bestowed upon it its approval—though with the proviso that churches to which it applied should be closed ' the moment any discourse was delivered directed against the constitution of the kingdom and in particular the Civil Constitution of the Clergy' (May 7, 1791). In the face of such a condition the task of the non-juring preacher was certainly delicate. Still, the principle of toleration was recognized : and if only the National Assembly had persisted in this policy, the worst consequences of a disastrous step might have been avoided.

Even so, however, its concession was very far from being universally operative. A characteristic and very confusing feature of the whole Revolutionary period is the frequent discrepancy between the action of the central power at Paris and that of the local authorities which had to execute its decrees. The latter were by no means content to be the passive instruments of the former. The municipalities of the towns, dominated as they often were by Jacobin influences, were especially inclined to be extreme in their views and arbitrary in their methods. Thus when, despite the decree of the Directory, the outrages on non-juring worshippers broke out afresh, the municipality of Paris applauded the action of the mob. In a number of departments, the more liberal provisions of the Assembly's decree of May 7th were simply ignored, and a policy of persecution substituted.

Meanwhile the King—now virtually a prisoner in Paris—was casting about desperately for some means of escape from his difficulties. Not the least of these arose out of the Constitution Civile. So far as his own practice went, he would have none of it. Its friends naturally expected the head of the State to attend the Constitutional worship, but this Louis would not do. Still more did his conscience forbid him to receive the sacraments from those whom he regarded as schismatics. When

Easter came, he tried to go to St. Cloud to receive
his communion from a non-juring priest. But the
mob gathered round his carriage and refused to let
him go. They believed that his pious intention was
only a pretext for getting away from Paris altogether, and probably they were not far wrong. In
any case there could be no doubt about the royal
intentions when, on July 20, 1791, the King and
Queen made their ill-fated flight to Varennes.
From that moment the monarchy had finally lost
the confidence of the nation : and its destruction
was only a matter of time.

The blow was no less fatal to the ' refractory '
clergy. When he quitted Paris, the King left
behind him a message implying that his religious
scruples were largely responsible for his desire to
escape from the capital. Henceforth the cause of
the non-jurors was identified more closely than
ever in the popular mind with the cause of political
reaction : and there is a marked increase in the
desire and tendency to persecute. The anti-clerical
section of the Assembly loudly demanded a decree
of proscription against the *réfractaires*. But the
majority declined the responsibility, though they
were quite willing to turn a blind eye when the
directories of various departments issued similar
decrees on their own behalf. Shortly afterwards,
on September 30, 1791, the Constituent Assembly
came to an end. One of its last acts had been to
decree the annexation to France of Avignon and
the adjacent County of Venaissin, which for more
than four centuries had formed part of the patri-
mony of the Holy See. The decree was indeed no
more than the recognition of an accomplished fact,
for the inhabitants had sent the papal vice-legate
packing more than a year before.

CHAPTER III

PERSECUTION AND REVIVAL
1791–1801

THE second of the three Assemblies of the
revolutionary period, the ' Legislative,' was
of a very different complexion from its predecessor.
In the Constituante the moderates had been a
majority : in the Legislative they found themselves swamped. The partisans of persecution
were thus masters of the situation, and at once
demanded the internment of all curés and *vicaires*
who had not taken the oath. In vain two commissioners, Gallois and Gensonné, sent by the Constituante into La Vendée to appease the distur-
bances there, pleaded on their return for a policy
of concession and toleration. For a moment indeed
the Assembly seemed inclined to listen. But on
November 29, 1791, it definitely committed itself to
a policy of persecution. A decree was passed by
which all ecclesiastics who had not obeyed the previous decree of November 27, 1790, were to take the
'civic oath' at once. Those who refused to do so were
to be deprived of their pensions and to be reputed
' suspect of revolt against the law and of evil intentions towards the fatherland.' As such they were
put under the surveillance of the authorities : and
if convicted of having fomented religious disturbance, were liable to be imprisoned for two years.
Further, the right of hiring churches for worship
was to be withdrawn from ecclesiastics who had
refused the civic oath.

The decree was sent up for the royal sanction. This time Louis was resolved to be firm. He rejected it. But once again the local authorities took the law into their own hands : and in forty-three departments the veto was disregarded and the decree put into execution.

Meanwhile in Paris the more advanced revolutionaries were in the ascendant. In March, 1792, the King was forced to accept a ministry composed of the party called ' Girondins.' Whatever the virtues of the Girondins may have been, toleration was not one of them. The liberty for which they were so enthusiastic was never allowed by them to extend to the Catholic religion. Through all their deadly struggle with the Jacobins, the sacred cause of persecuting the non-jurors never failed to unite the two rival parties in a common action. The situation was exacerbated still further by a fresh brief issued by the Pope on March 19th, excommunicating all clerics who, having taken the oath, failed to retract it within sixty days. On May 2nd a deputy demanded the deportation of the non-juring clergy *en bloc* : and on May 27th the Assembly passed a decree which at least went a considerable way in this direction. By this any non-juring ecclesiastic could be deported on the demand of twenty active citizens of the same canton, if the advice of the directory of the district was in accordance therewith. Any such ecclesiastic who returned to France was to be imprisoned for ten years.

A week later another decree was passed dismissing the royal guard. The two decrees were sent up for the royal sanction together. But the Court had now determined on a counter-stroke. War had been declared against Austria in April, and had opened disastrously for the Revolution.

The King seized the opportunity of getting rid of his Girondin ministry (June 13th), and on June 19th he refused his sanction to the decrees. The immediate result was the insurrection of June 20th. A far more serious insurrection followed on August 10th, when the Tuileries were stormed, and the royal family were forced to take refuge with the Assembly. The Paris Commune and the 'Mountain' had triumphed : the Revolution entered on its extreme phase. The King was suspended : and the Assembly at once decreed that the rejected decrees should be put into execution.

But the measure of May 27th was already regarded as insufficient. The deportation of non-juring priests must no longer depend on the public spirit of local patriots : it must be the fate of every non-juror as such. A concession was first made to tender consciences by a change in the form of oath (August 15th). Henceforth the formula was to run, ' I swear to maintain liberty and equality or to die in their defence '—no allusion, explicit or implicit, being made to the Constitution Civile. Having thus given to the clergy an opportunity (of which many of them were willing to avail themselves) to withdraw their opposition, the Assembly on August 26th passed its decree. By this all priests who had not taken the oath or had retracted it were to leave the kingdom within fifteen days. After the expiry of that period the non-juror still on French soil was to be deported to Guiana.

The savage decree was executed without delay. All over France priests were seen wending their way towards the frontiers and exile. The authorities neglected no opportunity of venting their spite upon them ; the populace insulted and robbed them. Many were slain. For before the eyes of patriots there shone the bright example of the

'September massacres' just consummated in Paris
(September 2, 1792), when those who had been imprisoned for suspected complicity with the invader
— the majority being non-juring priests — were
butchered in cold blood like rats in a drain.

The Legislative Assembly now in its turn gave
way to the Convention (September 21, 1792). The
first act of the new Assembly was to abolish the
monarchy. The trial and execution of the King
were not long in following. Religion fared no
better at its hands. On March 18, 1793, the penalty
which a non-juring priest incurred by returning to
France was changed from imprisonment to death :
and, on the following April 23rd, the decree of
August 26, 1792, was made applicable not only to
the secular clergy but to the regular as well—even
lay brothers and members of teaching orders being
included.

In passing judgement on these measures, as on
other savageries of the extreme Revolutionary phase
we must in justice remember the situation in which
France at the moment found herself. Fear always
tends to make men cruel : and Anatole France's
wonderful reproduction of the atmosphere of the
period in *Les Dieux ont Soif* helps us to realize
that the ' Reign of Terror ' held its sway not less
in those who perpetrated, than in those who
suffered, its enormities. The Revolution stood face
to face with an avenging coalition of armed Europe :
and for the moment there seemed small hope of
conjuring the peril. To make things worse, the
west of France chose this desperate crisis in the
national fortunes to flame out into the famous
' Revolt of La Vendée ' (March, 1793)—a movement which was to show that a capacity for atrocious deeds was not a Jacobin monopoly. It would
be absurd, of course, to lay the blame for this

insurrection at the door of the Catholic Church. But the Royalist and Catholic causes were so inextricably intertwined that it was not—and still is not—easy to distribute the responsibility for a movement designed to serve the interests of both. Nor is it possible to deny that many of its most active agents were non-juring priests. Human motives are generally mixed : and if the Assembly did not punish for purely political reasons, neither did the clergy as a body suffer for purely religious offences. Yet of the ' crimes ' which brought upon them their doom the great bulk of the individual victims were doubtless innocent.

It appearing impossible henceforward to take more rigorous measures against the non-jurors than those actually in operation, the Convention turned now its attention to the Constitutional Church. So long as it was a convenient stalking-horse for the persecution of Catholics, this institution had enjoyed the favour of the extreme revolutionaries. But now it had served its purpose. Its abolition, however, was not contemplated immediately. When, on November 16, 1792, Cambon proposed the suppression of the salaries of the constitutional clergy, Danton had spoken against the motion. ' The intention of the Convention,' he said, ' is not to destroy but to perfect.' In other words, the faith and practice of the Constitutional Church were by gradual steps to be assimilated to those of the fanatical anti-Christians who now ruled France. In two directions in particular the ' perfecting ' process was to be effected—divorce and the marriage of priests. The former had been declared legal by the Legislative Assembly on August 30, 1792. As to the latter, the Convention did not at first go so far as to make it compulsory. But any priest who married was sure of its enthusiastic support against ' aggrieved parishioners': and when a bishop (Lindet) took a wife, its delight knew no bounds. Another constitutional bishop, Fauchet, who forcibly expressed his disapproval of clerical marriage was bitterly denounced : and on July 19, 1793, the Convention passed a decree punishing with deportation any bishop who tried to prevent a priest from marrying. The constitutional clergy had been already deprived by the Legislative Assembly of the *état civil*, which was entrusted to the municipalities instead (September 20, 1792). They were now forbidden to keep ' registers ' of any kind or to demand before giving the nuptial benediction any conditions other than those required by the civil law.

After the fall of the Girondins (June 2, 1793), the Jacobins had secured the passing by the Convention of a new ' constitution ' guaranteeing freedom of worship and payment of their salaries to the constitutional clergy (June 27, 1793). This constitution, however, was simply an anodyne to lull the alarms and scruples of the more moderate members of the Assembly. The real intention of the Mountain was very different. On September 16, 1793, all episcopal salaries above six thousand livres were reduced to that sum. It was also decreed that no ecclesiastic might receive simultaneously a salary and a pension. A few weeks later all nuns who had not taken the oath were expelled from the hospitals, their places being taken by ' citizenesses known to be attached to the principles of the Revolution.' Meanwhile the commissioners of the Convention were running amok in the provinces. The Terror had begun. The laws against the non-juring clergy were ruthlessly put into operation : and those of the laity who sympathized with them were imprisoned as ' suspect ' and ' very attached to fanaticism,' or crippled by ruinous fines. At the same time the way was prepared for the final snuffing-out of the Constitutional Church. The ex-Oratorian Fouché (notorious later as Napoleon's Minister of Police) particularly distinguished himself by his antireligious activities as representative of the people in the Central and Western departments. In Paris atheism was running riot. The Assembly, while not making a formal decree, allowed the Commune to abolish the Constitutional worship. The Commune's example was followed throughout France. On November 7th a disgraceful scene was enacted in the presence of the Assembly, when the wretched Gobel, Bishop of Paris, and many others of the constitutional clergy solemnly apostatized. The carnival of atheism reached its climax in the Feast of Reason at Notre Dame on November 10th when a dancer of the opera, arrayed as ' Goddess of Reason,' took her seat upon the highaltar and received the adoration of the multitude.

But now Robespierre intervened. As a disciple of Rousseau he was no atheist, but a fanatical devotee of the *Être Suprême*. Moreover, he was of Rousseau's opinion that the atheist is anti-social and should be punished with death. Accordingly Hébert and Chaumette, the loathsome pair who had inspired the recent orgies, were sent to the guillotine. The Cult of Reason gave way to the Cult of the Supreme Being. The *Fête de l'Être Suprême* was celebrated on June 8, 1794, when Robespierre pontificated, the cynosure of all eyes in a ' sky-blue coat ' and carrying a ' bouquet of flowers and wheat-ears ' in his hand.

The change was doubtless for the better, but it did not mark any improvement in the lot of either of the rival clergies. Nor did the fall of Robespierre and the Thermidorian reaction (July 27, 1794) bring any immediate relief. The men who succeeded to power after the collapse of the Terror were less bloodthirsty than their predecessors, but neither more religious nor more moral. Paris gave itself up to an orgy of licentiousness in which the claims of religion and the dictates of justice and humanity (so far at least as the non-juring priests were concerned) were alike forgotten. The laws against the *réfractaires* were not repealed. It is true that the death-penalty was no longer exacted : but deportation remained the fate of any priest denounced for *incivisme*. In the midst of the general chase after pleasure the unhappy priests who languished in prison or were still awaiting transportation in the crowded, fetid, fever-ridden hulks at Rochefort were conveniently lost sight of. Of eight hundred and twenty-seven priests deported to Rochefort only two hundred and eighty-five survived.

The honour of being the first to call the notice of the Convention to these poor wretches belongs to an unknown deputy, who, in November, 1794, demanded their release. In the following month the Constitutional Bishop Grégoire renewed the demand. The same orator, on December 21, 1794, boldly proclaimed the principle of religious liberty. ' A people,' he said, ' which has not freedom of worship will soon be without freedom at all.' His plea remained ineffectual for the moment. The Convention voted the previous question. But Grégoire's speech, printed and circulated as a pamphlet, produced a strong impression on public opinion.

An important step in the right direction had been already taken when, on September 18th, the Assembly decided to abolish the *salaire des cultes*. ' The French Republic,' ran the decree, ' no longer pays expenses or salary for any form of religion.' Henceforth all religious denominations were on the same level : and the way was thus laid open for granting equal liberty to all.

The demand for this was renewed in a famous speech by Boissy d'Anglas, on February 21, 1795. It is true that he was careful to disclaim any tenderness for religion itself. He did not conceal his own hatred and contempt of Christianity, which he regarded as ' a superstition destined to disappear before the religion of Socrates, Marcus Aurelius, and Cicero.' But this happy consummation must be the effect of a gradual process of enlightenment, not of persecution, which could only delay its coming. ' The best way of slaying the Church is to grant it a disdainful toleration.' Put in this way, the principle advocated made an irresistible appeal to the audience : and the ' law of 3 Ventôse ' was passed on the spot. The exercise of every form of religion was to be free from disturbance : but the Republic was neither to pay salary to, nor provide accommodation for, any. The worshippers were to be subject to the surveillance of the authorities : but the surveillance was to be confined to *mesures de police et de sûreté*.

The freedom thus restored to the Church was of a sufficiently restricted kind : yet at least it was an immense improvement on the situation that had preceded it. The effect was seen immediately in a remarkable revival in both the Constitutional and non-juring Churches. It was not to be supposed, however, that persecution was at an end. If the law had become liberal, the legislators had not. The familiar denunciations of ' fanaticism ' were still heard from the benches of the Convention. One speaker described the non-jurors as ' infamous mountebanks.'

Over the greater part of France, the operation of the law was greatly hampered by those who administered it.   Only in Brittany and La Vendée was a more generous policy adopted.   General Hoche, charged with the pacification of the latter region, went at once to the heart of the matter. ' If,' he said to Carnot, ' we do not admit the principle of religious toleration, we must give up all hope of peace in this country.'   By acting on this principle, he achieved the most satisfactory results.

But the Convention declined to listen to the logic of facts.   By the decree of 20 Fructidor (September 6, 1795) deported priests returning to France were condemned to perpetual banishment.   On the other hand, the principle of the law of 3 Ventôse was not disturbed.   In fact, by that of 11 Prairial (May 30, 1795), it received a considerable extension.   The free use of unalienated churches was conceded to citizens on payment of a money rent and on condition that no one should officiate who had not previously declared his ' submission to the laws of the Republic.'   The test was much less stringent than that previously exacted.   Further, those priests (the majority) whose conscience forbade them to take it might still exercise their functions in private houses.   The freedom thus accorded was limited in certain points by an elaborate law of September 29th (7 Vendémiaire) on the *police des cultes*, which codified the existing legislation on the subject.   But the main principle was not disturbed.

While thus according to the rites of the Catholic Church a ' disdainful toleration,' the Convention did not lose sight of the necessity of providing something better in their place.   Such was the aim of the project introduced on February 5, 1795,

for the observance of *fêtes décadaires*. By means
of these the extreme Republicans hoped to gratify
at once their hatred of Christianity and their passion for the decimal system. The Christian Sunday
was to go, along with the Christian seven days'
week. In place of the latter was to be set up a ten
days period called a *décade,* with the tenth day—
the *décadi*—marked by ' civic festivals for the
solemnizing of the pure worship which is celebrated under the open sky.' Sad to say, this
religion made-to-order failed to take hold. The
Christians adhered to their Sunday : the non-
Christians found the *fêtes décadaires* merely ridiculous with their ' civic repasts,' at which the praises
of the Republic were sounded with wearisome re-
iteration and to the accompaniment of such insipid
rites as ' the presentation of a rose to innocence.'
The Convention therefore, while applauding the
sentiments of the promoters, refused to give the
décades legislative force. In the Constitution of
the Year III, one of its last works, it reaffirmed the
principle that ' Every man is free in the exercise
of his religion.' But the proscription of the *réfractaires* was maintained : and just before its dissolution the Convention reimposed the death penalty
for any deported priest who should return to
France.

    The same duality of attitude—the result of the
unhappy confusion between religious opinions and
political that marked the time—persisted under
the Directory. The non-jurors were immune from
prosecution as Catholics : but as Royalist suspects
they were still under the ban of the law. No
doubt most of them heartily desired the overthrow
of the Republic—and very naturally. It seems
impossible, too, to deny that not a few of the priests
who, after the collapse of the Terror, flocked back

to France profited by the greater leniency of the new government to plot and preach against it, or that the savage measures of retaliation perpetrated by insurgent Royalists in various parts of France were made with clerical sanction, if not at clerical instigation.   Yet it is permissible to believe that it was not to conspire against the existing régime but to minister to their derelict flocks that the great majority dared to brave the terrors besetting their return.   In any case a policy of generosity seemed to hold out the best hopes of internal peace for France.   The bulk of moderate opinion was rapidly inclining to this view.

Unfortunately, the government was in the hands of men who hated Christianity for its own sake. Of the five Directors four had no religion at all. The fifth, La Réveillère-Lépeaux, was a patron of the new sect—based on the doctrines of Rousseau— called the Theophilanthropists.   Everything was done to assist this new religion : but the general public remained profoundly indifferent.   ' The meetings,' it was reported, ' are not well attended. The new cult does not seem destined to have a long career.'   When La Réveillère-Lépeaux complained to Talleyrand of its slow progress, the latter re- plied :   ' Jesus Christ died for His religion : you must do something similar for yours.'   This kind of witness to conviction, however, the Theophilan- thropists preferred to leave to the Catholics.   Nor were these latter left unprovided with facilities for the purpose.   A decree passed by the Assembly (May 6, 1796) condemning to deportation, and to death if he returned, any priest who had not taken the oath to accept the Constitution Civile fell, indeed, to the ground owing to the refusal of the second legislative Chamber, the Council of An- cients, to confirm it.   But this did not prevent some thirty priests from being executed during 1796 on the strength of previous decrees.

The triumphs of the Army of Italy under the young Bonaparte in the same year seemed to hold out the prospect of meting out to the Pope himself the fate of his faithful clergy in France. Not only was the Holy See deprived of large sums of money and of priceless works of art, but the Directory demanded that he should retract the various briefs by which he had condemned the Constitution Civile on pain of the complete extinction of the temporal power if he did not. The Pope indignantly rejected the proposal and prepared for the worst. Fortunately for him Bonaparte was wiser than those who employed him. The Directory's proposal was tacitly dropped : and by the Peace of Tolentino (February 19, 1797) the Pope got off with the cession of the Legations and the payment of an indemnity of thirty million francs.

The elections of 1797 seemed to herald the approaching collapse of the Directorial régime. The moderate and conservative parties were considerably strengthened : and in consequence the majority both in the Five Hundred and the Ancients passed from the Left to the Right. The new spirit of the legislature was exhibited in a speech of Camille Jordan on June 16th in favour of complete religious liberty for the Catholic clergy. Ten days later (June 26th) a measure was introduced repealing the laws imposing deportation or imprisonment on priests guilty only of refusing to swear submission to the laws of the Republic. This was fiercely denounced by the extremists of the Left : but, supported by a magnificent speech from the youthful Royer-Collard, it passed the Five Hundred and soon after (August 24, 1797) received the assent of the Ancients also.

A new era seemed to be opening for the Catholics when their hopes were again dashed to the ground. Eleven days after the adoption of the above measure by the Ancients the *coup d'état* of 18 Fructidor (September 4, 1797) riveted the Jacobin yoke once more on the French nation. A kind of recrudescence of the Terror followed. Again the guillotine claimed its victims, though less comprehensively than in '93. The laws against the non-juring clergy were once more put into operation : and many suffered the penalty of deportation—called by the ominous name of *guillotine sèche*. To the oath of ' submission to the laws of the Republic ' was added an oath of ' hatred to royalty.' Above all, the observance of the *fêtes décadaires* was made compulsory. It was even proposed to prohibit formally the keeping of Sunday. This fell to the ground : but everything was done to make its observance difficult. Even the Pope was *fructidorisé*. An anti-French riot in Rome was made the excuse for taking the aged pontiff from his own city (February 25, 1798) and transporting him to France, where he died in captivity at Valence in 1799.

The triumph of the Republic over the Church seemed complete. But the Directory in its turn was to learn that ' it is not good to make martyrs.' The Catholic West once again rose in revolt : difficulties thickened about the corrupt and divided administration : and with Bonaparte's return from Egypt and the *coup d'état* of Brumaire (November 9–10, 1799) the whole wretched edifice collapsed.

From this dreary record of grudging toleration alternating with renewed persecution it is a relief to turn to the slow but sure revival of religious feeling in France which, in spite of all difficulties, succeeded in maintaining itself from 1794 onwards. This revival of course suffered severely from the schism which divided French Catholics into two sharply-opposed camps. The Constitutional Church, conscious perhaps of the weakness of its position, was willing enough to make overtures to its rival : but the non-jurors scornfully refused all dealings with it. They even condemned their opponents to eternal damnation. Yet side by side the expansion of the two Churches went on. Even at the height of the Terror a considerable number of the non-juring clergy still refused to quit the soil of France, exercising their ministry in cellars and garrets where a handful of the faithful laity gathered together at dead of night in momentary expectation of surprise. As the tumbrels lumbered along the streets of Paris with their loads of victims towards the guillotine, priests concealed in the crowd or standing in a window would by a gesture signify the absolution that the Church never refuses to its penitent children in the hour of death. Even on the scaffold itself Louis XVI was attended by his confessor, the heroic Abbé Edgworth.

Such devotion inevitably produced a profound impression on all who were not utterly blinded by hatred of Christianity. It reaped its reward after the Terror had passed. Robespierre fallen, a large number of the priests who had fled into exile returned to Paris. They were still under the ban of the law : but the frequent renewal of the proscriptive degrees against them suggests that these were not always very drastically enforced. Their number was increased by the many who now retracted the oath. The non-juring Church no less than the constitutional profited by the toleration accorded by the law of 3 Ventôse. At Paris no difficulties were put in the way of its worship.

Large numbers, we are told, attended service on Easter Day, 1796 : and still larger numbers the following Easter. On May 29, 1797, the Church of S. Roch was reopened : and soon after the Bishop of St. Papoul ordained seventy priests. In the provinces the non-jurors met with similar success : though here they seem to have been more liable to the spasmodic violence of popular fanaticism. It was, however, in the West that the influence of the non-juring clergy reached its zenith. They were the soul of the Vendéan revolt both at the time of the Terror and during its renewal in the last phase of the Directory. The expansion of the non-juring Church was temporarily checked by the Fructidorian persecution : none the less, its members continued to worship in secret. When after Brumaire it emerged once more from the catacombs, it had attained an importance with which the triumphant Bonaparte found it advisable to reckon.

The Constitutional Church had meanwhile undergone a similar process of renewal under the wise direction of Grégoire. His task was not an easy one. The record of the Constitutional clergy under the Terror had been far from brilliant. Many of them, no doubt, like Grégoire himself, had accepted the Constitution Civile from perfectly respectable motives. Not a few had suffered grievously for their fidelity to Christianity. But many too were the mere *canaille* of the ecclesiastical body, time-servers and sycophants who had taken the oath because they thought it would pay them to do so, or from fear of the consequences if they did not. It was among them that the apostasies of 1793–4 occurred, which provided so deplorable a contrast to the heroism of the *réfractaires*.

The first task then of Grégoire and his associates after Thermidor was one of purgation. The priests who had apostatized or taken wives were weeded out. Their next duty was to reorganize what remained. New bishops and pastors were provided. An ecclesiastical journal called *Annales de la Réligion* was founded, together with a *Societé de la Philosophie Chrétienne* for the dissemination of religious literature. The churches were again thrown open : and the faithful began to flock back to the deserted altars. On August 15, 1795, divine service was once more celebrated in poor, dilapidated Notre Dame.

The policy of the Directory certainly did not err on the side of generosity even at the periods when it was least hostile. Churches and presbyteries continued to be pulled down ; and petty molestations were the order of the day, especially in the shape of local attempts to compel observance of the *décadis*. The State no longer providing salaries or paying pensions, the bishops and priests were compelled to live in the utmost poverty. In the dark days following Fructidor the Constitutional Church suffered persecution along with the nonjurors, though in a less acute form. Yet all this helped rather than hindered the good work. ' You will no longer be tempted,' wrote Grégoire, ' to rely on the arm of flesh. God alone will be your support.'

In 1796 there were services in more than thirtytwo thousand parishes. The Constitution Civile was tacitly dropped. Attempts were made to effect a reconciliation with the Holy See on the basis of the Gallican Articles of 1682,[1] and to bring about a

---

[1] As these ' Articles,' issued by the General Assembly of the clergy of France, in the course of the struggle between Louis XIV and Innocent XI, are frequently referred to in this work, it may be useful to set them forth here in an abbreviated form :

1. S. Peter and his successors, vicars of Christ, and likewise

reunion with the non-jurors. At a National Gallican Council held at Paris in August, 1797, definite
proposals were made to this end and embodied in
a *décret de pacification*. By this the authority of
the Pope as the head of the Church was recognized :
and it was proposed that when there were two
bishops, constitutional and non-juring, for one
diocese or two curés for one parish the senior
should be recognized. A request was made to the
Holy See for an Oecumenical Council to settle disputed questions.

These proposals came to nothing owing to the
intractable opposition of the *réfractaires* : but the
attitude they betrayed was hopeful for the future.
Of this in due course Bonaparte was to take
advantage when he set himself to effect by force
that religious pacification which could not be
achieved by voluntary means. His frequently
vaunted claim of having effected *le relèvement des
autels* cannot be substantiated. The revival of re-

the Church itself, have received from God power in things spiritual and pertaining to salvation, but not in things temporal
and civil. . . . Consequently kings and princes are not by the
law of God subject to any ecclesiastical power, nor to the keys
of the Church, with respect to their temporal government.
Their subjects cannot be released from the duty of obeying
them nor absolved from the oath of allegiance. . . .

2. The plenitude of power in things spiritual which resides
in the Apostolic see and the successors of Peter is such that at
the same time the decrees of the Oecumenical Council of
Constance . . . remain in full force and perpetual obligation. . . .

3. Hence the exercise of the Apostolic authority must be
regulated by the canons enacted by the Spirit of God. . . . The
ancient rules, customs, and institutions received by the
realm and Church of France likewise remain inviolable. . . .

4. The Pope has the principal place in deciding questions of
faith, and his decrees extend to every church and all churches :
but nevertheless his judgement is not irreversible unless confirmed by the consent of the Church.

ligion was already an accomplished fact when he seized the reins of power : or he would have left the matter severely alone. It was not the habit of Napoleon to concern himself with insignificant minorities. But the full advantage which he hoped to reap from officially recognizing the Catholic religion could not be secured so long as the schism in its ranks continued. This schism therefore the First Consul set himself to terminate : and by means of the Concordat of 1801 the object was successfully achieved.

CHAPTER IV

CHATEAUBRIAND AND ' LE GÉNIE DU CHRISTIANISME '

TWO events, virtually coincident in time, may serve as indices of the effective revival of Catholicism in France at the opening of the nineteenth century. The one is the Concordat, the significance of which in this respect has been already briefly indicated. The other is Chateaubriand's famous work *Le Génie du Christianisme*—begun just as the eighteenth century passed into the nineteenth and published in 1802. Intended as a piece of Christian apologetic, this book cannot, as such, be taken very seriously. But its appearance is profoundly significant in its relation to a change that was coming over the mental and spiritual attitude of the cultivated literary class in Western Europe. The expression of that change is known as the Romantic Movement. The *Génie du Christianisme* represents Romanticism applied to the sphere of religion.

Nothing could have been more unsympathetic to the peculiar genius of Catholicism than the atmosphere of the eighteenth century, which in consequence exhibits itself in all countries as the ' glacial age ' of the Church. A revealed religion must always tend to subordinate reason to faith : its deepest mysteries are beyond strictly rational proof. But the eighteenth century was above all rationalistic, and rationalistic in the peculiarly

arrogant manner of an age upon which has not yet
fallen the shadow of reason's conceivable in-
sufficiency to solve every problem in heaven and
earth. Youth is always cocksure, and the science
of the eighteenth century was decidedly young.
No doubt it was just the determination to subject
everything to a rigorous intellectual analysis that
gives the century its importance in the story of
human progress. It was the work of the eighteenth
century to prepare the way for the astounding
scientific achievements of the nineteenth. Reason
had to be set free to do its own work in its own
way free from the trammels of theological interference. But all progress is fated to be one-sided.
It is not surprising, therefore, that the eighteenth
century intellectuals should have refused to set
any limits to the sphere of reason and should have
regarded Faith as synonymous with superstition.

The eighteenth century indeed—or at least the
first half or two-thirds of it—was more remarkable
for mind than for soul. It was an age singularly
devoid of moral and spiritual enthusiasm. ' Enthusiasm ' was a term of reproach, meaning what
we should call fanaticism. The flight of such inspiration as it had was nearly always on a low wing.
Its art faithfully reflects its character. Finish and
delicacy it has in a remarkable degree, together
with a certain solid magnificence in its larger productions. But it makes no attempt to soar or
aspire. Its characteristic products in ecclesiastical
architecture are in England the churches of Hawks-
moor and Gibbs, on the Continent the Jesuit
churches of the period with their ' elegant ' decora-
tion, frescoed cupolas, and thoroughly worldly atmosphere. As for the cathedrals bequeathed to it
by the Middle Ages as the supreme triumph of their
faith and art, their vastness and solidity defied

demolition : but the age did the best it could by
sweeping away the lesser features—roodscreens,
altars, stallwork, and stained windows—and covering up with classical panelling what it could not
destroy.   Such was the fate of Notre Dame at the
hands of Louis XIV (1699–1714) and of the authorities who removed the bulk of the mediaeval glass
in 1741.

Time was bound to bring a reaction : and a
reaction at last came.   But not at first in the direction of a love of the Middle Ages or of Catholic
sentiment.   The primary note of the age was
artificiality—in literature, in art, in manners. Now
an artificial society is bound sooner or later to
produce by opposition a prophet of the ' simple
life.'   Such a prophet—the greatest of his kind—
arose in France in Jean Jacques Rousseau.   It is
scarcely possible to exaggerate the influence of this
man upon the thought and life of his own generation, and, still more, of those that followed. More
than any one else he is the father of the modern
world.   That world has indeed little cause
to be proud of the character of its progenitor.
History provides no parallel to so vast an influence
wielded by so unpleasant and even despicable a
character.   But the vastness of the influence is
indubitable.   Rousseau's teachings as to the *Con-
trat Social* inspired the French Revolution and its
unfathomable consequences.   In the theories of
Émile he is the father of modern educational
method.   His matchless style is the starting-point
and the perennial inspiration of modern French
prose as opposed to the prose of the *Grand Siècle*.

The key to all his teaching may be summed up as
' the return to Nature '—or more precisely to what
Rousseau believed to be ' Nature.'   He came upon
the close hothouse atmosphere of the Paris

salons like a breath of fresh mountain air from his own Savoy. And just because he taught men to abandon convention and go back to Nature he is able to claim paternity to the most widely divergent movements. That is the paradox of Rousseau. He gave the impulse to the Revolution, but equally to the Counter-Revolution. Chateaubriand and de Maistre are his descendants, no less than Robespierre. For Nature is not one-sided but many-sided.

Rousseau's preference, too, of emotion and sentiment to reason made for the dethronement of the latter from its insolent eighteenth-century supremacy. Again, with all its perversity and weakness of moral fibre, his character was fundamentally religious. The religion of the ' Savoyard Vicar ' may be shallow, vague, and unsatisfying : but it was real as far as it went, and appealed to sides of human nature that even eighteenth-century infidelity could not destroy. And when once the reaction against the eighteenth century was set in motion, it found its own channels. The classic tradition resuscitated at the Renaissance began to lose its power and slowly but steadily petered out. The glamour of the Middle Ages, the love of the strange, the aspiring, the transcendental took its place : and the Romantic Movement began.

In this movement Chateaubriand was the first great figure. Alike in manner and in matter he represents something new in the literature of France and of Europe. His *Atala* marks the beginning of the modern sensibility to nature, not in her tame, cultivated form beloved by the eighteenth century but in such wild grandeur as that of the American primeval forest in which the scene of the tale is laid. So again *René* first struck the note of sentimental, introspective pessimism so characteristic of much nineteenth-century literature—' Byronism ' as it is sometimes called from its great English exponent. Finally in the *Génie du Christianisme* (of which both *Atala* and *René* are parts, published before the main work appeared) we see the dawn of the new appreciation of Catholicism, particularly on its poetic and aesthetic side, which played so great a part in the Romantic Movement in France and Germany, which in England found a voice in the novels of Sir Walter Scott, and through him (as Newman admitted) was a chief source of inspiration of the Oxford Movement.

François René de Chateaubriand, like his great successor Lamennais, was a Breton—like him, too, a native of St. Malo. He was born of an ancient and aristocratic but impoverished family in 1768. He himself, in his *Mémoires d'Outre-Tombe*, has given a wonderful picture of the scenes and impressions of his youth. Even to-day Brittany retains far more of the spiritual atmosphere of the Middle Ages than any other part of France. In the eighteenth century this mediaeval quality of its life and faith was altogether unimpaired. From his cradle the boy was surrounded by the tender symbolism of the Catholic faith. His foster-mother, ' La Villeneuve,' dedicated him in infancy to the Virgin. Assisting on winter nights at the Salut in the old cathedral at St. Malo, ' when in the pauses between the hymns the Christmas gales rattled the windows and shook the vaulted roof,' he experienced, he says, ' an extraordinary feeling of religion.'

In every way the circumstances of his boyhood were such as to develop the dreamy, romantic side of his nature to the fullest extent. The grey expanse of those western seas was ever before his eyes : around him stretched the wide, bare spaces of the Breton landscape. The home where his youth was spent, with short interruptions for educational or other reasons, was the old manor of Combourg, a vast dilapidated place alive with all the mysterious enchantments of the Middle Ages. The scant attention and sympathy of his parents drove him in upon himself. His only confidant was his fourth sister Lucile. It was she who first stimulated him to give literary expression to his thoughts and feelings. But a sudden doubt as to his gifts caused him to cease writing : and deprived of this outlet his passionate and moody temperament became more than ever the prey of morbid fancies. He attempted suicide.

At last he fell desperately ill and lay long between life and death. During his convalescence he finally decided against an idea, entertained but half seriously, of becoming a priest and took a commission in the army instead. While in Paris in this capacity he began to frequent literary circles and himself published a poem. The great events of 1789 were just beginning when he set out on a journey to America, acquiring there the materials and local colour used by him later in *Atala*. Returning to Paris in 1791 to find the revolutionary extremists in the saddle, he escaped to Coblentz and joined the *émigré* army. He was wounded before Thionville : then his company broke up and he took refuge in England, remaining there for several years.

His resources were of the slenderest. How was he to make a living? The idea of doing literary work suggested itself to him, and he set to work upon a book of which the first volume (the only one published) appeared in 1797 with the title *Essai Historique sur les Révolutions*. In this he revealed himself as under the sway of eighteenth-century sceptical thought and also as a strong admirer of Rousseau. He admits that his master's principles had ' covered France with ruins ' : yet he says, ' I preferred to condemn the human race rather than the citizen of Geneva.' Still there is none of the acrimonious hatred of Christianity characteristic of eighteenth-century infidelity. ' The essay,' says Villemain, ' was not the work of a bigoted sceptic but of a storm-tossed seeker after truth.'

That the young man's scepticism was only skin-deep was shown by the circumstances of his conversion. It was while he was in London that he learned of his mother's death by a letter from his sister Julie, who spoke of the grief caused to the dying woman by her son's *Essai*. The effect upon him has been described in characteristic fashion by himself : ' The idea of having poisoned the last days of the woman who bore me filled me with despair. . . . I only found relief from this trouble when the thought came to me of expiating my first book by a religious work.' Such was the origin of the *Génie du Christianisme*. A similar account is given in the preface of the book itself : ' These two voices proceeding from the tomb ' (Julie too had died soon after writing her letter), ' this death which seemed an interpreter to death itself, overwhelmed me. I became a Christian. I did not yield, I admit, to any mighty supernatural illumination. My conviction came out of my heart. I wept and I believed.'

Was the conversion sincere ? The question has been much debated, especially since the appearance of Sainte Beuve's damaging book, *Chateaubriand et son groupe littéraire*. In this work Sainte Beuve seems to set himself deliberately to discount what he had apparently come to regard as the excessive enthusiasm displayed in his essay on Chateaubriand published in the *Revue des deux mondes* in 1838— the essay that contains the famous description of the reading of the manuscript of the *Mémoires* in Mme Récamier's apartment in the Abbaye-aux-bois. According to him the author of the *Génie du Christianisme* was ' an Epicurean with a Catholic imagination—sensual in life and at bottom sceptical in heart.'

Our judgement on the matter will perhaps depend largely on the view that we may have formed of the character of Sainte Beuve. There is at least no doubt as to the strong anti-Christian bias of the great critic in his later years, nor as to his unworthy love of garbage for its own sake. It is also possible to hold that he was jealous of Chateaubriand's fame, glad to attack an illustrious figure whom he had flattered as a living patron but now defamed as a dead rival. If, however, we put all prepossessions on this point on one side and consider only the evidence alleged, it is hard to acquit Sainte Beuve of injustice and prejudice.

The question has been made the subject of an elaborate monograph by Abbé Bertin on the *Religious Sincerity of Chateaubriand.* In this Sainte Beuve's subtle innuendoes are carefully examined and refuted. The abbé then goes on to show how nowhere has Chateaubriand allowed himself to say a word against the dogmas of the Catholic Church. Few other things escaped his criticism : but these at least were always sacred. His was a nature that soon tired of things : more and more as life went on he became the victim of an immense ennui and disillusionment. Yet if he tired of all else he never tired of religion. If belief in all else failed him he still believed in religion. ' Obstinate Catholic as I am,' he says, ' there is no Christian so believing

and no man so unbelieving as I.' ' Outside of
religion,' he says again, ' I have no belief.' Certainly his character was far from perfect. It is his
faults that give Sainte Beuve's attacks their sting.
He had the sensuous nature that usually accom-
panies an ardent imagination and the artistic
temperament. ' It is certain,' says a warm apologist, Mr. W. S. Lilly, ' that his life was unsatisfactory in its sexual relations.' He was ever a dangler
after petticoats, and his senile passion for one
fascinating siren was not unjustly qualified by
Barbey d'Aurévilly as ' ignoble and revolting.' He
was also egotistic and self-conscious to an amazing
degree. Yet a man (especially perhaps a Frenchman) may be genuinely religious without being
morally faultless : and to do him justice, Chateaubriand was never slow to admit his failings. Moreover, his bad traits must be balanced against his
good. Few have questioned his honesty and disinterestedness in political matters, and that is
much to say of a statesman of his generation.

It seems reasonable, then, to conclude that the
conversion of Chateaubriand was sincere. On the
other hand, his religion did not perhaps go very
deep. It was the aesthetic side of Christianity that
chiefly attracted him—its appeal to the romantic
instinct and the sense of beauty. His interest in
the intellectual aspects of religion was slight, nor
had he any overwhelming moral enthusiasm. This
weakness of Chateaubriand's Christianity is also
the weakness of his apologetic. The *Génie du
Christianisme* undoubtedly played an important
part in helping on the reaction from eighteenth-
century infidelity. But that is not to say that it
has much intrinsic value. Intellectually its reasoning is surprisingly feeble and shallow. It is in fact
simply an exposition of the poetic and artistic

aspect of Christianity which was what really
attracted Chateaubriand himself. It has been well
said that the author never seems to be quite sure
whether he is dealing with the truth of Christianity
or only with its beauty. If the proof of the former
is incomplete the latter is brought in to clinch the
argument. Further, Chateaubriand allows himself
considerable latitude in the use of the term Christianity. Often he seems to be concerned less with
the ' Genius of Christianity ' than with the ' Genius
of the Middle Ages.' Legend and folk-lore are
freely drawn upon by way of embellishment. Yet
if in this sense he expands his subject unduly, in
another sense he unduly contracts it. Christianity
means for him Catholicism and Catholicism only.
He entirely ignores the vast mass of Christian life
and experience outside the Roman allegiance. It
is not that he would deny the right to Protestants
to be called Christians, but merely that their kind
of Christianity does not interest or appeal to him.
This attitude is partly the result of his Breton birth
and upbringing : ' *Il est à naître,*' he quotes some-
where, ' *qui ait vu Breton bretonnant prêcher autre
religion que la catholique.*' But it is due, no doubt,
chiefly to the aesthetic deficiencies of Protestantism—its Puritan fear of the beautiful, its dislike of
ceremonial pomp, its austere intellectualism.

The plan and purpose of the *Génie du Christianisme* has been explained by the author in his first
chapter. The times, he says, demanded a new
apologetic. That of the Christian writers of the
eighteenth century was obsolete. They had postu-
lated a divine revelation : but contemporary
scepticism refused to admit anything of the sort.
Thus the task of the apologist is ' no longer to
prove that Christianity is excellent because it
comes from God but that it comes from God

because it is excellent.' The 'sophists,' i.e. the eighteenth-century *philosophes*, had maintained that
Christianity was ' a cult born in the heart of bar-
barism, absurd in its dogmas, ridiculous in its
ceremonies, the sworn foe of art and letters, of
reason and beauty.' As against this it was necessary and possible to prove that on the contrary
' of all religions which have ever existed the
Christian is the most poetic, the most human, the
most favourable to liberty, to art, and to letters ;
that the modern world owes to it everything from
agriculture to the abstract sciences, from hospitals
for the needy to the temples built by Michelangelo
and decorated by Raphael. It must be shown that
there is nothing more divine than its morality,
nothing more attractive and majestic than its dogma, its doctrine, and its worship. In a word, all
the enchantments of the imagination and all the
interests of the heart must be enlisted in behalf of
religion, which they had previously been used to
assail.' If it be argued that ' there is danger in
approaching religion from a human point of view,'
Chateaubriand replies by the question, ' Will
Christianity be less true because it appears more
beautiful ? '

The work is divided into four sections. The
first is headed ' Dogmas and Doctrines.' The
author here departs in some measure from his plan
and attempts a vindication of the main doctrines
of the Christian faith on conventional lines. The
attempt, it must be admitted, is neither profound
nor convincing, giving the impression of a candidate for holy orders serving up under examination
the confused product of a hasty and miscellaneous
reading of current text-books. The author in fact
is not really interested in this section : he only puts
it in for the sake of completeness. When he reaches

the second part—' Christian Practice '—he is more at home.   His main thesis is now to be developed. It is certainly ambitious—nothing less than to prove that both in literature and art human achievement has been greater since Christianity than before it, and that this is directly the effect of Christianity.   The second part deals with this argument as it relates to poetry, the third in its reference to the fine arts and literature.   An eloquent book on ' the harmonies of the Christian religion with the scenes of nature and the passions of the human heart ' concludes part iii.   But it is when he comes to the fourth and concluding part— on Christian worship—that Chateaubriand really finds his opportunity.   The rites and ceremonies of the Church and the character of the clergy, secular and regular, are described with all the orchestral magnificence of the great artist's style. It is all, of course, very *couleur de rose*: but Chateaubriand is frankly a special pleader, and at the worst his picture is no more one-sided than the disparagements of the *philosophes*.   The book concludes with a summary of ' services rendered to society by the clergy and by the Christian religion ' —including hospitals, education, agriculture, law and government.   The last chapter draws a horrifying picture of ' what the state of society would be to-day if Christianity had not appeared,' and comments incidentally on ' the alarming symptoms produced by the irreligion of the revolutionary régime.'   ' For ourselves,' says the author, ' we are convinced that Christianity will rise triumphant out of the terrible testing-time that has recently purified it.'

The book was published in the face of doleful misgiving on the part of the author's friends. Mme de Staël said, with reference to the chapter on 'Virginity,' ' *Ah ! notre pauvre Chateaubriand, cela va tomber à plat.*' That eminent preacher, the Abbé de Boulogne, consulted by a publisher, replied, ' If you want to ruin yourself, print that.' There was the possibility, too, that Bonaparte might object to its publication. But he had just concluded the Concordat : and thought that the book might win support for his handiwork—though (Chateaubriand tells us) he ' later repented of his mistake.'

The book appeared and had a resounding success. It excited, of course, the bitter hostility and scorn of the unbelieving world. But the Catholics were delighted to see the war carried so bravely into the enemy's camp. Chateaubriand's fervid championship and the Concordat together filled them with new dreams of still greater triumphs. As to the general intellectual society of the time, if not convinced by Chateaubriand's arguments, at least it found its interests taking a new direction. It had been ' jolted out of the eighteenth-century rut.' Its members, says Chateaubriand, ' were no longer nailed down by an anti-religious prejudice, but allowed themselves to examine any and every system, however absurd, even though it might be Christian.'

Vain as he was, Chateaubriand was not unaware of the shortcomings of his work. Writing his Memoirs many years later, he admits that if he had been writing it then he would have written it differently. But at least he had given the first impulse to a movement that was to go on working and expanding through the nineteenth century and beyond.

CHAPTER V

THE CONCORDAT OF 1801

W HAT was Napoleon's religion ? Or had he indeed any religion at all ? Such data as exist
may be interpreted in more than one way. There is
a famous anecdote which represents him as stretch-
ing out his hand to the star-lit heavens and saying,
' Someone must have made *that*.' And there is the
equally famous tribute to the divinity of Jesus
Christ uttered at St. Helena, ' I know something of
men, and I tell you that Jesus Christ was not a man.'
In his will he declared that he died ' in the Catholic,
Apostolic, and Roman Church, in the bosom of
which I was born.' But if he professed Catholicism he showed little ardour in practising it. In
many ways he was a typical child of eighteenth-
century scepticism. Actually, his attitude towards
religion seems to have been determined mainly
by a sense of its political value. It was a guarantee
of social order, a useful instrument of police. For
him atheism was ' a principle destructive of all
social organization, which takes from man his
consolations and all his hopes.' ' One does not
argue with such people, one shoots them (*on les
mitraille*).' So again he said to Roederer :

How is one to secure morality ? There is only one way—to
re-establish religion. Society cannot exist without inequality
of fortune, and inequality of fortune cannot exist without
religion. When a man is dying of hunger by the side of a
man who is full-fed, it is impossible for him to accept this
difference unless there is an authority which says to him
' God wills it thus.' There must be poor and rich in this world,
but hereafter in eternity the division will be made differently.

It is scarcely an exalted conception of religion which thus degrades it from an end into a means. But Napoleon was capable of going still further and prostituting it to become a mere instrument of his own personal ambition. From this point of view he was not even particular as to what religion he professed. When he was in Egypt he showed a marked enthusiasm for Islam. He surrounded himself with eminent Mohammedan Imams, and gave it to be understood that it was quite possible that he himself might become a convert to the teachings of the prophet. When, however, he became First Consul Catholicism appeared to him the card to play. '*Vous trouverez,*' he said, '*quel parti je saurai tirer des prêtres.*'

He did not adopt this solution without careful consideration. There were three candidates for his suffrage — Protestantism, the Constitutional Church, the Catholic Church. But Protestantism was too weak, the Constitutional Church too novel and discredited. Generally speaking, a Frenchman must be either a Catholic or nothing. So Catholicism should have his protection, though room might be found for the Constitutionals on terms. Already he had dreams of being Emperor, and the Pope was a necessary party to their realization. As the Altar had been the sturdiest pillar of the Throne under the old régime, so it might be under the new. Louis XIV had been the ' eldest son of the Church.' He would be the same. A Church rich, splendid, and influential, but with all its dignity and influence strictly subordinated to the interests of autocracy—this was his idea, as it was the idea of many ' most religious ' monarchs before him.

It was under the sway of such motives that he undertook the establishment of the Concordat. A new Pope had recently assumed the tiara (March 14, 1800), elected at Venice in the room of the *peregrinus apostolicus*, Pius VI, who had died a prisoner of the Directory at Valence. The choice made was a severe blow to Austria. She had just won from the French the three Legations of Bologna, Ferrara, and Romagna, ceded by the Pope to the Directory by the Peace of Tolentino, and she meant to keep them. With this object she had pertinaciously intrigued for the election as Pope of the signatory of the Tolentino treaty, Cardinal Mattei. The election of Cardinal Chiaramonti (who assumed the title of Pius VII) disappointed her in this : but she did not abandon her main purpose.

Immediately after his election, the new Pope was met with a demand for the formal cession of the coveted territory. Politely but firmly he refused, with a warning that ' the Emperor was putting into his wardrobe garments which would not only quickly perish but would communicate the moth to his own garments.' The prophecy was fulfilled almost as soon as spoken. Marengo was fought and lost (June 14, 1800), and the Emperor Francis found himself bereft not only of the Legations but of all his Italian dominions besides. Under the circumstances he was graciously pleased to make the Pope a present of the former. But the victorious Bonaparte had naturally his own views as to that.

Master of Italy as a result of his victory at Marengo, Bonaparte showed himself anxious to do all he could to conciliate Catholic opinion. In his proclamations to the Italians he spoke respectfully of the Pope and the Church, and he was careful to explain that his former contemptuous language about such things in writing to the Directory must not be taken too seriously. He had only

used the language he thought his correspondents
would like. In France too, since becoming First
Consul, he had obtained the abrogation of the
laws restricting religious liberty. But the most
explicit declaration of his policy had been made
immediately before Marengo in a famous speech to
the assembled curés at Milan.

' Persuaded,' he remarked, ' that this religion [Catholicism] is
the only one which can produce a real happiness to a well-
ordered society and strengthen the bases of a government, I
assure you that I will apply myself to protect and defend
it at all times and by all means. I shall know how to punish
whosoever offers the slightest insult to our common religion.
. . . France has recalled it into her bosom. I cannot deny
that I have contributed largely to this excellent work. . . .
When I have an opportunity of conferring with the new Pope,
I hope I shall have the happiness of removing all obstacles
which might still stand in the way of the complete reconciliation of France with the Head of the Church.'

Such words were calculated to excite high hopes
in clerical bosoms. The situation was the more
promising because the new Pope was known to be
no bigoted reactionary, but had actually, in a
Christmas Day sermon preached while he was still
Bishop of Imola, spoken kind words of the democratic movement that proceeded from France. Soon
after his crushing victory over the Austrians Bonaparte expressed to the Pope through Cardinal
Martiniana, Bishop of Vercelli, ' his ardent desire
to effect a settlement of the ecclesiastical situation
of France,' at the same time outlining a scheme
which in its main essentials was identical with that
ultimately adopted (June 25, 1800). The Pope
was delighted with the First Consul's proposal to
negotiate, whatever he may have thought of his
terms. He appointed Mgr Spina, Archbishop of
Corinth *in partibus*, as his envoy. No doubt Cardinal Martiniana had hoped to fulfil the role of

intermediary himself, but, as the Abbé Maury
unkindly remarked, ' he had no head.' Without
delay Spina set out for Vercelli, which had been
fixed upon by Bonaparte as the place of rendezvous.
On reaching Florence, however, he found a letter
awaiting him to say that the First Consul had gone
to Paris, and bidding him follow him thither. Before
doing so, Spina felt it necessary to ask the Pope's
authorization. This was accorded: and he was
given Father Caselli, a learned theologian, to be
his companion and adviser in what might well
prove a risky venture.

Before giving some account of the protracted
and complicated negotiations which issued in the
famous Concordat of 1801, it may be well to define
the situation as it presented itself to each of
the contracting parties. Bonaparte, it must be
repeated, desired to make the Church the abettor
and instrument of his schemes of personal rule.
For this reason, it was necessary to keep it as
much under his control as possible. Now the control of the Church by the civil power had been
precisely the object of the promoters of the Constitution Civile. Thus, as a settlement of the problem
of Church and State, the Constitution Civile—or
something much like it—would suit the First Consul's turn very well. Moreover, it had the advantage of being actually at work, and it was regarded
as part of the revolutionary settlement, which he
had no desire to disturb—at least at this stage of
the proceedings. On the other hand, the Constitutional Church laboured under the immense dis-
advantage of being regarded by the Holy See as a
heretical and schismatical body—in fact as no
Church at all. This view was also that of the
French non-juring Catholics whom, even more
than the Constitutionals, Bonaparte wished to rally

to his cause. For him they were always the genuine Church. His aim therefore was simple— to secure the papal sanction for a settlement which was in its broad outlines that of the Constitution Civile, but with the important difference that it was no longer the people but himself who was to appoint to the chief ecclesiastical offices. Such a settlement might well rally Constitutionals and non-jurors alike—the former because the arrangements of the Constitution Civile were not discarded, the latter because these arrangements had been recognized and sanctioned by the Holy See.

But would the required sanction be given ? For the Pope the Constitution Civile was something ' impious,' had been indeed solemnly condemned as such by his predecessor. He would have much preferred that it should be ignored altogether and a return made to the ecclesiastical settlement of the *ancien régime* with all its drawbacks. Unfortunately Bonaparte decreed otherwise ; and, Bonaparte's position being what it was, the Pope could only make a virtue of necessity.

The situation, however, was not without its compensating circumstances—for the Papacy, if not for the cause of Catholicism in France. For what else was Bonaparte asking of the Pope but a tremendous act of spiritual absolutism ? Bonaparte himself summed up the situation in a celebrated phrase : ' If the Pope had not existed it would have been necessary to create him for the occasion.' In no other way could a spiritual sanction be provided for changes so drastic as those which the Revolution had made in the organization of the French Church. The bishops of the old régime had throughout declined absolutely to recognize those changes ; and those of them who still survived were not likely to resign in order that they might be perpetuated. Yet resign they must if Bonaparte's plans were to be carried out—either voluntarily or, failing this, under compulsion. Here only the Pope could help. He might ask them to resign, or if they still refused he might depose them.

This is precisely what the Pope, in the sequel, did. Such an assertion of the complete subordination of the episcopate to the Pope was calculated to rejoice the heart of an Ultramontane. No doubt this consideration helped to decide the Pope in favour of Bonaparte's wishes. Yet the awkward fact of a surrender to civil dictation remained, and first Spina and afterwards Consalvi did their utmost to limit the proportion of the dose. Their efforts, however, as we shall see, were not very successful.

As soon as Spina reached the French capital negotiations began. The First Consul's representative (or rather mouthpiece, for Bonaparte kept the negotiations strictly in his own hands) was the Abbé Bernier, a somewhat sinister personage who had played a leading part in the royalist movement in La Vendée but was now following enthusiastically in the wake of the rising star. Bonaparte had no illusions as to the character of his agent. ' I know,' he said, ' that he is a rogue, but I have need of him.' Working in the background, too, was Talleyrand, who, as a renegade bishop and the husband of Madame Grand, was hardly likely to be over-eager for the re-establishment of Catholicism in France. He himself claims in his *Memoirs* that he ' largely contributed to that result.' But Cardinal Mathieu suggests that if so it can only have been as the *advocatus diaboli* ' contributes ' to the canonization of a saint. Certainly his attitude throughout the negotiations was little calculated to conciliate Roman susceptibilities.

Frequent *tête-à-tête* consultations took place between Bernier and Spina at the latter's lodgings in the Hotel de Rome. The theological expert, Father Caselli, much to his chagrin, was not allowed to be present. The basis of the discussion was furnished by the proposals of Bonaparte which had been transmitted to the Pope through Cardinal Martiniana. The First Consul made five demands : (1) that all existing bishops should resign, and, if they refused, should be forcibly deposed ; (2) that the Church should renounce all claims to the ecclesiastical property that had been converted into *biens nationaux* ; (3) that the number of sees should be largely reduced ; (4) that the choice of bishops should be left in the hands of the French Government ; (5) that the clergy should be required to take an oath of loyalty to the Constitution of the Year VIII.

The terms were hard, and Spina struggled hard to obtain concessions. But Bonaparte was inflexible. The papal envoy had to give way on practically every point. At last, on November 26, 1800, a *projet de Concordat* was presented to him by Bernier with an intimation that the Government ' strongly desired its acceptance.' Spina, however, demanded certain modifications, whereupon a revised draft was presented which was in some ways even less favourable to the Church than the first. A third and a fourth draft followed, and on the appearance of the latter Spina was curtly told by Talleyrand that he must sign it immediately. Spina replied that the Pope had not empowered him to sign anything. Talleyrand merely repeated his demand, with threats if it was not complied with. In despair Spina then made a personal appeal to the First Consul. This was successful, and he was allowed to send a courier to Rome for advice before any decisive step was taken. Talleyrand, however, contrived to delay the courier, who only left on February 26, 1801, taking with him not the fourth but a fifth draft of the Concordat.

By this time, in order to hasten on the negotiations, Bonaparte had chosen someone to represent him at the Court of Rome—a certain very shrewd and honest diplomat called M. Cacault, who described himself as a *révolutionnaire corrigé.* He arrived in Rome on April 8th to find his master's draft under consideration. Bonaparte was urgent that a decision should be arrived at as soon as possible, as he desired to celebrate at the same time a peace with Austria and a peace with the Church. Anxious to oblige him, Rome displayed a quite unusual haste. ' We shall do more than walk,' wrote the Cardinal Secretary of State, ' we shall fly.' The effort was immense. ' Every word costs drops of blood,' complained the same writer.

The Pope and Cardinals found several modifications in the French Government's proposals necessary. These were embodied in an amended draft which was forwarded to Paris together with a letter to the First Consul. At the end of this the Pope declared that he ' had accorded all that conscience could permit.' ' We are bound to tell you that, whatever it may cost us, we absolutely can concede no more.'

The letter and the accompanying draft reached Paris on May 23rd. But it was too late. In the meantime Bonaparte's wrath had boiled over. On May 12th he had made Spina the victim of a terrible scene at Malmaison : and for the next week Talleyrand had bombarded the unfortunate prelate with a hotter and hotter fire of threats and reproaches. At last, on the 19th, the French Jove launched his thunderbolt. A letter was written by Talleyrand to Cacault which amounted to an ultimatum. After saying that the Court of Rome ' could do perfectly well what was required of it if it chose,' and that ' the Government was determined to have nothing less than its own way,' it went on : ' In consequence, citizen, I have the First Consul's formal order that your first step in regard to the Holy See must be to ask of it within five days a definite decision on the *projet de Concordat* and on that of the bull in which the convention is to be inserted.' If within that time the two drafts were adopted then all would be well : but if not, Cacault was to inform the Pope that ' his presence having become useless for the purpose of his mission,' he was setting out at once for Florence. As Florence was the head-quarters of General Murat, the meaning of this was fairly obvious.

The Papal Secretary of State at this time was the Cardinal Ercole Consalvi. This remarkable man, the foremost ecclesiastical diplomat of his age, had been Secretary of the Conclave which elected Pius VII. It was at his suggestion and by his skilful management that a three months' deadlock was terminated by the election of Cardinal Chiaramonti, who on becoming Pope insisted on making his supporter Cardinal-Deacon and Secretary of State. Confronted with the task of re-starting and reorganizing the whole machinery of administration after an interregnum of several years, Consalvi set himself to work with energy. But he had scarcely been the Pope's Prime Minister for more than a year when the negotiations concerning the Concordat began. After Cacault's arrival he and Consalvi had naturally to see much of one another, and, being both of them conciliatory and moderate men, they became excellent friends. The advantage of this was seen when the French Government's ultimatum arrived on May 28th. On being told of it by Cacault, the poor cardinal (who was ill in bed) was plunged into the utmost agitation. The Holy Father was not less perturbed. ' All is lost,' he exclaimed, ' if Cacault goes away.' He even discussed the possibility of taking refuge in Spain. In conversation with Cacault he urged that his letter to Bonaparte (which must have arrived by this) was bound to have altered the situation. Could he not remain ? Cacault could only reply that his instructions were absolute and irrevocable. On the other hand, the Pope's conscience forbade him to accept the draft as it stood.

The situation seemed desperate when Cacault came to the rescue. Let Consalvi, he suggested, go at once to Paris to conduct the negotiations in person. The cardinal (according to his own account) was by no means enthusiastic at the prospect, but consented to carry Cacault's suggestion to the Pope. The Holy Father received it favourably, and it was settled that Consalvi should start at once. Meanwhile the secret conferences between the French minister and the Quirinal had been the subject of much gossip. It was feared that the revolutionary malcontents at Rome might interpret Cacault's departure as a proof that a definite rupture had occurred and provoke an outbreak. Here again Cacault's tact suggested a way out. Consalvi and he would leave Rome in the same carriage and would travel together as far as Florence, where Cacault would remain while the cardinal pursued his way to Paris.

The suggestion was carried out. Consalvi reached Paris late at night on June 20th, and next morning solicited an audience with the First Consul. Bonaparte fixed the following day for this. It took

place at the Tuileries in the presence of the Ministers of State and the personages of the Court ' in
gala costume.'

Bonaparte told him that his former impression
of him as an ' enemy of France ' had been removed,
but at the same time expressed his inability to
accept the changes in the *projet de Concordat* that
had been suggested from Rome.   The cardinal, he
said, should be presented with another *projet* containing the only changes he could admit.   ' It is
absolutely essential that you should sign it within
five days.'   Consalvi protested in vain that he had
no power to accept any alteration in the substance
of the Pope's amended draft.   Bonaparte merely
repeated, ' You will sign within five days or the
whole negotiation will be broken off and I shall
adopt a national religion,' and dismissed the cardinal with a nod of the head.

The negotiations began at once, Bernier again
acting as Bonaparte's representative.   The discussions centred mainly round the first article of the
Concordat, defining the status of Catholicism in
France and the relation of the Government towards
it.   The Pope had originally desired that it should
be recognized as the State religion, but had accepted
instead Bonaparte's phrasing, ' the religion of the
great majority of Frenchmen.'   Certain more explicit guarantees, however, were demanded, including a formal profession of adherence to the Catholic
religion by the Government.   This stipulation not
being included in a seventh draft presented by
Bernier on June 25th, Consalvi, Spina, and Caselli
hastily set to work to draw up a counter-draft.
Talleyrand's only comment on the result of their
frantic labours was that ' it made things worse
than before.'   Fortunately the Minister for Foreign Affairs left Paris on June 30th to undergo a

cure at Bourbon.   After this the negotiations went
on more easily.

On July 2nd, in an interview with Consalvi at
Malmaison, Bonaparte explained his reasons for
objecting to any profession of Catholicism on the
part of either the Government or the Consuls,
while declaring that neither he nor they ' had ever
renounced the religion in which they were born.'
Consalvi replied that he must first consult the Pope
before signing what was required of him.   But this
Bonaparte refused to allow.   He also alluded sig-
nificantly to the National Council of the Constitutional Church which had assembled in Paris a
few days before, saying, ' When one cannot come
to terms with *le bon Dieu* one comes to terms with
the devil.'

Next day the negotiations with Bernier were
resumed.   At last the two parties seemed to have
reached an agreement as to Article 1, and a formula
was drawn up which was accepted on both sides.
The resulting draft was submitted to the First
Consul.   He refused to accept it as it stood and
demanded sundry modifications.   Consalvi, however, stuck to his guns and obtained important
concessions.   The Consuls (not the Government)
were to declare themselves Catholics, and the
Catholic worship was to be ' publicly ' exercised.
In regard to the latter, however, Bonaparte insisted on the addition of the words ' in conformity
with the *règlements de police* which the Government
shall deem necessary,' at the same time explaining
that this qualification was merely imposed ' in
view of the circumstances of the time,' and related
to ceremonies outside the churches only.   Consalvi
thereupon suggested that the formula should take
the following form.   ' Its worship shall be public,
in conformity however, in view of present circum-

stances, with the *règlements de police* which shall be
judged necessary for public safety.' This final
version was transmitted to the First Consul on
July 12th. Bonaparte did not reply and expressed
no opinion. But Bernier was informed that the
First Consul had appointed citizens Joseph Bonaparte, Cretet, and Bernier to sign an agreement
with Cardinal Consalvi, the Archbishop of Corinth,
and Father Caselli. The following day in the
Moniteur the following announcement appeared :
' M. le Cardinal Consalvi has been successful in
the mission to the Government with which he
had been entrusted by the Holy Father.'

What occurred at the subsequent meeting of
plenipotentiaries has been variously narrated. Consalvi in his well-known *Memoirs* has not hesitated
to charge the First Consul with a calculated act of
bare-faced fraud. According to him, the document presented to him *at the meeting itself* for
signature as a copy of the Concordat proved, when
he ran his eyes over it, to be not the agreement
decided on, but the original scheme of the French
Government rejected by the Pope. He therefore
refused to sign, and the negotiations had to be
begun all over again. But research in the Vatican
archives has considerably shaken belief in the
accuracy of the *Memoirs*. They were written by
the cardinal during his enforced exile at Reims in
1812, when their author was not in a very amic-
able mood towards his imperial persecutor. For
many years they remained unpublished. When at
length in 1864 they were given to the world under
Crétineau-Joly's freely-interpreted editorship, their
damaging presentation of the First Napoleon was
eagerly seized upon by the enemies of the Third.
But even at that time their accuracy was impugned, and the researches of Count Boulay de la

Meurthe and others have abundantly justified this scepticism.

The despatches written by Consalvi to Cardinal Doria immediately after the event are still extant, so that it is possible to arraign the Cardinal Secretary of State as a witness against himself. Whether he deliberately falsified the facts or was merely the victim of a bad memory we shall not attempt to decide. In any case the actual facts in the present instance are now known to have been as follows.

On July 13th, Consalvi received from Bernier a letter intimating that he and his co-signatories were authorized to sign the Concordat. At 5 p.m. the same afternoon (i.e. three hours before the time fixed for his meeting with Bonaparte's plenipotentiaries), he received a second communication enclosing the *projet* that was to be signed. On examining it he found that it was an entirely new draft. Among other changes, the concession made as to the profession of Catholicism by the Consuls was withdrawn and the clause regarding ' publicity of worship ' was maintained in the form originally suggested by Bonaparte. Thus the *Memoirs* are right in stating that a new draft was substituted at the last moment, but they are wrong in alleging that there was any deliberate sharp practice. The explanation indeed was simple. Talleyrand, whose ' cure ' for rheumatism had not prevented him from following closely the course of events, had intervened at the eleventh hour to thwart what he considered an excessive complaisance on his master's part.

Under the circumstances, Consalvi did the only possible thing and wrote to Bernier to express his surprise and to demand the execution of the terms which had been agreed upon. At eight o'clock that evening the four negotiators met at Joseph

Bonaparte's *hôtel*. The points in dispute were once more fought over one by one. For twenty hours a *guerra terribile* raged. In the end Consalvi once more succeeded in extracting important concessions. The Catholicism of the Consuls was admitted, and publicity of worship was to be ' in conformity with the *règlements de police* which the circumstances of the present time necessitate.' When agreement had at length been reached, Consalvi insisted that the French plenipotentiaries should sign the new draft. They pleaded that they dared not do so without consulting Bonaparte first. Having gone to the Tuileries for this purpose they soon returned with rueful countenances. Bonaparte had flown into a passion and thrown the draft into the fire. '*Je veux mon texte,*' he cried, ' *ou c'est fini.*' He also told Joseph to inform the Pope's envoys that if they did not sign they might go away.

It was now 2 p.m. and at 5 Consalvi was due to attend a banquet at the Tuileries in honour of the *Fête Nationale,* at the end of which it had been intended to announce the successful conclusion of the Concordat. Between two and four o'clock Bernier and Joseph Bonaparte strained every nerve to induce Consalvi to submit : but all was unsuccessful and Consalvi went to the banquet undefeated. In the *Memoirs* Consalvi says that the moment he entered the room Bonaparte exclaimed loudly, ' Ah, M. le Cardinal, you have chosen a rupture, be it so.' This is not borne out by his despatch to Cardinal Doria in which he says that Bonaparte ' welcomed him politely.' However, there seems to have been a scene of some kind, and the furious tirade which the *Memoirs* attribute to Bonaparte is perhaps only a little exaggerated. ' I will act by myself : I have no need of the Pope.

If Henry VIII, who had not a twentieth part of my
power, was able to change the religion of his country, much more can and will I.   In changing the
religion of France, I will change it in almost the
whole of Europe, everywhere where my power
extends.'   Then, turning to the Prime Minister of
Austria, Cobentzel, who was standing by, he said,
' I take you as judge.'   ' Accepted,' said Consalvi
promptly : and at once began to explain his case to
Cobentzel.   Dinner interrupted their conversation,
but afterwards Cobentzel said he thought he had
found a satisfactory formula.   Neither Consalvi
nor Bonaparte objected to this, and the latter
consented to the holding of a final conference.

This conference began at noon on July 15th, and
lasted till midnight.   The discussion was again
concentrated on Article 1.   After much argument
Consalvi obtained the addition of the words *pour
la tranquillité publique* to the phrase *en se conform-
ant aux règlements de police*.   When agreement
on this and another article had been reached the
cardinal again proposed that the agreement
should be signed immediately.   With some hesitation Joseph agreed, and next day the First Consul
gave his approval.

In view of its importance and the prolonged discussions concerning it, it may be advisable to
insert here the final form assumed by the first
Article, together with the preamble before it :

The Government of the French republic recognizes that the
Catholic, Apostolic, and Roman religion is the religion of the
great majority of Frenchmen.

His Holiness recognizes likewise that this same religion has
drawn, and still expects at this moment, the greatest advantage and *éclat* from the establishment of the Catholic religion
in France and from the personal (*particulière*) profession of it
made by the Consuls of the Republic.

In consequence . . . they have agreed as follows :

Art. i.   The Catholic . . . religion shall be freely exercised
in France and its worship shall be public in conformity with
the *règlements de police* that the Government shall deem necessary for public tranquillity.

In addition to the first Article the chief provisions of the Concordat were the following.   The
Holy See, in concert with the Government, was to
make a new delimitation of dioceses (2).   The
Pope was to ask the existing holders of sees to
resign ' for the sake of peace and unity.'   If they
refused their places were to be filled up all the same
(3).   As regards the appointment to vacant sees—
both now and after—the First Consul was to
nominate within three months, the Pope giving
canonical institution according to the ancient forms
(4 and 5).   Before assuming office the bishops
were to take a simple oath of fidelity to the Government (6).   The right of nominating to parishes
was secured to the bishops, who must however
appoint persons approved of by the Government
(10).   The Pope undertook that neither he nor his
successors would trouble in any way the occupants
of alienated ecclesiastical property (13).   A suitable income was guaranteed to bishops and curés
(14).   The First Consul was to enjoy the same
rights and privileges in regard to the Holy See as
the pre-revolutionary Government (16).

Four days later (July 20th) Bonaparte received
Consalvi, who once more experienced a very disagreeable surprise.   Bonaparte announced to him
his intention of including several Constitutional
clergy among the new bishops.   ' But, General,'
remonstrated Consalvi, ' the Concordat did not
speak of the *intrus*.   There has been drawn up
in your name, an official note affirming that they
are not included under the term *évêques titulaires*
and, moreover, Cardinal Martiniana formally de-

clared to us that you would not take them into
account.' ' Doubtless,' replied Bonaparte, ' but
that was before the agreement : now that it is
signed I intend that they shall profit by it. What
must they do ? ' ' Retract,' replied Consalvi.
' Retract, M. le Cardinal, never will I ask that
of them. A man who retracts is a man dis-
honoured. You must arrange for them to return
to the Church without retracting.'

By Bonaparte's orders the six plenipotentiaries
held a conference to settle this and certain other
points. Consalvi would make no promises. He
merely undertook to bring the matter before the Pope
when he got back to Rome. He paid his farewell
visit to the First Consul on July 24th, but Bonaparte declined to address any remark to him. He
left Paris next evening, arriving in Rome on August
7th. The text of the Concordat had preceded
him, and was still under consideration by the Pope
and Cardinals when Consalvi reached Rome. He
was considerably nettled by the criticisms to which
his handiwork was being subjected in curial circles.
' They talk *bien à leur aise,*' he acidly remarked,
' but if they had been in my place, they would have
signed more readily than I.' On the other hand,
he had the satisfaction of knowing that the Pope
was veering more and more towards his point of
view. The terms of the Concordat were formally
brought before the Sacred College on August 11th,
the Pope presiding. Two articles only were called
in question—the much discussed first and the
thirteenth, which recognized the rights of those
who had purchased Church property. But in each
case a majority approved, and the Pope concurred.
The papal ratification was therefore accorded, and
a bull was drawn up (on lines laid down by the
French Government) announcing the Concordat

to the Catholic world (August 15, 1801). At the same time it was agreed that in accordance with Bonaparte's request a papal legate should be sent at once to Paris, and—again at Bonaparte's desire —Cardinal Caprara was appointed to the post.

The courier bearing the ratification and the bull reached Paris on August 27th, and on September 8th the First Consul affixed an imposing signature to the Government's act of ratification. This was carried back to Rome by the same courier. It had been expected that he would also bring the news of the official publication of the Concordat. But by this time Bonaparte had changed his mind. He was no longer anxious for a speedy publication, and began to make difficulties. The fact was that he had not yet had his pound of flesh.

The setting up of the new ecclesiastical organization had been taken in hand immediately after the signing of the Concordat. The first step was to get rid of the existing bishops : the second to appoint new ones. The former was quickly effected. As regards the Constitutional bishops the Pope had evinced a strong repugnance to addressing them directly. It was therefore permitted that he should demand their submission and resignation indirectly through Spina. The bishops in question were at first inclined to make objections : but a little pressure from Bonaparte soon brought them to heel. A second brief to Spina authorized the reconciliation, on terms, of priests who had married. To the non-juring bishops the Pope addressed a brief, gracious and affectionate in tone, in which he asked them to make the ' sacrifice ' of their sees ' for the preservation of unity.' But at the same time they were informed that if they did not do so—and at once— the Holy Father would ' have to resort to the necessary measures for removing all obstacles and assuring the good of religion '—in plain words, to depose them.

Those of the non-juring bishops who were in France and Italy obeyed, with a few exceptions, immediately. Those who had taken refuge in England or Germany were less amenable. A few of them did what they were asked : but the majority of them respectfully but firmly declined. The total number of refusals was thirty-eight. The Pope was thus forced on November 29, 1801, to issue the Bull *Qui Christi Domini vices* suppressing the one hundred and thirty-five sees of pre-revolutionary France and by implication therefore decreeing the deposition of their former occupants.

The effect of this recalcitrance was to call into existence the so-called *Petite Église*—a body which is even yet not completely extinct, though for a century it has had no bishop and for over eighty years no priest. The non-Concordatist bishops indeed remained in dignified and secure aloofness in their countries of exile until the Restoration, the majority of them not even refusing to give a provisory consent to their successors' exercise of authority. But in various parts of France—and notably at Lyons—small groups of unbending priests and layfolk pursued their religious existence apart, disdaining the churches and sacraments of the Concordatist Church and quite convinced that they were ' the only Catholics in the world.'

The filling of the vacant dioceses proved to be a more delicate matter. As his conversation with Consalvi had indicated clearly enough, Bonaparte insisted that members of the Constitutional clergy should be included among his nominees. The Pope would, of course, have preferred that they should be left out altogether : but if they must be included, he told Caprara to insist on their making a formal act of submission to the Holy See, and of repudiation of their previous position. To this Bonaparte objected. The acceptance of the Concordat should suffice.

The issue was raised immediately on Caprara's arrival in Paris. There could be little doubt as to the result. For a trial of strength with such a man as Bonaparte, Caprara was almost comically inadequate. His conduct throughout the negotiation betrays the strangest mixture of timorousness and complacency. In his despatches to Rome he repeats fatuously over and over again, ' The Pope must have confidence in me.' Yet he yields point after point. The pressure upon him was ceaseless—both from Bonaparte's underlings and (now and again) from the First Consul himself. At an interview at Malmaison the latter expressed himself with such violence concerning the Holy See that the poor old cardinal went away with his nerves quite shaken. On March 30, 1802, Bonaparte definitely informed Caprara of his intention to appoint ten Constitutionals among the new bishops. Caprara protested in vain, then declared that he would at least insist on the rigid performance of the conditions laid down by the Pope. On April 9th he was received by the First Consul in solemn audience. Next day the *Moniteur* inserted a form of oath which he was said to have signed, to the effect that he would ' observe the laws of the Republic ' and respect ' the liberties of the Gallican Church.' He himself, however, declared that he had *signed* nothing and that the oath tendered to him contained no mention of the Gallican liberties. Soon afterwards the nomination of twenty-two bishops was published, ten being Constitutionals. Caprara consented to institute them, but only on condition that they made a formal act of submission to the Holy See in terms which the cardinal legate himself was to prescribe. The bishops, however, refused to sign Caprara's formula. Once again Caprara, threatened with the non-publication of the Concordat as the alternative, gave in : merely entrusting Bernier, now Bishop-designate of Orléans, and the new Bishop of Vannes with the duty of bringing the bishops in question to a better mind. A few hours afterwards they announced that their brethren had ' given satisfaction ' and ' would abjure their schism and past errors.' A little later, however, the former Constitutionals denied having made any retractation at all! The Pope thereupon declined to grant their bulls of institution.

Whether they lied or Caprara's informants is a disputed question. In any case the chief obstacle in the way of the publication of the Concordat was now removed, and on Easter Day (April 18th) a solemn *Te Deum* was sung in Notre Dame, in joint celebration of the peace with England and the peace with the Church. Bonaparte was present, accompanied by his generals and the various *corps d'État*, whose attendance had been engineered by means of an ingenious if not very dignified trick.

The behaviour of the distinguished assembly, it was remarked, was not such as to suggest the impression that the new religious settlement was taken very seriously in the most important circles. The Corps Législatif indeed had received the Concordat, when presented for their sanction, with icy indifference : and its reception would have been less friendly still if it had not been accompanied by the notorious *Articles Organiques* which now first made their appearance.

For what Bonaparte had given with one hand he took away with the other. The concessions of the Concordat were made largely nugatory by the Organic Articles, the effect of which was to bind the yoke of the State more tightly than ever upon the neck of the Church. No written communications from the Pope of any kind whatever might be received in France without the authorization of the Government. His legates and representatives must receive the same authorization. The decrees of foreign synods, and even of General Councils, might not be published in France until the Government had examined and approved them. No Council—national, metropolitan, or diocesan— might assemble without the Government's permission. In the case of any abuse of their powers by ecclesiastical persons, recourse was to be had to the Council of State. Professors of seminaries were to teach the ' Gallican Articles ' of 1682. . . . No wonder Bonaparte had kept this halter up his sleeve, producing it only when the horse was caught and the Concordat an accomplished fact !

CHAPTER VI

THE BREACH WITH THE PAPACY
1802–09

THE brief honeymoon period which followed the conclusion of the Concordat was marked by an interchange of favours on both sides. The Pope allowed the First Consul to nominate five new French cardinals. The right of the Bourbon sovereigns to appoint *Cardinaux de Couronne* was thus revived in favour of the Consular Government, and Bonaparte found himself placed on the same footing as the old monarchies of Europe. The Pope also gave an unwilling consent to the First Consul's request that the obliging Caprara (now Archbishop of Milan as well as Legate) should be deputed to negotiate a Concordat for Italy. On his side, Bonaparte restored Ancona and Pesaro to the Pope, induced Naples to restore Benevento and Ponte Corvo, and allowed the Holy Father to appoint the Grand Master of the Knights of Malta. These mutual good offices were the more cheerfully rendered in that each party had an eye to favours to come. Bonaparte had already conceived the idea of setting up the Empire, and hoped to enlist the help of the Holy Father as an accomplice—or at least an accessory after the fact—by inducing him to come to Paris and crown in person the new Charlemagne. The Pope for his part was profoundly dissatisfied with the Organic Articles, but was not without hopes that his personal influence

79

with the ruler of France might induce the First Consul to withdraw or at any rate modify some of their most offensive provisions.

One of Bonaparte's first acts after the conclusion of the Concordat was to recall M. Cacault from Rome. The frank speech and unobsequious manner of the old diplomat (as of an equal to an equal) had begun to jar on his nerves. Cacault had already expressed himself bluntly about his master's ambition to be (as he put it) ' a sort of Henry VIII.' Bonaparte's imperial designs were certain to find his representative more critical still. Besides, the First Consul wanted to be represented at Rome by a personage of importance, who might revive the glories of the French Embassy in the days of Cardinal de Bernis, the last ambassador of the old régime. Fortunately the Sacred College already included a member of his own family—his mother's brother, Cardinal Joseph Fesch. To him therefore was entrusted the task of representing French interests at the Court of Rome.

Fesch's previous career had been sufficiently varied. Archdeacon of Ajaccio before 1789, he had embraced the principles of the Revolution and had acted as an official of the commissariat department in the army of Italy when it was under the command of his nephew. After the *coup d'état* of Brumaire he returned to the duties of the ecclesiastical state, and was appointed by Bonaparte to be Archbishop of Lyons. As commissary of war his way of living, it would seem, had not been untinged by the free and easy manners of the camp, but in his new situation he was careful to observe the rules of decency and decorum. He was made cardinal after the conclusion of the Concordat. His character was that of a man honest and well-meaning enough, but inordinately vain and not conspicuously endowed with intelligence. He was also more than ordinarily deficient in the diplomat's essential quality of tact. ' Go and be tactful,' was Bonaparte's parting word to him, but this was easier said than done.

It was probably with a view to supplementing his uncle's mental deficiencies that Bonaparte appointed as his Secretary of Embassy the brilliant young Vicomte de Chateaubriand, who had just sprung into fame with the *Génie du Christianisme*. Actually, however, no partnership could have been more disastrous. Between the respective abilities of Fesch and Chateaubriand there could be no comparison, but in the matter of vanity they were very equally matched. The result was that Chateaubriand despised Fesch, while Fesch was jealous of Chateaubriand. The secretary had entered upon his duties fully convinced that he would be able to conduct the affairs of the Embassy after his own fashion, and allowed himself a corresponding latitude of action. Fesch, however, had no mind to be treated as a mere figurehead. Soon a continuous stream of complaints about the conduct of the secretary began to pour towards the Foreign Office at Paris, while Chateaubriand confidentially informed the First Consul that his ambassador was not up to the level of his duties, and in a letter to his friend Fontanes referred to his chief as *notre imbécile*. The situation rapidly became so unpleasant that Chateaubriand asked to be relieved of his post. He was appointed Minister in the Valais and quitted Rome, to the infinite relief of Fesch, who was now free to make his own mistakes in his own way.

Fesch's first difficulties at Rome were concerned with Bonaparte's demand for the extradition of M. de Vernègues, a royalist *émigré*. Rome would

have liked to refuse, and pleaded that Vernègues
was really a Russian subject.   But a threatening
note from Talleyrand made it clear that she would
do well to give in : and the news of the murder of
the Duc d'Enghien drove the lesson home. The
Pope wept in conversing with Fesch about the fate
of that unfortunate prince. But he conceded the
extradition of Vernègues.

Having thus reduced the Pope (as he hoped) to
a sufficiently complaisant state of mind, Napoleon
now began to broach the question of the coronation.
A week before the passing of the *senatus consultum*
establishing the Empire (May, 1804) he suggested
to Caprara that as Pope Zacharias had come to
France to crown Pepin the Short, so Pius VII
should come to Paris to hallow the new Emperor
of the West, the founder of the latest French
dynasty.   It is hardly necessary to add that in
transmitting this request Caprara gave it his cordial
support.

The suggestion was not received very enthusiastically at Rome.   No doubt the habitual caution
of the curia hesitated to commit itself so deeply
in regard to what must still have seemed a hazard-
ous political experiment. And in any case the Pope
did not wish to appear too palpably dragged behind
Napoleon's triumphal car. Already his critics
were dubbing him ' Chaplain of the Emperor.'
Consalvi therefore pointed out in his reply that the
step suggested could not be entertained unless
' some interest of religion ' was to be served by it.
This point must be brought out in the letter of
invitation.   He also indicated various points on
which the Pope desired concessions to be made by
the French Government.

The receipt of this reply threw Caprara into despair. But his anguish was unnecessary. The Qui-

rinal was not prepared to insist on strict engagements, any more than Bonaparte was prepared to
give them. On the strength of a few vague promises the Pope—with the rather hesitating assent
of the Sacred College—declared his willingness to
fall in with the Emperor's wishes. Maury at once
protested on behalf of Louis XVIII. But this did
not prevent the same writer from inditing, a month
later, a letter breathing fervent devotion to the new
monarch of France.

The Pope left Rome on November 2, 1804, with
six cardinals in attendance. He had rather feared
that when he reached French soil, the unspent fires
of the anti-Catholic fury of the Revolution might
blaze out in hostile demonstrations against him.
But on this point he was agreeably surprised.
Everywhere he went—and notably at Lyons—he
was received with great popular enthusiasm.

His meeting with the Emperor in the Forest of
Fontainebleau (November 25th) is historic. The
worst side of Napoleon's character—the mingled
arrogance and self-mistrust of the parvenu—was
never more in evidence than on this occasion. His
one haunting fear was lest he should seem to con-
fess himself the inferior of any one in the world—
even of the Vicar of Christ. For this reason there
must be no official reception, but a meeting, as it
were, casual and accidental in the course of a
hunting-party. So too when, after embracing,
the two potentates entered the carriage to proceed
on their journey to Paris, they must enter simultaneously at opposite doors.

On the other hand, the Pope had no cause to
complain of the splendour of the preparations made
for him. He was magnificently lodged at the
Tuileries in a suite of rooms which were arranged
as a close replica of his private apartments in

Rome. The Emperor and the Imperial family lavished marks of graciousness upon him, and he had frequent opportunities of intimate conversation with the former.

Immediately before the coronation Josephine came to him and confessed that she and her husband had never been married by a priest. The Pope at once declared that he could not crown either of them unless they had first received the Church's benediction on their union. When he was informed of this the Emperor flew into a passion, but unwilling to face a hitch at the eleventh hour, he gave his consent. The imperial couple were therefore married at 4 p.m. on December 1st in the private chapel of the Tuileries by Cardinal Fesch. Napoleon, however, refused to allow the presence either of witnesses or of the curé of the parish. In this way he meant to leave the door open for a questioning of the validity of his marriage with Josephine, should a divorce appear to him at any time to be desirable.

The coronation took place at Notre Dame next day (December 2, 1804). The Emperor promised to ' observe the law, justice, and peace for the Church as for his people,' and ' to see that its Pontiffs enjoyed the respect and the honour due to them.' The Pope then proceeded to anoint the Emperor and his spouse, after which he invested the former with the various ornaments comprising the imperial regalia. The crown itself, however, was not to come from his hand—so Napoleon had at the last moment decreed, determined to give no handle to any possible assertion in future that it was the Pope who had invested him with the imperial dignity. Taking the crown from the altar the new Emperor placed it upon his head himself. He then took the other crown and placed it on the head of Josephine.

After the coronation, the Pope remained in Paris for some months longer. Napoleon never failed to be cordial and charming, but he declined to commit himself to anything beyond vague promises as to the points on which the Pope desired satisfaction. When Cardinal Antonelli, at the Pope's request, drew up a memorandum summarizing the papal demands, which included the restitution of the Legations, Talleyrand's talent for saying something while meaning nothing was brought into play. ' If God,' he wrote, ' accords to the Emperor the duration of life common to all men, he hopes to discover circumstances in which it will be possible for him to improve and extend the dominions of the Holy Father. On all occasions he will give him his assistance and support.' The Pope's other demands met with no better success. The Government declined to suppress divorce or to reimpose the old laws for the observance of Sundays and holidays. The obligation to teach the Gallican Articles of 1682 was retained, and no change was made in the Organic Articles. On the other hand, the Pope received the heartiest welcome from the faithful in Paris, and he had the joy of securing by his personal action the submission of those Constitutional bishops who had declined to give satisfaction in 1801. With these sources of gratification he had perforce to be content. He left the French capital on April 4, 1805, reaching Rome on May 16th. He had gained nothing of what he sought, while Napoleon had gained everything. The prestige of the Papacy had been impaired—and for no result. Joseph de Maistre, from his Sardinian embassy at St. Petersburg, did not spare him. ' The crimes of Alexander Borgia,' he wrote, ' are less revolting than this hideous apostasy of his feeble successor.'

Napoleon was not long in following the Pope to Italy. On May 8, 1805, he arrived at Milan, and on the 26th of the same month he assumed the Iron Crown of Italy with the proud traditional words of the Lombard Kings, ' God has given it me. Woe to him who touches it.' Soon afterwards he issued a decree for the reorganization of the Church in Italy. The terms of this decree were criticized by the Pope. The Emperor made the blunt reply : ' I have sometimes told your Holiness that the Court of Rome is too slow-moving and follows a policy which though good in other ages is no longer adapted to the age in which we live.' None the less he gave hopes of some modifications in the terms of the decree. This made the Pope more content —the more so as the Catholic religion had been recognized as *réligion d'État* in the Italian Concordat, which it had not been in the French.

Unfortunately at this moment a subject of dispute arose which, touching as it did Napoleon's dynastic schemes, was to exacerbate considerably the relations between the French Government and the Papacy. The Emperor's brother, Jerome Bonaparte, had married at Baltimore, U.S.A. (December 24, 1803), a Miss Elizabeth Patterson— daughter of a merchant of that city. Such a mésalliance was a severe blow to the soaring ambition of the Bonaparte family, who sought to have it annulled. So far as the annulling of the civil contract went, no difficulty arose. Jerome being a member of the imperial house, the Emperor had the power to effect this on his own authority. But Napoleon wanted more. He desired the annulling of the religious marriage—for which purpose he asked the Pope to grant a bull. The Pope, after a careful consideration of the facts of the case, replied that ' of all

the motives which have been put forward there
is not one which permits us to content your
Majesty by declaring the nullity of the said marriage.' Napoleon was much annoyed by this reply,
but had to be satisfied with a decree of nullity issued
later on by the Diocesan Officiality of Paris (October 6, 1806). On the strength of this Jerome married Princess Frederika, daughter of the King of
Wurtemberg (August 22, 1807). The fact that the
princess was a Protestant provided an amusing
comment on the ground of ' disparity of religion '
alleged by Napoleon as a reason for the dissolution
of the previous marriage.

Disappointed by the Pope in this matter, Napoleon vented his spite by ordering General Gouvion
St. Cyr to seize Ancona on the pretext that it needed
security against an English attack (October, 1805).
Pius VII at once made a strong protest and demanded the evacuation of the town. To this protest Napoleon did not trouble to reply until after the
victories of Austerlitz and Friedland had put all
Europe at his feet. His answer (dated January 7,
1806) was an implied charge that the Pope had made
common cause with his enemies. He added, ' I
shall be the friend of your Holiness whenever you
consult merely your own heart and the true friends
of religion.' This letter was accompanied by one still
more insulting addressed to Cardinal Fesch, which
he bade his ambassador read in the presence of the
curia. ' I am religious, *mais je ne suis pas cagot.*
. . . Constantine separated the civil from the
military power, and I too can nominate a senator to
command in my name at Rome.' He called the
cardinals ' imbeciles,' and said, ' For the Pope, I
am Charlemagne.'

To all this the Pope sent a mild and conciliatory
reply, defending himself against the Emperor's

charges. Napoleon, however, refused to accept his explanations. The truth was that he bitterly resented the existence in the heart of his dominions of a single independent principality which refused to fall into line with his continental policy. Meanwhile Fesch was sending inflammatory reports to Paris. He had quarrelled with Consalvi and did all he could to blacken his enemy's character with the Emperor.

At last, on February 13th, Napoleon wrote to the Pope : ' My conditions must be that your Holiness shall have for me in temporal matters the same consideration that I have for you in spiritual matters. . . . Your Holiness is sovereign of Rome, but I am its Emperor. All my enemies must be yours.' He demanded the instant expulsion from the papal states of all English, Russian, and Swedish subjects, and of all persons attached to the Court of Sardinia, together with the closing of the papal ports.

The Pope replied (March 21, 1806) that he could not do what was required of him. As the common father of the faithful he must live at peace with all. In reply to Napoleon's claim to be Emperor of Rome he boldly asserted that 'the Sovereign Pontiff neither recognizes nor has ever recognized in his state a power superior to his own,' and that ' no Emperor has any rights over Rome.' Such language was not likely to appease the wrath of the Emperor, especially as Fesch was all the time diligently fomenting it. He accused Consalvi of being in league with the British Minister to Sardinia, Mr. Jackson. Napoleon demanded that Jackson should be arrested and that Consalvi should resign. He was by now fully determined to take the most drastic measures if he could not otherwise have his way, and to facilitate these he recalled Cardinal Fesch from Rome (April 18th) and put in his place M. Alquier, an ex-revolutionary and regicide who was at the time of his appointment ambassador to the Court of Naples. He could scarcely with decency make a Prince of the Church the agent of the measures which were before long to horrify the Catholic world. Nor (to do Fesch justice) was the Cardinal prepared to go all lengths.

As a warning to the Pope of what he might do if he chose, he occupied Civita Vecchia (May 6th) and made a grant of the duchy of Benevento to Talleyrand and of Ponte Corvo to Bernadotte. Consalvi now became thoroughly nervous, and in the hope of placating the Emperor, resigned the post of Secretary of State (June 17th). He had several times offered to do so already, but the Pope had refused his consent. Now, however, stung by the charge that he was Consalvi's *fantoccino*, the Holy Father waived his opposition. But so far from being conciliated by this step, Napoleon merely increased his exigencies. He again demanded the closing of the papal ports to English vessels. The Pope again refused. It was, he said, ' a matter of conscience ; and in that nothing can be got from us.' Even Alquier was impressed by the Pope's resolution, and wrote to his master urging moderation. But Napoleon's temper was up. He now began seriously to threaten to take away the temporal power. ' I will respect the Pope always as Head of the Church. But there is no necessity that the Pope should be sovereign of Rome. I will put at Rome a king or a senator and will divide his state into duchies.'

By this time the quarrel had been further complicated and embittered by a new subject of dispute, which was to assume growing importance as time went on. Certain episcopal sees had fallen vacant in the north of Italy, and Napoleon had appointed the persons who were to fill them. The Pope, however, refused to grant canonical institution, alleging the failure of the Emperor to fulfil the conditions of the Italian Concordat (September, 1806). At the same time, in his desire to meet the Emperor half-way, he suggested to the Viceroy of Italy, Eugène Beauharnais, that, though he could not accept the Emperor's nomination, he was willing on his own motion to appoint the Emperor's nominees. This failed to satisfy Napoleon, who, in a letter written from Dresden (July 22, 1807), indulged in violent and haughty language against the Pope.

Still anxious to be conciliatory, the Pope sent Cardinal de Bayane to Paris to arrange a settlement, having been given to understand that the choice of this negotiator would be that most acceptable to the Emperor. But while he was on his way, Napoleon suddenly ordered the occupation of a further slice of the Pope's dominions (September, 1807) and the detention of the cardinal at Milan, pending proof that his powers were really plenary : saying at the same time that the Pope must come into the system of France or he would appeal to a General Council. Pius at once recalled de Bayane—an act of defiance to which Napoleon replied by ordering General Miollis to march on Rome.

The order was immediately carried out. On the Feast of the Purification, February 2, 1808, while the Pope was celebrating High Mass in the Quirinal Chapel in the presence of the Sacred College, Miollis seized the Castle of S. Angelo and surrounded the Quirinal. The Pope ordered a protest to be placarded the same night on the walls of Rome and addressed a formal complaint to the members of the Corps Diplomatique. The Emperor now re-called Alquier and gave orders that the papal states should be divided into two governments. On February 25th the Pope addressed a note to the Emperor in which he vindicated himself from the charge of plotting against the Empire, and at the same time declared that he would entertain no negotiations so long as the occupation of Rome lasted. Napoleon paid no attention. His temper was roused : he was now fairly launched on the path of violence. He ordered the expulsion from Rome of the Neapolitan Cardinals and of those who were his own subjects, whether as Emperor or King of Italy. He gave elaborate instructions for the organization of the papal states into prefectures and sub-prefectures. When fifteen cardinals re-fused to leave Rome at Miollis' request, they were removed by force.

Pius renewed his protests and entreaties again and again. But it was all in vain—the Emperor only proceeded to worse extremities. The Ponti-fical Guard was disarmed, and on April 2nd he declared the provinces of Urbino, Ancona, Macera-ta, and Camerino annexed to the Kingdom of Italy on the explicit ground that ' the Pope had constantly refused to make war on the English.' The Pope made an elaborate reply to Napoleon's charges and rehearsed his own grievances. The Emperor still paid no attention. By his command the Noble Guard was disarmed and a number of the Pope's officers arrested. He also ordered the formation in the papal states of civic guards who were to wear the tricolour cockade.

The Pope then took a somewhat extreme step. On May 23rd he issued an instruction to the bishops of the recently annexed provinces forbid-ding his subjects to take any oath of fidelity and obedience to the usurping Government under pain of incurring the guilt of sacrilege, or to accept any employment which would involve organizing or consolidating its power. At the most, they might swear not to take part in any conspiracy against the Government, and to be subject to it in all that was not contrary to the laws of God and of the Church. To this proceeding Miollis retorted by a step still more extreme. By his orders (June 11th) two officers entered into the apartments of the Cardinal Secretary of State (Gabrielli), searched his papers and ordered him to retire within two days to his bishopric of Sinigaglia. The Pope was deeply incensed, and at once appointed Cardinal Pacca to the vacant post. The first act of the new Secretary was to make a protest against the unlawful arrests made in the papal states. Cardinal Fesch also ventured to interfere with his terrible nephew on the Pope's behalf, but was severely snubbed for his pains. When he warned the Emperor of the possible effect of his policy on the destinies of the Empire, Napoleon recommended him to take ' cold baths ' as the best remedy for terrors so imaginary. Miollis soon wearied of the reiterated protests of Pacca, and decided to get rid of him too. On September 6th an officer came to order him to depart immediately to his native place under escort. The Pope, informed of this, at once descended to the Secretary's apartments. 'I command,' he said, 'my Ministers not to obey the orders of an unlawful authority, and to follow me into my apartment to share my captivity.' With these words he led Pacca away. Miollis retorted by ordering more arrests, including that of Cardinal Antonelli, Dean of the Sacred College.

For the time being Napoleon's preoccupation with the revolt in Spain prevented him from taking further decisive action in regard to the Pope. But his wrath continued to rise. In the early months of 1809 he was only waiting for the successful issue of his new campaign against Austria to launch a final blow. Having entered Vienna, he signed (May 17, 1809) in the imperial camp outside that city the decrees which incorporated the papal states in the French Empire, declared Rome an imperial free town, and assigned to the Pope an annual income of two million francs. The decrees also alleged that the union of the spiritual and the temporal power had been a source of continuous discord, and that the circumstances allowed of no alternative to the course that was being taken.

A copy of these decrees was posted in Rome on June 11, 1809. The same day the Pope's reply appeared in the form of a Bull of Excommunication. This bull had been kept in readiness for some time, and now made its appearance upon the walls of the principal Roman churches. Its terms were as follows :

> By the authority of God Almighty, by that of the Holy Apostles Peter and Paul, and by our own, we declare that all those who since the invasion of Rome and of the territory of the Church . . . have committed acts of violence (*attentats*) against the ecclesiastical immunities and against the temporal rights of the Church and the Holy See—all their agents, fautors, counsellors, or adherents—all those who have facilitated the execution of these violences and have executed them themselves—have incurred the greater excommunication and other ecclesiastical pains and censures inflicted by the sacred canons, and . . . we excommunicate and anathematize them afresh, declaring them deprived of all privileges and indults.

The Pope also, by a brief dated June 12th, sent an official intimation of his excommunication to the Emperor, declaring that ' Napoleon I and all his adherents, fautors, and counsellors have incurred excommunication.'

This brief is important in view of Napoleon's repeated assertion that he himself was not touched by the excommunication, and of the pronouncement made to the same effect by his Minister of Religions, M. Bigot de Préameneu, after an examination of the terms of the bull, undertaken at the Emperor's request. Napoleon indeed was by no means so indifferent to the spiritual censures of the Vicar of Christ as he thought fit to pretend. It is unlikely indeed that he himself ascribed much virtue or importance to pains and penalties of a spiritual kind. But if he did not believe in them, other people would. His motives in concluding the Concordat showed what political importance he attached to a correct status in the eyes of the Catholic world. And equally his action during the years that followed exhibits a keen desire not to allow this status to be jeopardized.

His first instinct, however, was to strike back. He was not the man to be defied by those whom he contemptuously called *la prêtraille*. The order was given to arrest the Pope. ' *Plus de ménagements,*' he wrote to Eugène Beauharnais. ' He is a furious madman who must be shut up.' Miollis entrusted the unpleasant task to General Radet, who was summoned from Tuscany for the purpose. The arrest was carried out in the middle of the night of July 5–6th. Its circumstances have been minutely described by Cardinal Pacca in his *Memoirs*. Just after dawn the cardinal was awakened with the news that the French were in the palace. He at once sent to arouse the Holy Father, who put on his robe and stole and went into the Audience Chamber. Meanwhile the doors of the pontifical apartments had been broken down with axes. Presently General Radet entered, followed by a number of French officers. After a pause of

several minutes, during which both parties stood
face to face in perfect silence, the general, ' pale
and with a trembling voice, addressed the Pope.
He said that he had a painful duty to perform, but
. . . he was compelled to intimate to His Holiness
on the part of the Emperor that he must renounce
the temporal sovereignty of Rome and the pontifical states, and,' he added, ' in case of the non-
compliance of the Holy Father with the proposition
he had further orders to conduct him to General
Miollis, who would indicate to him the place of his
destination.' The Pope replied that he had not the
power to renounce what did not belong to himself,
and went on, ' This dominion the Emperor, even
though he cut our bodies in pieces, will never obtain
from us.' He added, ' Are we to go alone ? '
' Your Holiness,' said the general, ' may take with
you your Minister, Cardinal Pacca.' Pacca then left
the room to put on his cardinal's habit, after which
the two old men left the palace together. In the
Piazza they found Radet's carriage waiting for
them. When they were inside both doors were
locked (the blinds had been previously nailed down)
and the carriage drove away, the general sitting on
the box. It drove as far as the Porta del Popolo,
where post-horses were waiting.

The Pope now saw that he was to be taken from
Rome, and reproached Radet with his untruthful-
ness in saying that he would take him to Miollis.
He also protested against being thus removed
without his suite or even a change of clothes.
Radet replied that some of his attendants would
shortly bring him anything he required. A few
minutes later the Pope asked the cardinal whether
he had any money. The two prisoners then turned
out their pockets, and discovered that the Pope
had one papetto (10*d.*) in his possession and the

cardinal three grossi (7½*d*.). 'Thus,' says Pacca, 'the Sovereign of Rome and his Prime Minister set forth upon their journey literally in apostolic guise.'

As the blazing July day wore on, the heat within the carriage became terrific. Just before midnight, after a journey of nineteen hours, the party reached a small inn at Radicofani, where they passed the night. The journey was resumed the following evening, and next morning the travellers reached the Chartreuse of Florence. Here the Pope was lodged in the identical room in which Pius VI had been detained ten years before. Immediately on his arrival, the Grand-Duchess of Tuscany, Napoleon's sister Elisa, sent a chamberlain to present her compliments. But further reflection seems to have convinced the lady of the risk she ran of compromising herself in the eyes of her formidable brother, for in the middle of the night another messenger came from the same quarter demanding that the Pope should continue his journey immediately. At the same time Pacca was informed that he would not be allowed to accompany his master any further.

By this time the fatigues and discomforts of the journey had made the Pope ill, but no heed was taken of this. He was driven towards Genoa, while Pacca and his nephew were conducted to Alessandria. On July 14th the Pope also arrived at Alessandria, and remained there the two following days, but Pacca was not allowed to see him. At last permission was sent for him to rejoin the Pope's suite, but only on condition that he should follow a prescribed distance behind. Through Savoy the party made its way to Grenoble, remaining there from July 22nd to August 1st. Here, though now on French soil, the Holy Father received the same enthusiastic welcome as had greeted him in his passage through Italy. From Grenoble by way of Avignon, Aix, and Nice he journeyed to Savona, a small town on the gulf of Genoa, which was to be the term of his wanderings for the present. The episcopal palace was assigned to him as a permanent place of residence. By Napoleon's strict command, no mention was made of the Pope's removal in the newspapers. The *Moniteur* of August 9th, however, permitted itself the following allusion in the form of an alleged letter from Grenoble, dated August 1st : ' There is much concern about an *unknown animal* which has passed through here : the traces it has left lead to the supposition that it was a *reptile of extraordinary size.*' The credit for this amazing piece of vulgarity belongs presumably to Fouché.

A few hours after the departure of the Holy Father from Grenoble, Pacca was informed that he was to be placed under arrest and must leave that place immediately. Next morning he was removed to the mountain fortress of Fenestrelles, grimmest and most solitary of state prisons. Here he was treated with the extremity of rigour, occupying a miserable chamber and being forbidden to hold communication with any one. Permission to write was refused him, and when he asked for a book to read he was given a volume of Voltaire ! The same prison contained other ecclesiastical prisoners, and though these were at first few in number, their number rapidly increased as time went on and Napoleon's animosity against the Church and the clergy grew more fierce.

For the mighty ruler of France would recognize no *imperium in imperio.* If he did not spare the Pope himself, still less was he prepared to tolerate opposition, or even any claim to independence, on the part of the French clergy. He was determined to exact the price of the Concordat, reckoned according to his own estimate, to the uttermost farthing. In making a pact with the Church, he had sought not the Church's interest but his own. If the French Church was willing to accept this situation and become the accommodating tool of his policy, its representatives could count on being treated with unfailing courtesy and consideration. The tone both of the Emperor's letters and of his conversation with the bishops when on progress through France left nothing to be desired. Cardinals and bishops were no less welcome at the Tuileries than they had been at Versailles in the majestic days of Louis XIV. The Emperor's free-thinking marshals and generals had to give them precedence, however little they might like it. But in return their subservience was expected to be unlimited and absolute.

For this reason as time went on Napoleon showed an increasing preference for the surviving ecclesiastics of the *ancien régime*. In the days when the Concordat was still young, policy dictated that the nominees to bishoprics should be chosen partly from the Constitutional, partly from the non-juring, clergy. But as Napoleon's imperial pretensions became more pronounced and his firmer mastery allowed him to give freer course to his personal inclinations, the Constitutionals more and more dropped out of the running. Their revolutionary antecedents were an offence. Men who had opposed a King might oppose an Emperor. From the time of his coronation onwards Napoleon's bishops were chosen, as far as circumstances allowed, among members of old aristocratic families or those who had shown special devotion to the old order. 'It is only,' he said, 'the men of ancient family who know how to serve.' M. de Boulogne owed his bishopric of Troyes largely to his having been a favourite preacher at the Court of Louis XVI. So, too, when Cardinal Maury decided to throw in his lot with the imperial fortunes, the heartiest welcome awaited so desirable an acquisition. His birth was certainly not aristocratic, for he was the son of a cobbler. But as the Abbé Maury he had been a protagonist of the monarchy in the days of the National Assembly, and he had been one of Louis XVI's most trusted counsellors until his consuming ambition and an avarice that was almost insane led him to desert a master whose fortunes seemed by then to be desperate. At the same time Napoleon was under no illusions as to his worldliness and lack of moral fibre. He was a useful tool—no more. Of one of his Court sermons Louis XVI had said : ' If the abbé had only said a word about religion, he would have discoursed on every possible subject.' Napoleon was not likely to be less perspicacious.

It seemed, indeed, impossible to enjoy the Emperor's favour and his esteem at the same time. He would not use you unless you would be his slave. Yet if you became his slave he despised you. Almost the only ecclesiastic whom he respected was the venerable Abbé Émery, Superior of the Seminary of Saint-Sulpice—and this because Émery, as Talleyrand admitted, was never afraid to say what he thought. Yet for this very reason Émery was never given any preferment, nor did the Emperor's admiration save the abbé's beloved seminary from being dissolved. Napoleon's sins were too often against the light.

It would seem that the majority of bishops raised small opposition to the Emperor's plans for making them useful. They may not have liked what they were told to do, but they knew better than to disobey. The subject of their sermons and their charges were carefully prescribed for them by the Minister of Religions. Sometimes they were called upon, like Balaam, to curse the enemies of their master. The zeal of their Catholic flocks was to be inflamed against the Protestant English or the Orthodox Russians. Tears of indignant sympathy were to be drawn on behalf of ' our brethren, the persecuted Catholics of Ireland.' The praise of the good and glorious ruler of France must be incessantly sounded. ' You must praise the Emperor more in your charges,' said the Prefect of Police to M. de Broglie, Bishop of Ghent.

The sermons of priests were not less carefully supervised than the charges of bishops. ' Inform M. Robert, priest of Bourges,' wrote the Emperor to the Minister of Religions, 'of my displeasure. He made a very bad sermon on the 15th of August.' Those clergy who incurred the imperial disapproval were arrested and incarcerated either in a convent or in a prison. This imprisonment was unaccompanied by any form of trial, and, once under lock and key, many of the unfortunate victims remained shut up until the fall of the Empire, unless death anticipated their release. All ecclesiastical newspapers were suppressed, with the exception of the strictly censored *Journal des Curés* : and even this failed to satisfy the Emperor, who described it as ' written in the worst possible spirit, contrary to the liberties of the Gallican Church, and the maxims of Bossuet.'

Napoleon did not even hesitate to invent new feast-days. A Sunday was to be set apart for the annual celebration of the Emperor's coronation and the victory of Austerlitz : and August 15th—

the Feast of the Assumption—was ordered to be observed as the Feast of Saint Napoleon! Even the glories of the Mother of God had to pale before those of the Conqueror of Europe. Notwithstanding this, the bishops greeted the imperial commands with an enthusiasm which was at least well-feigned. M. d'Osmond, the Bishop of Nancy, urged the formation of pious associations in honour of the new saint. The only difficulty was that no one knew who St. Napoleon was. Application was made to Paris for information, with the result that, through the good offices of Cardinal Caprara, Catholic devotion was enriched by a legend which made it appear that among the martyrs of the time of Diocletian had figured a Neapolis or Neopolus whose name had been transformed in the Italy of the middle ages into Napoleone.

But Napoleon was not content with inventing saints. He aspired also to formulate the faith of the Church. One of the Organic Articles had provided that ' there shall be only one liturgy and one catechism in all the churches of France.' The task of providing the one universal catechism was at once taken in hand. After an abortive attempt by a theologian attached to the papal Embassy in Paris, the work was entrusted to a commission which took as a basis the catechism of Bossuet. Napoleon had no fault to find with Bossuet's theology, but he deemed his catechism insufficiently explicit on the one point which he really cared about—the duty of subjects towards their sovereign. As Portalis put it, this section was insufficient to ' bind by a religious sanction (*réligieusement*) the conscience of the peoples to the august person of the Emperor.' Napoleon therefore set to work with Caprara to concoct an entirely new section which should be really adequate to his ideas on the subject.

Caprara had received strict injunctions from Rome to lend no countenance to any such lay trespassing on the doctrinal preserve. ' It does not belong to the secular power,' wrote Consalvi, ' to choose or dictate to the bishops the catechism which it wishes to have.' But Caprara was flattered, as usual, by the imperial condescension, and simply ignored the prohibition—for which he was never forgiven. On May 5, 1806, the *Journal de l'Empire* announced the early publication of the catechism, which duly made its appearance, and was imposed on the whole Empire by a decree of August 4th in the same year.

The section to which Napoleon had devoted his special care (Leçon VII, *Suite du Quatrième commandement*) is too lengthy to be transcribed here in full, but a quotation may serve to indicate its quality. The answer to the question, ' Why are we bound by all these duties towards our Emperor ? ' begins thus : ' First of all, because God, Who creates empires and distributes them according to His will, while showering gifts upon our Emperor both in peace and in war, has established him as our sovereign, has made him the minister of His power and His image on earth. To honour and serve our Emperor is therefore to honour and serve God Himself.' It was also laid down that those who failed in their duty towards him ' would render themselves worthy of eternal damnation.'

CHAPTER VII

THE POPE AT SAVONA AND THE CARDINALS AT PARIS
1809-11

THE arrest and imprisonment of the Holy Father passed without protest from the Governments of Europe. Of Catholic countries, Austria had just been once again beaten to her knees: Spain and Naples were under the Napoleonic yoke : while the non-Catholic powers did not care enough about the Pope's misfortunes to take any action. The Catholic episcopate, too, kept silence, with the sole exception of the bishops of Dalmatia, who were a somewhat negligible quantity. In Rome the administration of General Miollis was popular with the aristocracy and *bourgeoisie*. The former even sent a deputation to the Tuileries to lay their fulsome homage at the conqueror's feet. But the common people regretted the papal régime, while (as was only to be expected) the clergy were irreconcilably hostile to the new Government. For them the French occupation was sacrilege pure and simple. The Cardinals, indeed, had been tolerably complaisant, most of them obeying the Emperor's summons to Paris and taking a pension from his hands. But the lower officials would not touch a penny of Napoleon's money. Further, the confusion between the spiritual and the temporal powers, which had been natural under the old régime, had become anomalous and intolerable under the new, and gave rise to insoluble difficulties.

Meanwhile, the Pope's attitude at Savona was one of passive yet uncompromising resistance. He would not receive the pension provided for him. He ignored the splendours and the honours with which Napoleon sought to surround him. He was always courteous and did not fail to express his thanks. But he would take nothing for himself and expected his followers to imitate his example. He had been a monk all his life previously to his assuming the tiara. He now became a monk again. He fed on vegetables and a little fish. He never left his room except to go into the tiny garden outside his windows or to say mass in his private chapel.

As for the institution of Napoleon's nominees to the vacant bishoprics, he would make no concessions whatever. Almost immediately after his departure from Rome, the Emperor (who was at Schönbrunn and still ignorant that his order for the Pope's removal had been executed) had so modified his demands that he no longer required that his own name should be included in the bulls of institution. But the time for compromise had gone by. The violence done to the person and liberty of the Holy Father had altered the whole situation. On August 26, 1809, the Pope, writing from Savona, definitely announced that in the position in which he now was he could no longer recognize the Emperor's right to appoint bishops and must refuse to institute his nominees.

In the hope that it might find some way out of his difficulties, the Emperor resorted to the idea of constituting a committee called *Conseil Ecclésiastique*, with Fesch as president. This held its first meeting at the end of November, 1809, when various questions were put to it on behalf of the Government. The situation of the members was a delicate one. On the one hand, they were in mortal terror of offending the Emperor. On the other, they were anxious not to be stampeded by him into producing or countenancing a schism. In consequence, their answers to the Emperor's questions betrayed more adroitness than definiteness or courage.

The main questions they had to decide were two. First : ' Could the Pope arbitrarily refuse institution to the archbishops and bishops nominated?' In support of his action, the Pope had alleged, first, the religious innovations introduced into France since the Concordat ; secondly, the annexation of the States of the Church ; thirdly, the separation of the Holy Father from the Sacred College. In reply to the first ground the Council maintained that the innovations in question had been for the advantage of religion : in reply to the second, that ' the temporal power is for the Popes merely an accessory which is foreign to their authority.' They also denied that the invasion of Rome was a violation of the Concordat. So far they had given judgement for the Emperor. The third ground of refusal, however, proved less easy to surmount, and they could only lay it before the Emperor, 'who will feel all the force and justice of it.'

The second question was : ' Supposing that the Emperor caused the Concordat to be abrogated, what was to be done for the good of religion?' Here the Conseil demurred to the term ' abrogated,' preferring to say ' suspended.' But whatever the term employed, the question still remained—what was to be done ? The Conseil began by a historical excursus designed to show that the method of appointing bishops sanctioned by the Concordat— i.e. nomination by the Government, institution by the Pope—had not always been the rule. By the

Pragmatic Sanction of 1438 the people and chapter were to elect, while the metropolitan and provincial council confirmed. But it did not venture to suggest this or any other substitute for the method of the Concordat. It replied modestly that 'it has not the necessary authority to indicate the measures proper to take the place of the Pope's institution in the confirmation of bishops.' It could only suggest the convening of a National Council to deal with the problem.

This answer did not satisfy Napoleon, who insisted on his question being reconsidered. The Conseil set to work again : but could only renew their suggestion of a National Council. This, they thought, should respectfully remonstrate with the Pope as to his refusal to institute. If he still maintained his refusal, it must consider whether it was or was not competent to decide a new mode of institution. If it deemed itself competent, it should make a provisory arrangement ' with the intention of returning as soon as possible to the Concordat.' If it did not think itself competent, then it must demand the summoning of a General Council, ' the only authority in the Church which is above the Pope.' If this appeared impossible, then it might decide that institution by the metropolitan, or (if the bishop-designate were himself metropolitan) by the senior bishop of the province, might be substituted for the papal bulls ' until such time as the Pope or his successor shall consent to the full execution of the Concordat.'

There remained the question of the Bull of Excommunication. This the Conseil decided to be invalid. Its replies were presented to the Emperor on January 11, 1810. One member, the saintly Émery, had refused to sign.

Meanwhile, another subject of dispute had arisen

to make what already seemed a hopeless situation more hopeless still. The movement which severed the Anglican Church from Rome had begun with an autocrat's resolve to take a new wife in place of an old. Here, as in other ways, Napoleon followed in Henry VIII's footsteps, though in less revolting fashion. We have seen how unwillingly he consented to a religious marriage with Josephine before his coronation, and also how careful he was to provide himself with a loophole for contesting its validity later if circumstances should make this desirable. As time went on and it became increasingly clear that Josephine could not provide an heir to the throne, the idea of a divorce became more and more tempting. The imperial family and entourage, too, exerted a constant pressure in this direction. It is to Napoleon's credit that he did not yield easily to this pressure. He had a genuine affection for his wife, which persisted in spite of their constant bickerings and his own infidelities. But about 1808 the thought of dissolving a marriage which had become a serious obstacle to his dearest ambitions began to take definite shape in his mind. The decision was finally taken after Wagram. It was on his return from Schönbrunn to Paris that he declared his intention to Josephine. The Empress fainted at the news, but knew better than to resist. On December 15th, 1809, husband and wife made a public declaration of their intention to separate, and this declaration received the formal consent of the Senate next day. Soon afterwards Josephine said farewell to the Court and retired to Malmaison.

The old wife had thus been disposed of. Who was the new wife to be ? In this case there was no Anne Boleyn for whom a way to the royal bed and throne had to be opened. The Emperor's motives were motives of policy, not of mere roving affection. He wished for an alliance which would enlarge and secure his prestige in the eyes of Europe. He seems first to have thought of a Russian archduchess, Olga, sister of the Emperor Alexander. The negotiation appeared to be on the point of succeeding when chance threw a still more flattering alliance in his way. A member of the Austrian Embassy at Paris let drop a hint that the Court of Vienna might not be unwilling to entertain the idea of a marriage between the victorious ruler of France and a daughter of the imperial house. The hint was at once communicated to Napoleon, who was immensely flattered and delighted. He, the Corsican parvenu, to marry the daughter of the Caesars—it was a consummation beyond his dreams. The negotiations with St. Petersburg were broken off, and an envoy despatched to Vienna without delay. By February, 1810, it had been finally decided that Napoleon should marry the Emperor's daughter, the Archduchess Marie Louise. The marriage with Josephine, however, still remained to be dissolved : and the austerely Catholic antecedents of the House of Austria made it necessary that this should be done in the most formal and correct manner possible.

Under ordinary circumstances, Napoleon would have applied to the Pope for such a dissolution. It was generally admitted that matrimonial cases involving sovereigns lay in the exclusive competence of the Holy See : and Napoleon himself had adopted this course in the first instance in regard to the marriage of Jerome Bonaparte. But the feud between the Pope and the Emperor rendered any application of the kind difficult, if not impossible. Napoleon therefore looked round for an alternative, and consulted the Arch-Chancellor, Cambacérès, on the question.

Cambacérès gave his opinion that a sovereign might have recourse to the same tribunal as was resorted to by his subjects under similar circumstances. This was all very well : but unfortunately no such tribunal was now in existence. Could not, however, one be improvised for the purpose ? Without delay three different ' officialities ' were called into being, called ' diocesan,' ' metropolitan,' and ' primatial ' respectively. The case was first brought before the Diocesan Officiality of Paris. The members of this had an interview with Cambacérès, who with an explicitness which left nothing to be desired instructed them in what they were expected to do. Their initial feeling was one of astonishment and horror. First they pleaded that such a case was reserved to the Sovereign Pontiff : then they sought to transfer the appalling responsibility to the shoulders of the *Conseil Ecclésiastique.* It was all in vain. They then declared that they would only consent to hear the case if the *Conseil Ecclésiastique* recognized their competence. This condition was conceded : and on January 2, 1810, the Conseil pronounced the Officiality competent. The case came up for hearing on January 8th. The sentence was to be given with the utmost despatch: no lingering over technicalities would be tolerated. ' What ! ' Cambacérès had said, ' you wish to follow forms ? I have been a lawyer : forms kill the essence of things ' (*les formes tuent le fond*). The grounds on which a dissolution was demanded were three : the absence of the parish priest, the lack of the required number of witnesses, and the non-consent of the Emperor. The last was too exquisitely absurd for even the Officiality to allow it to pass. But the two other grounds were admitted : and on the strength of these it was declared that ' the marriage between the Emperor and King Napoleon and Josephine de Beauharnais must be considered as null and invalidly contracted.'

The Metropolitan Officiality was next asked for its opinion. This went one better, and solemnly declared that the mighty conqueror of Europe had been married to his first wife against his will !

Armed with this decision, and more than ever master of Europe after the Peace of Schönbrunn, Napoleon felt that the moment was come to ' finish off the Roman business.' On February 17, 1810, a *senatus consultum* was passed by the Senate declaring that the States of the Church were formally annexed to the Empire. It was also decreed, by Article 7, that ' the Prince Imperial shall have the title of King of Rome.' (In view of the fact that Napoleon's second marriage had not yet even taken place this may seem a trifle premature.) In a letter sent soon after to the Pope, Napoleon thus delivered himself :

The triple tiara is a monstrous product of pride and ambition entirely contrary to the humility of a Vicar of Jesus Christ. The irascible principles of those who surround Your Holiness would have done much harm if God had not given me calm and a true knowledge of the sublime principles of our religion. . . . You will have enough of cares and occupations when you agree to confine yourself to spiritual affairs and the direction of souls. I have the duty (*mission*) of governing the West, do not you meddle with it. . . . I recognize you for my spiritual chief, but I am your Emperor.

With the exception of a few aged men whose feeble health forbade their removal, all the Cardinals were by this time in Paris. Towards the end of 1809, those who were then still in Rome had received a letter from the Minister of Religions ordering them to go to the French capital, where a

pension of thirty thousand francs would be paid
to each of them. Among them were Consalvi and
di Pietro, who replied that they could not leave
Rome without the Pope's leave. As for the pension, the orders of His Holiness forbade them to
accept it. Their objections were unheeded : and
on December 9th the two Cardinals, bowing to
necessity, left Rome. At Paris, Consalvi determined to lead a very retired life, abstaining as much
as possible from all social functions. He knew that
many of his fellow Cardinals were less scrupulous
and were perpetually frequenting the festivities
of the capital. But the Pope had given his instructions, and he felt bound to observe them even if
others did not. He also refused the pension, which
had been accepted by all the Cardinals who had
arrived in Paris before him. Di Pietro and two
other Cardinals joined in this refusal.

Soon after reaching Paris, the newly-arrived
Cardinals—twenty-seven in number—were presented to Napoleon by Fesch. Having saluted Consalvi, the Emperor remarked, ' It must be confessed
that I made a mistake in turning you out. If you
had continued to occupy your post, things would
not have gone so far.' His purpose was obvious :
he wished to create an impression (as possibly he
wished to convince himself) that the Pope's course
of action was unsupported by Consalvi. Consalvi
thought it necessary to nip the attempt in the bud.
' Sire,' he said, ' if I had remained in my place I
should have done my duty.' The Emperor proceeded to suggest to Cardinal di Pietro that the
entire Sacred College being now in Paris, they ought
to see whether they could not make a proposal
towards ending his dispute with the Pope. He
would give them leave to meet for the purpose—
or the chief among them. ' See that in the number

is included Cardinal Consalvi, who if he knows
nothing about theology knows a good deal about
politics.' The Cardinals accordingly held a consultation, in which Consalvi took the lead. He
saw through the Emperor's crafty intention of
driving a wedge between the Cardinals and the
Pope, and set himself to frustrate it. Under his
inspiration a reply was drawn up stating that the
Cardinals, being separated from their head, could
not frame any plan or draw up any proposal,
especially in questions on which the Pope had
already pronounced. They could only unite their
supplications to that of His Holiness, and entreat
His Imperial Majesty to listen to them. Cardinal
Fesch conveyed this reply to the Emperor, who
tore it into fragments and flung it into the fire.

In this matter the Sacred College had shown an
united front. The occasion of the Emperor's marriage, on the other hand, was to divide them into
two sharply contrasted sections. The marriage was
announced a few days after Consalvi's arrival in
Paris. There were at this time twenty-nine Cardinals in the capital, including Caprara, who was
childish and dying, and Fesch, who was to officiate
at the wedding as Grand-Almoner of France.
What was to be the attitude of the Cardinals towards the marriage ? It was historically indisput-
able that the matrimonial causes of sovereigns
had always been regarded as the exclusive concern
of the Pope. On this ground thirteen Cardinals
(including Consalvi and di Pietro) decided that
they could not recognize the violation of the rights
of the Holy See involved in the sentence of the
Officiality, by being present at the marriage. On
the other hand, they did not wish to put an open
slight upon the Emperor. The senior of them,
Mattei, therefore went to Fesch, and while inform-

ing him of their decision, suggested that any awkward consequences might be avoided if the Cardinals were not invited personally but only a few of them—as was to be the case with the Senate and Corps Législatif. Fesch was exceedingly annoyed and tried hard to persuade the Cardinals to change their minds. Failing in this, he went to see the Emperor. On his return he reported that the Emperor had been very angry and absolutely refused to adopt the suggestion made.

The time of the wedding (April 1, 1810) was now drawing near. It was announced that there would be four different ceremonies : on Saturday, the presentation of the principal Corps d'État; on Sunday, the civil marriage ; on Monday, the ecclesiastical marriage ; on Tuesday, the presentation of the dignitaries of the Empire. The Cardinals were invited individually to all of these. After consultation the thirteen decided that they could conscientiously attend the first and last, but not the second and third. On the Saturday evening, therefore, they all went to St. Cloud. While waiting in the Grande Salle, Consalvi saw Fouché, the Minister of Police, coming up to him. Having received from the Cardinal an admission of his intention to be absent from the wedding ceremony next day, Fouché pointed out the terrible consequences which such a course would entail. But Consalvi refused to modify his position. The civil marriage was performed at St. Cloud, the ecclesiastical at the Tuileries. The thirteen were absent from both. At the latter, three even of the fourteen Cardinals who had decided to attend failed to appear, sending messages of excuse at the last moment. In view of this they were considered as having been present. The thirteen, however, sent no excuse nor explanation at all.

When Napoleon entered the chapel his glance rested first on the seats reserved for the Cardinals. Seeing only eleven present, his eyes flashed with rage : but he said nothing. However, the explosion was only postponed. Next day the thirteen attended the reception. While they were waiting their turn in the antechamber, an officer came out of the Throne Room with a message from the Emperor that those Cardinals who had been absent from the wedding were to go home at once as he declined to receive them. All eyes were upon them as they made their way out through the crowded rooms. When the other Cardinals came into the imperial presence, Napoleon gave himself up to one of his carefully stage-managed ebullitions of rage, declaring Consalvi to be the chief culprit.

Next day those of the thirteen who were bishops were ordered to resign their sees at once. They obeyed subject to the Pope's approval. That night at nine o'clock the recalcitrant Cardinals had an interview with the Minister of Religions. Fouché was there, too, to greet Consalvi with an ' I told you so.' The Minister informed them that they had been guilty of treasonable conspiracy, especially in attempting to cast doubts on the legitimacy of the succession. As a punishment the Emperor deprived them of all their property, refused to recognize them as Cardinals any longer, and reserved to himself the right to take further action in regard to their persons. Consalvi replied that such treatment was unjust : they had acted straightforwardly throughout. The two Ministers appeared to be impressed with his arguments : and at their suggestion a memorandum embodying these was prepared for submission to the Emperor. The Minister of Religions took it at once to St. Cloud, but when he arrived there he found

Napoleon gone. He therefore informed the thirteen that he had no alternative but to carry the
imperial orders into effect. Their property was at
once sequestrated, and they were deprived of their
cardinalitial insignia. Hence arose the famous distinction between *cardinaux rouges* and *cardinaux
noirs.*

Two and a half months later (June), ten of the
thirteen were informed that they must leave Paris
within twenty-four hours for various places of exile
in France, among which they were to be distributed
in pairs, care being taken that each Cardinal should
have as his companion the one with whom he was
on the least intimate terms. Consalvi was sent to
Reims, and it was there that he wrote his *Memoirs.*
It is hardly surprising, under the circumstances,
that these exhibit not a little acrimony on the
subject of their writer's persecutor.

The Black Cardinals were not the only victims
of Napoleon's rapidly gathering wrath. The clergy
of the erstwhile papal states were, not unnaturally,
unwilling to accept either a compulsory teaching
of the Four Gallican Articles or a redistribution of
dioceses at the hands of the new Caliph of the West.
But the more the clergy objected, the more ener-
getically Napoleon developed his measures for
assimilating the ecclesiastical arrangements of the
Roman departments to those of the rest of his
dominions. ' If any difficulty were likely to arise
I have already,' he wrote, ' sent twelve thousand
men in three columns. I will send a hundred thousand if necessary.' For refusing to take the oath
of allegiance nineteen bishops were sent under
armed escort across the Alps, with many dignitaries
beside, while more than two hundred priests were
deported to Corsica.

The Pope and those of the clergy who supported

him must have been by now sufficiently aware of
the formidable consequences of provoking the imperial wrath.   But in spite of this the attitude of
the Holy See remained unchanged.   Napoleon's
nominees to the vacant sees were still awaiting the
papal institution, and without this they could
exercise no episcopal functions in their dioceses.
In order to meet the inconveniences thus entailed
Maury had already suggested that Napoleon should
do what Louis XIV had done before him under
similar circumstances, and have the vacant sees
administered by the bishops-designate, in the
capacity of vicars-general of their respective chapters.   But on consulting Bigot de Préameneu, the
Minister of Religions, Napoleon discovered that
this course had been already suggested to the
bishops concerned, who had ' betrayed an extreme
aversion for it.'   At the same time the Minister
expressed the opinion that if the Emperor insisted
they would obey.

However, Napoleon did not insist yet.   His
marriage with Marie Louise taking place at this
time, he thought that the occasion might provide
a good opportunity for the Court of Vienna to
mediate between himself and the Pope.   Vienna
was willing and appointed the Chevalier de Lebzeltern its agent for the purpose.   Lebzeltern's mission was entirely secret, having ostensibly to do
only with matters concerning Austria.   But he
carried with him a document in which Napoleon
had set down with engaging frankness his views
on Church affairs.   It began by premising that
' the Emperor has no need of the Pope.   *Tout est
d'accord de s'en passer.*'   The *Conseil Ecclésiastique*, it declared not quite accurately, had given
its opinion that the Emperor might convene a
Council, which should provide for the institution

of his nominees. On the other hand, the Emperor preferred a reconciliation with the Pope if this were possible. He suggested, therefore, that the Pope should consent to return to Rome and recognize the annexation of the papal states to the Empire. If he objected to this he might go to Avignon, where he would be treated in a manner befitting his dignity. Lebzeltern had an interview with the Holy Father at Savona on May 14, 1810. Pius received him cordially and expressed the utmost goodwill towards the Emperor personally. But he said he could do nothing until his communications were re-established with the faithful, and requested that he should be allowed the presence of *un Conseil* to advise him. As to surrendering the temporal power, he refused utterly to entertain the idea. On receiving Lebzeltern's report of his mission, Napoleon judged that the hour had not yet come to enter into a formal negotiation, but that such a negotiation was not out of the question. In order to pave the way, his next move was to send to the Pope two Cardinals, Spina and Caselli, both devoted to his own interests and both instrumental (it will be remembered) in the conclusion of the Concordat. The Pope showed no great haste or anxiety to see them, and when he did merely reiterated his demand for *un Conseil*. He was strongly opposed to the idea of going to Avignon, and still more to that of going to Paris— which was what Napoleon himself really desired. If he could not go to Rome he would remain at Savona. Before he could enter into negotiations the Emperor must send him two Cardinals whom he could trust.

Informed of the Pope's attitude Napoleon at once made up his mind. He would do without him. Instructions were sent to four of the bishops-

designate to repair to their dioceses. As Fesch
refused to take possession of the vacant see of
Paris (to which he had been nominated) without
the Pope's approval, Napoleon appointed in his
stead Cardinal Maury, who was less burdened by
scruples. This appointment forms the subject of a
well-known anecdote, probably apocryphal. When
Fesch refused to take the archbishopric Napoleon
began to threaten him, saying, 'I will force you into
it.' 'Sire,' replied Fesch, '*potius mori*.' 'Ah!
potius mori—rather Maury. Ah well, be it so, you
shall have Maury.'

A week later the Emperor appointed M. d'Osmond to be Archbishop of Florence. Both prelates were ordered to take possession of their sees
at once. They did so. But the Pope now judged
the time come to raise his voice in protest. Asked
by the Chapter of Florence what should be its attitude towards the new archbishop, he replied by a
brief declaring that the custom and canons of the
Church forbade the election of the bishop-designate
of a see as vicar-capitular. The Chapter were enjoined to keep the brief strictly secret. But the
leading spirit in it, Canon Muzzi, who was a vehement opponent of the Napoleonic régime, spread
the news of it all over the city. The Grand-Duchess
Elisa (Napoleon's sister) sent for him, but he declined, as he put it, to 'discuss theology with
ladies.' In the end he and two other canons were
sent off to join Cardinal Pacca at Fenestrelles.

At Paris, too, events followed a similar course.
Maury was enthroned at Notre Dame on November 1, 1810. The vicar-general of the diocese
during the vacancy had been the Abbé d'Astros,
a nephew of Portalis (formerly Napoleon's Minister
of Religions) and decidedly of the stuff of which
martyrs are made. As soon as Maury had to exer-

cise his functions he found d'Astros thwarting
him at every turn. On Christmas Eve this valiant
champion went to dine with his cousin, a son
of the elder Portalis, and himself a Counsellor
of State. Going with his host into his study, he
showed him a brief which he had just received from
the Pope, addressed to Maury and denouncing his
usurpation. Portalis besought him to hold his
tongue. But the news of the brief soon spread
among the Paris clergy. It also reached the
police—indeed Portalis had thought it his duty to
drop a hint to the Prefect. Already, too, the police
had in their possession a similar brief addressed to
d'Astros and declaring all acts of the *soi-disant*
archbishop to be null and void.

Napoleon was furious—the more so as he had
given strict instructions that the Pope's correspondence should be subjected to the most rigorous
supervision. His rage boiled over at a great reception at the Tuileries on New Year's Day. The
Chapter of Notre Dame were present, having been
informed that their presence was required. After
Maury had paid his compliments Napoleon approached the canons : and standing in front of
d'Astros, said, ' There are some among you who
sow trouble in men's consciences and lift themselves up above authority.' Then to d'Astros, ' It
is you I mean, monsieur l'Abbé. Know that it is
necessary to uphold the liberties of the Gallican
Church. There is as much difference between the
religion of Bossuet and that of Gregory VII as
there is between heaven and hell.' Then laying
his hand on his sword he said, ' Remember that
I do not carry it in vain.'

This was not all. Before they left the Tuileries,
Maury told d'Astros that the Minister of Police
desired to have some conversation with him and

suggested that they should go together in his carriage to the Minister's hotel. The unsuspecting d'Astros fell into the trap, and no doubt during the drive Maury reflected on the pleasantness of paying off old scores. When they arrived Savary asked him whether he had received a brief from the Pope. D'Astros replied that he had. Savary then told him that if he would resign nothing more would be said. D'Astros refused. ' Resign,' said the Minister, ' or you are my prisoner.' ' Then I am your prisoner,' came the calm reply. An attempt by a subordinate agent the same evening to extract from him how the papal brief reached him met with no better success. Napoleon had first declared that he would have him shot, but being dissuaded from this he exclaimed, ' Let him be cast into prison for the rest of his life.' He was at once taken to Vincennes, where he remained till the fall of the Empire.

Cardinals di Pietro and Gabrielli soon followed him thither. As for the younger Portalis, the Emperor seized the occasion of a Council of State to deliver a violent personal attack upon him. Against his charges of ingratitude and treason Portalis tried to excuse himself, but in vain. The Emperor went on relentlessly, ' The duties of a counseller of state towards me are immense. You have violated them. You are no longer such. Go away, and never appear here again.' Portalis at once quitted the room in such confusion and terror that he left his hat and portfolio behind. In vain did the Minister of Police explain to the Emperor the steps the accused man had taken to intimate the existence of the papal brief. No heed was taken. Portalis was exiled from Paris and placed under police surveillance.

But the chief offender in Napoleon's eyes was

the Pope. He wrote to Prince Borghese a letter which was one long scream of invective against ' this ignorant and atrabilious old man.' ' The Pope,' he complained, ' has profited by the freedom (*sic*) I have allowed him to sow rebellion and discord among my subjects.' He instructed the Prince to inform him that he was absolutely forbidden to correspond with any Church or any of the Emperor's subjects. ' The prefect or some one else will tell him that I no longer recognize him as Pope and that he ceases to be the organ of the Church. Since nothing can make the Pope sensible, he shall see that I am strong enough to do what my predecessors have done and depose a Pope.' The Pope's surgeon, chaplain, and personal attendants were arrested and sent to Fenestrelles. His apartments were entered at dead of night and his papers searched and seized. He was deprived of his desk, his pens, even of his breviary and his purse. As though this were still not enough, a captain of gendarmerie, Lagorse, went to him by Napoleon's command and demanded the Fisherman's ring. The Pope was deeply moved, but handed it over without a word. Before giving it up, however, he was careful to break it in half—presumably to prevent the concoction of forged documents in his name.

Terrified by d'Astros' fate, the Chapter of Notre Dame hastened to dissociate themselves from his action and make their peace. At Napoleon's own suggestion, they presented to him on January 6th at the Tuileries an address drawn up by Maury and the Emperor in collaboration, in which they expressed their ' intense affliction ' at their colleague's action and intimated that they had deprived him of his position as vicar-general. They declared their unfaltering adhesion to the Gallican liberties and affirmed that the custom of the Church of France gave the chapters the right of conferring on bishops-designate their capitular powers. Napoleon in reply expressed his satisfaction and delivered a lengthy speech in which he inveighed bitterly against the Holy See. He ended by saying that if the Pope solemnly promised to do nothing against the Articles of 1682 he might return to Rome. But he added, ' If S. Peter were to return to the world, it is not to Rome he would go.' Next day he asked the chapter to forward their loyal address to the Pope. It was not sent.

CHAPTER VIII

THE NATIONAL COUNCIL AND THE CONCORDAT OF FONTAINEBLEAU
1811-14

IN January, 1811, a new *Conseil Ecclésiastique* of nine members was formed by order of the Emperor, Fesch again acting as president. On behalf of Napoleon, Bigot de Préameneu propounded to it two questions :

1. ' All communications between the Pope and the Emperor's subjects being interrupted at present, to whom is it necessary to resort in order to obtain the dispensations formerly accorded by the Holy See ? '

2. ' Seeing that the Pope obstinately refuses to grant bulls to the bishops nominated by the Emperor to fill vacant sees, what is the lawful means of giving them canonical institution ? '

In its reply the Conseil began by deploring the ' interruptions ' alluded to. In answer to the first question, it gave its opinion that the bishops had, within their own dioceses, the power to give dispensations and absolutions as required. In regard to the second it suggested that as the Pope refused the required bulls without any canonical reason for his refusal, the simplest course would be the addition of a fresh clause to the Concordat by which the Pope should be bound to give institution within a fixed time, failing which the right of institution should devolve on the council of the province. If the Pope rejected this he would justify in the eyes of Europe the entire abolition of the Concordat and the recourse to another means of conferring canonical institution. In conclusion the Conseil recommended the Emperor to summon a National Council to consider the whole question.

Such a solution of his difficulties had long been present in Napoleon's mind, and he was of opinion that the time had now come to resort to it. But the Bishop of Nantes, the adroit Duvoisin (a member of the *Conseil Ecclésiastique*), persuaded him to allow one more assault to be made upon the Holy Father's constancy. A deputation of bishops (such was the plan) should be sent to the Pope to obtain if possible his consent to the insertion in the Concordat of such a clause as the Conseil had propounded. The Emperor was not very enthusiastic : and his instructions to the deputation suggest that he did not wish the negotiations to succeed. In any case he had no intention of awaiting the issue of them before convening the National Council. He hoped and believed that the knowledge that this was hanging over his head would make the Pope disposed to a policy of concession all along the line. June 9th was fixed as the date for the Council to meet : Notre Dame as the place. Letters of summons were addressed to the bishops of the French Empire, the Kingdom of Italy, and the Confederation of the Rhine.

The bishops chosen to negotiate with the Pope were three—Barral, Archbishop of Tours ; Duvoisin, Bishop of Nantes ; and Mannay, Bishop of Trèves. A fourth bishop, the Bishop of Faenza, joined them later at Savona. Before starting the three had an interview with the Emperor, who authorized them to sign two agreements—the one relating to the institution of bishops, the other to the Pope's future position. The former was to provide that if the Pope would consent to institute the Emperor's nominees, or, after a delay of three months, authorize the metropolitan to do so, the Concordat should be re-established. The second would permit the Pope to return to Rome on condition that he took the oath prescribed for ecclesiastics by the Concordat—or if he refused, he might reside at Avignon on engaging to do nothing against the Gallican Articles. Napoleon also instructed his emissaries to use the imminence of the Council for all it was worth and to avoid showing their hand until the Pope had given some signs of being willing to treat.

No means of disposing the Holy Father towards the imperial desires was neglected. At the Emperor's bidding some thirty of the French bishops wrote to him to urge the disastrous effects of his resistance and entreat him to abandon it. At the same time the Pope's gaoler at Savona, the Prefect Chabrol, was enjoined to use every possible device for acting upon his prisoner's mind. The prefect acquitted himself of his task with a consummate and almost fiendish ingenuity. He had discovered that for all his obstinacy, the Pope was (as he put it) ' accessible to sensibility ' : and now he was to act on the knowledge. Already the unhappy pontiff was entirely cut off from the outside world. His ignorance of what was happening in it was complete. His friends had been removed : even pens and paper were denied him. His health inevitably suffered from his confinement and isolation. Deprived of any one to advise him, he was left a helpless prey to his own self-questioning.

The bishops reached Savona on May 9th. Pius received them graciously, but once again declared that he could do nothing ' without his natural counsellors.' When told of the impending Council, he remarked that his concurrence was necessary. A parley between the envoys and the prefect resulted in the decision to employ ' all appropriate measures ' to convince the Holy Father of the ' uselessness of having advice before making up his mind.' To this end the assistance was enlisted of the two men who had most opportunities of seeing the Pope in the intimacy of his solitude—his private physician, Dr. Porta, and Lagorse, the Commandant at the palace. With their help (as he himself put it in a letter to Bigot de Préameneu) the prefect hoped ' to ascertain what the Pope might let fall in familiar conversation and to be able to make known to him in a discreet though unofficial way what it was desirable for him to know in order to facilitate the negotiations.' His expectations were not disappointed. Porta played his part to perfection—' the Pope's physician serves us marvellously,' wrote the prefect appreciatively. Nor did the Emperor fail to reward the devotion of his spy.

The second interview of the bishops with the Pope took place on May 12th. The Holy Father again complained of the absence of his ' natural counsellors.' The bishops therefore, ' *avec quelques détours de modestie*,' offered themselves as a substitute. But the Pope declined their services as ' insufficiently disinterested.' A further conversation took place the same evening in the garden attached to the Pope's residence. But at neither interview, as the bishops mournfully confessed in a letter to the Minister of Religions, were they able to gain anything in regard either to the institution of bishops or anything else. Next day they handed to the Pope a written note drawn up by Duvoisin. But he refused to receive it.

The bishops having failed, the prefect determined to see what he could do. On May 14th he saw the Holy Father and expressed his surprise at his continued refusal. When his victim renewed his request for *un Conseil* he replied, ' Your *Conseil* shall be restored to you when you have made your pronouncement.' He warned him that every one (' posterity and history ' included) would blame his refusal. The Pope merely replied that it was a matter of conscience. The prefect next tried the effect of entreaty. But all his eloquence was in vain in the face of ' this incredible obstinacy.'

Next day (May 15th) Porta informed the prefect that the Pope's health was suffering. He slept little, and his pulse showed him to be ' in a state of profound agitation.' These encouraging tidings spurred on the prefect to fresh efforts. He renewed his persuasions, as did the bishops : but for the moment without visible result. On May 18th, however, he was able to report a very different story. He had warned the Pope, he wrote, that ' the Emperor's habit was to propose and not to accede. Any concession which was not complete would leave things as they were. It was only by good manners that he could obtain anything from his Majesty.' He also bade the Pope remember that ' the Emperor could obtain from his Council more than he demanded at that moment.' The Pope seemed to be impressed, and said that he wished to see the bishops in order to find out if an arrangement could be made. ' I noticed,' wrote the prefect complacently, ' that the Pope was resisting less from conviction than from an *amour-propre* which disguised itself under the form of conscientious scruples.'

A further interview between the bishops and the Pope took place immediately. The Pope complained of his ' head ' being ' tired ' and postponed the interview till the evening. Next day (May 19th) his favourable attitude was maintained, and a rough draft of a note was drawn up. This note was submitted to the Pope, and at his suggestion various changes and omissions were made in it. The general tenor was to make the Pope promise, first, to give canonical institution to the Emperor's nominees both in France and Italy, and, secondly, to send bulls of institution within six months, failing which he authorized the metropolitan of the province to confer it in his name.

' It is more than we had hoped for several days,' wrote the bishops joyfully the same night (May 19th). So no doubt it was. Unfortunately for them, however, the Pope did not sign the note, and thus it must always be a matter of controversy how far he definitely accepted its terms or how far he merely regarded it as representing a certain stage in the negotiations. In any case the note was with his consent left on the chimney-piece of his apartment, and very early next morning (May 20th) the bishops started on their triumphant journey to Paris bearing with them a duplicate copy of it.

That same morning the Pope rose early after a sleepless night and asked the captain of the palace if the bishops had left Savona. Learning that they had, he requested to see the prefect. While awaiting his arrival, he betrayed intense agitation, declaring that he had not paid proper attention to the bishops' note and could not accept it. He then proceeded to make a multitude of corrections in the note which he held in his hand. The corrected document was handed to the prefect when he arrived. Chabrol tried to calm him, but without effect. The Pope implored him to send a courier to overtake the bishops and instruct them to delete the last article. The prefect promised to write. Next day the Pope's agitation continued. He said that owing to a sleepless night he had been *à moitié ivre* during his last interview with the bishops, and was most anxious that it should be clearly understood that he had considered the note handed to him by them not as a treaty or as the preliminary of a treaty, but as *une sorte d'ébauche* (a sort of rough draft).

Some days after this the Pope's health was still affected, and Porta discerned in him ' all the signs of a hypochondriacal affection ' (May 26th). When the prefect mentioned to him the coming National Council he made no reply. After a long silence, he merely said, ' Fortunately I have signed nothing.' A little later (May 30th) the prefect was able to report that ' the mental alienation has passed away and the physical indisposition is less serious,' but he adds, ' everything shows that support is needed for a weakened mind and a self-tormenting conscience '—for which reason he ventured to suggest that the Pope must be surrounded by a council ' as wise as it is firm in order to keep him continually in the same resolution.'

The awkward fact, however, remained that the Pope had disowned the note. This fact the bishops did not dare to conceal either from themselves or from Napoleon, however much they might seek to persuade the outside world that ' they had obtained from the Pope much more than they had hoped and that everything was about to be settled.' The Emperor was very angry. Clearly nothing was to be obtained from the Pope, and no other course now remained but to see what the National Council could do towards solving his difficulties.

The Council was originally to have met on June 9th, but in consequence of the baptism of the King of Rome, Napoleon's new-born son, the opening was

postponed till June 17th.   On the previous day the
Emperor delivered a speech to the Corps Législatif
which revealed the imperial thoughts pretty clearly.
He attacked the Temporal Power as the main
cause of the separation of half Europe from the
Church of Rome, and took credit to himself for
having ' put an end to the scandal for ever.'   ' If
the Popes,' he declared, ' have at heart the interests
of religion they will wish to sojourn frequently at
the centre of the affairs of Christendom.   It is thus
that S. Peter preferred Rome even to a residence
in the Holy Land.'

On June 17th, then, the members of the Council
met in the archiepiscopal palace under the shadow
of Notre Dame.   The bishops present numbered
ninety-five, fifty-three French and forty-two Italians (the number slightly increased later).   Fesch
opened the proceedings by singing the Mass of the
Holy Ghost.   He had insisted that the presidency
belonged to him by right as Primate of the Gauls
and Archbishop of the most ancient see in France
(Lyons).   The sermon was delivered by the Bishop
of Troyes, M. de Boulogne, reputed the most eloquent preacher of his time.   His discourse had
been previously submitted to the president, at
whose suggestion certain passages were suppressed.
But the preacher in delivering his sermon re-
inserted them, and thus the assembled fathers listened, with delight or dismay according to their
individual views, to a passionate protestation of
loyalty to the Holy See, ' that corner-stone, that
key of the vault, without which the whole edifice
would fall in upon itself.'   ' That see,' proceeded
the preacher, ' may be displaced, it can never be
destroyed.'   Mass over, the bishops repaired to the
place prepared for their sessions, and the decree
was read declaring the Council open.   Each bishop

in turn responded *Placet*—the Archbishop of Bordeaux with the proviso ' saving the obedience due to the sovereign pontiff.' Fesch then pronounced upon his knees a profession of faith which included a solemn oath of obedience to the Pope. The same oath was taken by all the bishops in turn.

The bishops had decided to hold their second session on June 19th. But on their arrival they found no president, and the session had to be postponed till next day. The explanation of Fesch's absence was a hurried summons by the Emperor in connection with a criticism by the *Conseil Ecclésiastique* on the draft of a speech to be delivered to the Council by Bigot de Préameneu containing scandalously unfair charges against the Pope. The interview has been graphically described by Talleyrand in his *Memoirs*. ' By what right,' asked the Emperor of his uncle, ' do you take the title of Primate of the Gauls ? What ridiculous pretension ! And further without asking my permission ! I see your cunning. You desire to make yourself big, sir, in order to attract attention to yourself, in order to prepare the public for a still higher elevation in the future. You wish to make Europe believe that I desire to see in you a future Pope. A fine Pope forsooth !' The Emperor then diverted the vials of his wrath upon the fathers of the Council, whom he called traitors for having taken an oath of obedience to his enemy. ' Gentlemen,' said he, addressing Fesch and the other bishops present, ' you wish to treat me as though I were Louis le Debonnair. Do not confuse the son with the father. You see in me Charlemagne. *Je suis Charlemagne, moi*—Yes ! I am Charlemagne.'

Next day (June 20th) the postponed meeting—the first ' general congregation '—took place. On either side of the president—grim watchdogs of the civil power—sat the two Ministers of Religions for France and Italy. The imperial message was read ' amid a profound and respectful silence '— a silence, however, which was by no means without an element of temper. It began with a violent diatribe against the Pope and ended with a peremptory statement of the Emperor's wishes. ' His Majesty desires that bishops shall be instituted in accordance with the forms in force before the Concordat, so that a see may never be vacant for more than three months.'

Next day a commission was appointed to draw up an address to the Emperor. ' This commission,' said a secret report to the Government, 'is not at all constituted in a satisfactory manner. The prelates of a known devotion have few voices in it.' At its first meeting Duvoisin of Nantes produced a form of address which had been previously submitted to the Emperor and constituted (to use d'Haussonville's phrase) ' *une véritable traité de théologie d'Etat.*' De Broglie of Ghent—the *enfant terrible* of the Council—at once protested, amid the applause of his brethren. When Duvoisin tried to justify himself the president caustically observed, ' It is for you, my lord, to present *our* ideas to the Emperor.' After much acrimonious discussion, an amorphous composition was produced which satisfied nobody. This was presented to the Council on June 26th.

Suddenly the Bishop of Jericho, suffragan of Münster, rose and besought the Council to demand the setting at liberty of the Pope. His appeal was supported by the Bishop of Chambéry. De Pradt, Archbishop of Malines and a toady of the Emperor's, thought such a course undignified, but the others stuck to their guns. The assembly, too, was sympathetic until Fesch ventured to remind them that it would certainly displease the Emperor, after which they contented themselves with voting that the wish of the Council should be entered upon the minutes. A discussion of the address followed, which was continued next day. In the end Duvoisin's original draft was so altered and defaced that Napoleon declined to receive it. In consequence the solemn reception of the Council by the Emperor was abandoned.

Meanwhile another commission was engaged in framing a reply to the imperial message of June 20th. Its discussions were lengthy and animated and, in their results, far from gratifying to the Emperor. When his mouthpiece, Duvoisin, asked the commission to express an opinion whether the Council might consider itself competent to pronounce on the question of canonical institution without the intervention of the Pope, it replied in the negative by eight votes to three. A second question indicating a solution of the problem on lines similar to those suggested by the *Conseil Ecclésiastique* was also negatived. ' It is all over,' groaned Fesch. A petition was then signed asking the Emperor for leave to send to the Pope a deputation to explain the deplorable state of the Church and to confer with him on the means of remedying it (July 5th).

The following evening Fesch had an interview with Napoleon and informed him of the decisions of the commission. His first exclamation was, ' I will break up the Council.' Then, changing his mind suddenly, he said, ' It is I myself who will get you out of the difficulty. I will settle the whole thing.' Thereupon, calling the Secretary of State for Italy, M. Aldini, he dictated to him the basis on which the report of the commission must

be founded. These included a categorical statement that the Pope had accepted the note which
the three bishops had brought from Savona. He
further dictated the form which he desired the
decree of the Council to take—to the effect that if
the Pope had not given institution within six
months the metropolitan of the province should
give it.

Armed with this document, Fesch met his colleagues of the commission the following day (July
7th). They were already in a somewhat chastened
mood, for it had come to their ears that the
Emperor was determined to have his will, if not in
one way then in another. His statement as to the
concessions made by the Pope produced a still
more profound impression. It was generally agreed
that it entirely altered the situation. When the
Cardinal put the Emperor's draft before his brethren, calling it ' an inspiration of God,' two only
ventured to maintain their demand for a further
deputation to the Pope. By next day, however,
the majority had once more become suspicious of
the genuineness of the alleged papal concessions,
and on the question being put again, voted in favour of a deputation. When Fesch reported this
volte-face the Emperor took the news more calmly
than might have been expected. But the calm did
not last long. At the next general congregation
of the Council (July 10th) the report of the commission was read, after which Fesch declared the
congregation adjourned till July 12th. That evening Napoleon's mood had entirely changed. He
raged and stormed, calling the bishops ' ignorant
and obstinate ' and declaring that he knew more
about these matters than they did. Finally he
declared that he would dissolve the Council immediately, and signed a decree to that effect on the

spot. Two days later the three ringleaders of the opposition, the Bishops of Ghent, Troyes, and Tournai, were arrested on the charge of having ' perverted the minds of their colleagues ' and were imprisoned at Vincennes.

In execution of a threat already communicated to the bishops, Napoleon now referred the question at issue to a lay commission under the presidency of the Grand Juge. This commission reported upon the controversy between the Emperor and the Pope in a sense entirely unfavourable to the latter, declared that the custom of the Church of France indubitably permitted the solution of the difficulty proposed by Napoleon, and made suggestions as to the procedure to be adopted in giving it practical effect. The Arch-Chancellor Cambacérès approved the report, but advised the Emperor to wait and see what line the bishops would ultimately take. To this advice Napoleon assented. A letter had just arrived from Chabrol hinting that the Pope might well accept the Savona note after all, nor was the Emperor without hope that the fathers of the Council might in any case still be made pliable to his will.

The Council, as a body, had certainly proved recalcitrant. But what the bishops had refused to accept collectively they might be induced to accept individually. ' Our wine,' said Maury, ' has not been found good in the cask. You will find it better in bottles.' Napoleon took the hint. Each bishop in turn was asked for his adhesion to the Emperor's draft decree. To help him to make up his mind he had the advantage of a private interview with one of the Ministers of Religion, who lavished promises or threats upon him as circumstances requited, and did not disdain the assistance of the Minister of Police. At the same time

the Emperor redoubled his persecutions of religious
and priests, just to show what he might do if
he liked. By July 26th eighty archbishops and
bishops had yielded. Fesch still held out, but his
courage was rapidly oozing away. Next day the
Ministers of Religion assembled the bishops who
had signed, and formally asked for their adhesion
to the imperial wishes. ' A general movement of
satisfaction and devotion,' they reported later,
' such as it would be impossible to express, mani-
fested itself in the assembly.'

Assured now of an obliging attitude on the part
of a majority the Government ordered the Council
to reassemble on August 5th, with an intimation
that ' His Majesty has decided to restore his confidence to the Council and has persuaded himself
that the majority of its members are animated by
the sentiments of obedience and love which they
owe to their sovereign.' The decree on which it was
to be asked to vote was couched in the following
terms :

1. Conformably with the spirit of the sacred
canons, archbishoprics and bishoprics may not
remain vacant for more than a year together. In
this space of time nomination, institution, and
consecration must all take place.

2. The Emperor shall be asked to continue to
nominate to vacant sees conformably with the
Concordat, and those who are nominated shall
apply to the Pope for canonical institution.

3. In the six months following notification to
the Pope, the Pope shall give canonical institution
conformably with the Concordat.

4. Six months having expired without the Pope
according canonical institution, the metropolitan
(or failing him the senior bishop of the province)
shall proceed to the institution of the bishop

nominate, or, where the vacant see is metropolitan, the senior bishop shall institute.

5. The present decree shall be submitted to the approval of the Pope, and with this object His Majesty shall be asked to allow a deputation of six bishops to go and ask him to confirm the decree.

When the bishops—or rather those of them who still remained in Paris—reassembled on August 5th their decision was a foregone conclusion. Fesch presided, despite a previous declaration that nothing but an escort of four fusiliers would lead him to the chair. This time he espoused the opinions of the majority. The decree was put to the vote and accepted, without any discussion, by a majority of eighty to thirteen. The Archbishop of Tours had previously read a report of the Savona negotiations in which the Pope's acceptance of the note was again asserted without any mention of his subsequent retractation. No doubt this had its effect in quieting the scruples of the fathers, and the lie may count in their defence. Yet if there was on the Emperor's side the will to deceive, we cannot acquit the bishops of a certain willingness to be deceived. However we regard the matter, a defection so wholesale is hardly calculated to increase our respect for the French episcopate of the period. Some years after the Restoration a bishop of the majority was seeking to excuse himself to Cardinal Pacca. ' But, your Eminence,' he expostulated, ' even the best horse stumbles sometimes.' ' Perhaps,' replied Pacca dryly, ' but a whole stable . . . ! '

The decree having passed the Council, the next step was to send a deputation to the Pope to ask him to confirm it. Actually two deputations were sent : the one consisting of cardinals, the other of bishops. The purpose of the Government in sending the former was doubtless to obviate a renewal of the Pope's complaint that he was deprived of his ' natural counsellors.' The bishops took with them a letter signed by the members of the Council in which that assembly was described as ' a fresh proof of the Emperor's zeal for the interests of religion and of his respect for canonical forms.' Of their own attachment to the see of Peter they hoped that His Holiness ' would see a new proof in the decree which we have passed.' ' It is based,' they wrote, ' upon the dispositions which your Holiness has shown to the bishops who had the honour of visiting you three months ago, and which are contained in a document written under your eye of which you have allowed them to retain a copy.'

Before leaving Paris the episcopal envoys received from Bigot de Préameneu the imperial instructions—justly described by Talleyrand as *de nature à rien concilier*. The Pope's approval of the decree must be ' pure and simple.' ' You will refuse to receive [it] if the Pope wishes to give it with reserves.' In this case ' you will declare that we have returned to the common order of the Church, and canonical institution has devolved upon the metropolitan without the intervention of the Pope.'

The Cardinals left for Savona August 20th, the bishops the next day. Meanwhile instructions had been given to send to Savona Mgr Bartalozzi, Archbishop of Edessa, an old friend of the Pope, who (it was thought) would help him to make up his mind in the right way. As an inducement to him to play his part properly, he was arrested on crossing from Italy into France and conveyed to Vincennes. Here he remained a prisoner for a fortnight, being then informed that he had been arrested by mistake. The lesson was not lost upon him.

Both deputations, as well as Bartalozzi, were greeted by the Pope ' in friendly fashion.' The Council's decree he received ' with affability.' However, his scruples remained. He was not averse from approving the decree in substance, but he desired to cast its provisions into the form of a brief. The wording of this caused much discussion and the negotiations moved very slowly. Ultimately the brief was satisfactorily drafted, and the five articles of the decree appeared in it with certain slight alterations. The Pope, however, insisted that if the metropolitan instituted he should do so ' in the name of the sovereign pontiff,' to whom he should be compelled to forward a formal account of his action. On September 20th Chabrol was able to report that the affair might be regarded as happily terminated. The brief was at once sent to the Emperor, who acknowledged its receipt but said that he could do nothing in the matter till he had consulted the Council of State. Meanwhile he charged the bishops at Savona to obtain from the Pope the institution of the bishops who had been nominated more than six months, and then return to Paris immediately. Having issued these instructions Napoleon at once set out for Holland to superintend the preparations for his Russian expedition—somewhat to the consternation of the bishops at Savona, who, not knowing exactly what to do next, were reduced to playing backgammon and reading a *History of Naples*.

Napoleon, indeed, was still in doubt as to what he should do with the Pope's brief now he had got it. He referred it to the Council of State, asking them to make a report upon it. Meanwhile he would at least turn it to account in getting his

nominees instituted. The bishops at Savona
were informed that he would not receive them
unless they brought with them the bulls for all the
vacant sees. They were also told to remind the
Pope that ' all ' included the sees of the erstwhile
papal states. When the report of the Council
appeared, it pronounced the brief unsatisfactory
in several respects. Napoleon therefore ordered
it to be sent back to Savona to be altered.

But the Pope's scruples were increasing rather
than diminishing. He was beginning to see that
the more he yielded the more he would have to
yield. He started to renew his demands for *un
Conseil*, and once again the Archbishop of Tours
had to report that ' matters show little advance.'
In vain did the bishops and Chabrol strive to
remove his objections. On November 17th the
Pope dictated to the Cardinals a note declaring that
in his brief he had conceded all that was asked of
him. As for the Emperor's new demands, ' he
could not take any decision without the assistance
of *un Conseil convenable.*'

This was defiance. Napoleon's rage boiled over.
He determined to make the clergy pay for the
obstinacy of their head. On the ground that their
bishops were disloyal the bursaries granted from
the imperial exchequer to the seminaries of six
dioceses were suppressed, and exemption from
military service was refused to the young ecclesiastics of the same dioceses. The three bishops
who had been imprisoned at the time of the
Council were compelled to resign their sees, and
were exiled to different places. The Emperor
was determined that if the Pope would not bend
he should break. He wrote to the bishops a letter
explaining why he could not accept the brief.
These objections they were asked to communicate

to the Pope. If they were not met the brief would be rejected. The Pope, however, still refused to yield on the subject of the Roman sees. He had made sufficient concessions, and he would make no more.

It was now January, 1812, and the bishops were becoming desperate. They propounded a new note which they presented to the Pope as an ultimatum, warning him of the terrible consequences of a refusal. The prefect added warnings of his own. ' Your Holiness must take the sole responsibility for what will happen.' For his only reply the Pope wrote to the Emperor (January 24, 1812) a letter in which he explained his grounds for refusing what was asked of him, and renewed his demand for the assistance of the entire Sacred College. Having done this he told the Cardinals and bishops that he was willing to see them, but that they must not mention the brief or his letter to the Emperor again. His mind was at last made up, and the immediately visible result was an extraordinary improvement in his health and spirits. On January 28th the bishops received orders to leave Savona. Terrified at having to go back to Paris with their mission unfulfilled, they induced Chabrol to make one last effort with the Pope. But the only result was finally to convince the prefect that no further means of persuasion could succeed in changing his determination.

To the Pope's letter the Emperor vouchsafed no ostensible reply. But his fury found an outlet in a letter written by his instructions to the bishops at Savona by Bigot de Préameneu. In this they were told to inform the Pope that the Emperor regarded the Concordat as abrogated, and would permit no intervention by him in the institution of bishops. The letter ended with the blunt suggestion that the Pope should resign in favour of 'a man stronger in head and principle.' It did not reach Savona till after the bishops' departure; but unwilling that its lessons should be lost, Chabrol read it to the Pope on February 19th. The Holy Father, he reported subsequently, 'was very much moved. But I do not think he has been shaken, so great is his obstinacy.' Two days later a second attempt was equally unsuccessful. To the prefect's prophecy that in the end Christendom would demand that the Pope should resign 'for the good of all,' the Holy Father replied that he would never resign. On February 23rd the prefect formally notified the Pope that 'the brief of September 20th not having been ratified, the Emperor regarded the Concordat as abrogated and would no longer allow him to intervene in any way in the institution of bishops.'

A month later (March 21st) Napoleon wrote from Dresden that as the English threatened to make a descent on the coast of France it would be wise to remove the Pope to a 'place of security.' He therefore enjoined Chabrol to send him to Fontainebleau. Actually, however, nothing was done until June, when the prefect received definite instructions to carry the plan into effect. No time was lost. The journey began the same midnight. By the Emperor's order the Pope assumed the garb of an ordinary ecclesiastic. He suffered much on the journey and nearly died at the top of the Mont Cenis pass. When the party arrived at Fontainebleau (June 19th) no preparations had been made. The Pope had to accept a lodging with the *concierge* while the so-called 'Apartments of Anne of Austria' were got ready for his occupation.

Having got the Pope conveniently under his hand Napoleon gave a first turn to the screw. He ordered the Archbishop of Tours and three other bishops, together with the Red Cardinals, to go to Fontainebleau and urge the Pope to make the desired arrangement. But the Pope merely reiterated the demand which he had never ceased to make at Savona, that he must first be set at liberty and be allowed the advice of his counsellors. He continued his solitary mode of existence, spending his days in prayer or in the study of religious works. ' Never did an eighty year old nun,' wrote Lagorse contemptuously a little later, ' *bien cagotte et bien caillette*, employ herself in her cell in occupations more mystical and trifling than those of the Pope.'

Meanwhile that cosmic tragedy, the expedition to Moscow, was being enacted. Of the magnificent army which crossed the Niemen on June 24, 1812, only a few thousands of broken men were to return. So enormous a reverse, with all its incalculable consequences, might make even a Napoleon pause. Faced with the defection of unwilling allies abroad, he saw it all the more necessary to close the ranks at home. He knew that his feud with the Pope had strained the loyalty of Catholics almost to breaking point. At Christmas, therefore, he sent a friendly message to the Holy Father and suggested an arrangement. ' For my part,' he wrote, ' I am very disposed to it, and it will depend entirely on your Holiness.'

The Pope sent a friendly reply, and shortly afterwards Duvoisin arrived at Fontainebleau at the head of a fresh deputation with the Emperor's terms in his pocket. These were sufficient to prove that, however much Napoleon might desire and need a reconciliation, his pride would make no concessions to secure it. Besides accepting his demands in the matter of episcopal institution, the Pope was to promise to do nothing contrary to the Gallican Articles, to reside at Paris, and to nominate henceforth only one third of the Sacred College (the Catholic sovereigns were to nominate the rest). He was also to condemn by a public brief the action of the Cardinals who had absented themselves from the Emperor's wedding, and to allow the Emperor to nominate the bishops of the former papal states.

These requirements were read to the Pope, who appeared to find some of them very distasteful and renewed his request for the assistance of the Sacred College. He continued to delay a decision until worry and the persistent pressure to which he was subjected caused his health again to give way. Deeming the victim at length on the verge of collapse, the imperial matador thought the time come to administer himself the *coup de grâce*. On January 19, 1813, he gave orders for a hunting-party in the Forest of Melun. Suddenly at midday he leapt into a carriage and drove to Fontainebleau. That evening he strode abruptly into the papal apartments, where he found the Pope conversing with the Cardinals and bishops of the deputation. He embraced the Holy Father, who welcomed him even tenderly and consented to a discussion of the issues between them. The conversations lasted for five days, during which Napoleon plied the Pope hard, though the allegation that he stooped to personal insult and violence has no foundation on fact. At last, wearied and almost stupefied, the Pope abandoned his resistance, yet not until he had secured the withdrawal of several of the Emperor's most obnoxious demands. Turning an imploring glance upon the Cardinals, he braced himself to sign a document which described itself (the point is important) as ' designed to serve as a basis for a definitive arrangement.' The Cardinals made no sign, and the signature was subscribed. The Emperor signed his own name immediately below (January 25, 1813).

This so-called ' Concordat of Fontainebleau ' comprised ten articles, of which the following were the most important. The Pope should exercise his pontificate in France and in Italy in the same manner as his predecessors (1). The pontifical domains were declared exempt from all taxation, and a revenue of two millions per annum was to be provided for the Pope in compensation for those domains which had been alienated (3). The Pope must give canonical institution within six months, failing which the metropolitan or senior bishop of the province should institute (4). The Pope was to be allowed to nominate to ten bishoprics in France and Italy. The six suburbicarian sees were to be re-established and the Pope was to nominate to them (5 and 6). The Propaganda, the Penitentiary, and the Archives were to be established in the place of residence of the Holy Father (9). The clerics and laymen who had incurred the Emperor's displeasure by reason of recent events were to be restored to favour (10).

This Concordat, it must be repeated, was intended as a mere preliminary draft—or at least the Pope so understood it. But the Emperor was determined to regard it as a full-blown treaty. As such he communicated it to the Senate, and as such he sought at once to have it put into execution. Pacca and his fellow-prisoners were released, and the Black Cardinals notified that they were at liberty to rejoin the Pope. This they did with all speed. But when they reached Fontainebleau they found the Holy Father a prey to the blackest melancholy. He bitterly reproached himself with his weakness, and even denied himself for a time

the privilege of saying mass.   Naturally the arrival
on the scene of the most intransigent of the
Cardinals did nothing to allay his scruples.   When
Pacca expressed his admiration for his heroic
courage he exclaimed, ' And yet we have ended by
rolling in the mire.'

A series of secret conferences followed between
Pope and Cardinals, resulting in the decision that
the Pope should write a letter to the Emperor
retracting the concessions he had made.   Such
were the precautions necessary to keep the letter
secret that it took several days to write it.   But on
March 24th the Pope gave it to Lagorse, requesting
that it might be forwarded to the Emperor at
once.   In it he expressed his ' intense remorse and
repentance,' and declared ' in all apostolic sincerity
that our conscience is invincibly opposed to the
execution of divers articles contained in the document of January 25th.'   After Lagorse had depart-
ed, the Pope summoned the Sacred College and
read a statement that he considered both the Brief
of Savona and the alleged Concordat of January
25th as ' null and of no validity.'   Having thus
unburdened his conscience, the Holy Father
suddenly became calm and cheerful as he had not
been for a long time.

The Pope's letter must have come as a most disagreeable surprise to Napoleon.   But he restrained
his native irascibility, and merely told Bigot de
Préameneu to keep it a profound secret.   He then
asked the bishops to make one last effort to induce
the Pope to put the Fontainebleau Concordat (of his
retractation of which they of course knew nothing)
into execution.   By his orders, too, Maury went
to Fontainebleau on March 29th.   But the Pope
received him coldly and refused to listen to his
protestations and warnings.   Soon afterwards in-

structions reached Fontainebleau that access to the Pope was to be severely restricted, and that the Cardinals were to remain there only on condition that they did not interfere in affairs in any way nor write any letters. On April 5th Cardinal di Pietro was arrested and taken to Auxonne, where he was placed under police surveillance. But neither violence nor threats prevented the Pope from formally protesting, in an allocution to the Sacred College, against the two decrees by which the Emperor had declared the Fontainebleau Concordat binding. He expressed the hope that no metropolitan would venture to act in accordance with its provisions. But if this hope were falsified he declared all institution so given to be null and void, and both institutors and consecrators to be schismatics. At the same time he asked the Cardinals to draw up a bull embodying the arrangements for a Conclave in case of his death.

On April 25th the Emperor had gone to Mayence to take command of the Army of Germany. Just before his departure he had nominated bishops to the sees of Troyes, Tournai, and Ghent, and instructed the Minister of Religions to see that they were instituted with all possible speed. Until this could be done Bigot de Préameneu asked the chapters to give powers of administration to the bishops-elect. The chapter of Troyes first obeyed, then refused, then withdrew its refusal. But the chapter of Tournai declined to give the powers asked for until the resignation of the former bishop had been accepted by the Pope. When, too, the Bishop of Ghent entered his cathedral to take possession of it he found the choir empty. Napoleon retorted spitefully by ordering the Ghent seminarists to be conscripted for the army and sent to Magdeburg. On August 14th he gave instructions to have the canons of Tournai arrested. However, at both places the resistance was maintained. The Emperor was equally obstinate despite the uncertainties of the future and a dying message from Duvoisin, ' I implore you to set the Holy Father at liberty.'

Hearing that a congress was to be held at Prague to discuss the possibility of settling terms of peace, the Pope sent a secret letter to the Emperor of Austria, asking for the restoration to him of the papal states. At this very time the recipient of the letter was himself putting forward a claim to be recognized as ' King of Rome '—such was the devotion of the House of Hapsburg to the Holy See. However, it mattered little, for the congress came to nothing and the war was renewed on August 11th. Napoleon's embarrassments rapidly increased, and in the later autumn he made fresh overtures to the Pope. But the Pope replied that neither time nor place was suitable.

Not to be deterred, Napoleon, in December, sent de Beaumont, Archbishop-designate of Bourges, to Fontainebleau, but the Pope refused to give him any reply. The Allies having crossed the Rhine, de Beaumont was again sent to Fontainebleau bearing a letter in which the Emperor promised to restore the papal states—which, by the way, had just been seized by Murat, King of Naples, on behalf of the Allies—and suggested the terms of an agreement. But the Pope replied that the restoration of his states, being an act of justice, could not be made the subject of any negotiation. He desired to return to Rome as quickly as possible, but he did not doubt that Providence would soon bring him there. Next day (January 21, 1814) the Emperor gave instructions to remove the Pope immediately to Savona. ' The adjutant of the palace will say that he is taking him to Rome, where he has orders to cause him to arrive like a bomb. Having reached Savona the Pope will be treated in the same way as before.' The idea was obviously to get the Pope out of the reach of the Allies, and meanwhile to await the issue of events. On January 23rd the Pope left the palace. Three days later the Cardinals were informed that they must quit Fontainebleau within four days. Pacca was sent to Uzès and placed under strict surveillance.

The Pope reached Savona towards the end of February, 1814. In all the towns through which he passed he was greeted by enthusiastic crowds. France was already preparing for a change of master. Learning that the Allies intended to restore the Pope to Rome and to ask the French Government to set him at liberty immediately, Napoleon resolved to make a virtue of necessity and gave instructions to Lagorse to take him on to Parma and there hand him over to the Neapolitan advance guards. The Pope left Savona on March 19th, and on the 25th reached Firenzuola and freedom. By slow stages he journeyed towards Rome, the faithful Pacca joining him on the way. At Cesena Murat asked him whither he was going. 'To Rome,' was the reply : 'nothing is more natural.' The King of Naples did not dare to prevent him. At last, on May 24, 1814, he entered once more into the beloved city. Surrounded by a train of children bearing gilded palms and crying Hosanna, amid the wild plaudits of the crowd, his carriage drawn by the arms of young Romans, the Holy Father passed through the Porta del Popolo and proceeded to S. Peter's, where he knelt in prayer before the tomb of the Apostles.

CHAPTER IX

THE RESTORATION
1814–17

I

A FAMILIAR saying has it that ' the Bourbons learn nothing and forget nothing.' Judged by this standard, Louis XVIII was a little less than worthy of his race. His selfishness and love of ease combined with his common sense to save him from any personal wish to push reaction to extremes. Like Charles II, he had ' no mind to go again on his travels.' He knew that, however little the Revolution had succeeded in realizing the hopes with which it had started, France would never allow its work to be entirely undone. Nor was he unmindful of the very precarious foundations on which the restored dynasty rested. The French nation is notoriously willing to suffer many things at the hands of a Government which will gratify its love of power and prestige. But the Government of the Restoration was a symbol, not of national glory, but of national humiliation. It was the child of defeat : it was imposed by, and existed on the sufferance of, the victorious powers. It is true that, for the moment, the bitter fruits of Napoleon's imperialism had made France more willing than usual to carry herself humbly and to purchase the boon of peace at any price. But it would not be wise to press too hard on the bruised reed. Thus if Louis XVIII had inherited after all the throne of

Louis XIV, he was far from having inherited his authority.   And no one knew this better than he.

But while the King gauged the facts of the situation thus accurately, the *émigrés* who had crowded back to the Tuileries in his wake by no means shared his perspicacity.   For them the hour of vengeance had tarried long : but it had come at last, and they were prepared to use it to the uttermost. Nothing less would be adequate in their eyes than the complete restoration of the *ancien régime*. True, the *Charte*, granted on his return in 1814 by the restored prince, had established a monarchy of the ' limited ' type and ostensibly perpetuated some at least of the gains of the Revolution.   But this was at best a regrettable necessity—a concession to the exigencies of the time to be withdrawn the moment circumstances permitted. And along with the reversal of the new order must go a relentless proscription of those who had established or supported it. The ' White Terror ' of 1815 in southern France was an earnest of what the partisans of the Revolution might look forward to when once their enemies were fairly in the saddle.

The spirit which dominated the *salons* of the Faubourg St. Germain was only too faithfully reflected in the breasts of the clergy.   It will be remembered that in 1789 the *bas clergé*, if not their wealthy and aristocratic superiors, had shown decided sympathy with the cause of reform.   But in 1814 the situation was very different.   The iron of persecution had entered into their souls.   The Church and the Revolution were henceforth deadly foes : no compromise could exist between them. One or other must prevail and extinguish its rival. To the clergy of the Restoration period the league between the Altar and the Throne was an article

of faith, a part of the necessary order of things.
The disastrous effects of the association were
clearly visible later and have only ceased to operate
in the lifetime of the present generation—indeed
it would be absurd to suppose that even now they
are extinct. But under the restored Bourbons a
whole-hearted alliance with the principle of Legitimacy seemed the one sheet-anchor of safety for
the Church.

It must be remembered that modern Ultramontanism was as yet hardly born. The monarchy was
still the natural and cardinal embodiment of the
principle of Authority. The conception of the
Holy See as supplying a focus round which, while
everywhere else Liberalism triumphed, all human
loyalties and longings for direction from above
might cluster, was still a thing of the future. Moreover, the older generation of clergy had inherited
the Gallican tradition of the *Grand Siècle*, with its
minimizing of the papal, its extravagant exaltation
of the royal, claims.

The first opportunity of the would-be restorers
of the old order was short lived. Napoleon returned
from Elba : and Louis XVIII and his entourage
vanished temporarily from the scene. But Water-
loo put them once more in possession of the situation. The elections of August, 1815, saw reaction
triumphant all along the line. The Chamber of
Peers, nominated by the Crown and composed in
great part of those who had held office under the
Empire, was compelled by sheer self-interest to
espouse a policy of moderation. But no such re-
straints held back the Chamber of Deputies. The
elections had been industriously manipulated : and
the bulk of the nation's 'representatives' were
drawn from the most intransigent class of all—
the lesser *noblesse* of the provinces.

The executions of Ney and Labédoyère—both of whom the Government would have gladly saved if it could—were quite insufficient to slake the thirst for blood of the ultra-Royalist majority. ' It is time to put a stop to clemency,' cried one deputy. The King and his Ministers did their best to restrain this vindictive frenzy. Their efforts were not altogether in vain : but they were forced to concede the perpetual exile of the ' regicides.' Thus, among others, disappeared from the scene the unspeakable Fouché, whose long career of vileness, in which he had espoused and betrayed every successive Government in turn, came at last to an end.

The reversal of the work of the Revolution included as a matter of course the lifting up of the Church from the state of abasement and poverty in which it had lain since 1790. The French aristocracy had returned from exile cured (at least as far as outward professions went) of the polite infidelity which had characterized it in the closing years of the old régime. Under the shock of a common misfortune a *rapprochement* between clergy and *noblesse* had been effected from both sides. The former had shed its liberalism, the latter its scepticism. The solidarity of interest between them was now recognized to the full.

Opinions, however, differed as to the precise measure in which wealth and privilege were to be restored to the Church. The more moderate Royalists were prepared to be satisfied with an augmentation of the beggarly stipends of the inferior clergy and the elimination from the Civil Code of those provisions which were most repugnant to Catholic feeling. The more zealous, on the other hand, demanded the reconstitution of the clergy as a corporation possessed of ample estates and exercising at least a large measure of its former control over education and the *état civil* of citizens. It was this diversity of aim which, combined with the unwillingness of the Government to allow clerical claims to be pressed too far, prevented those claims from being satisfied to the extent desired by the more ardent spirits.

Certainly, the champions of the Church in the Chamber left no stone unturned to secure for it the maximum satisfaction of its desires. The fullest possible advantage was taken of the provision of the Charte enjoining that before a bill could be brought before the Chamber the Government's *projet de loi* must be submitted to a committee of deputies for examination and revision. The ultra-Royalist majority were careful to pack these committees with persons of their own political complexion : so that when a report was made, it was frequently found to distort the Government's intentions almost beyond recognition. Meanwhile the Church repaid its debt by mobilizing all its resources in support of the cause of Legitimacy. The bishops in innumerable charges sang the epithalamium of the mystic marriage between the Altar and the Throne. ' Our true liberty,' proclaimed the Bishop of Troyes, ' is in the power of the King. . . . Religion is the constitution *par excellence*, the truly fundamental Charte that may take the place of all others.'

Now, too, appeared in the country districts those bands of *missionnaires* who employed all the resources of religious revivalism in the cause of political reaction. It was one of those moments when (as in 1871 and 1915) France experiences a somewhat transient renewal of religious feeling and interest. No pains were spared to turn the opportunity to account. The efforts of the *missionnaires* were first directed to the provinces of the west—always the most fertile field for Catholic influences. Missions were preached at Angers, Nantes, Orléans, and other towns. Rousing and highly emotional sermons were preached in the churches both morning and evening : and the mission reached its climax in a solemn renewal of baptismal vows, an act of self-consecration to the Blessed Virgin, and a general Communion. Finally, as a memorial of the mission just concluded, a huge cross was erected in some public place—possibly (such are time's revenges) on the identical spot on which a ' tree of liberty ' had been planted a generation before.

The *missionnaires* declaimed against the doctrines of the Encyclopaedists and the misdeeds of the Revolution, especially the spoliation of the Church. They drew terrifying pictures of the fate reserved in the next world for those who had shared the fruits of sacrilege. Their denunciations and appeals drew tears and sobs from many of their audience, and as they left the scene of their exertions the faithful would press round and try to obtain a small portion of their linen or clothing as a kind of relic. Sometimes, too, their converts would bring volumes of Voltaire and Rousseau in their possession to the place of assembly, where the books were solemnly committed to the flames.

Such methods were obviously well adapted to impress the minds of the populace. Nor would it be at all fair to think of them as dictated by purely political or worldly aims. To a great extent the motives of those who employed them were genuinely religious, however much the desire to save souls might be mingled with aims less purely spiritual. In the same way we should not pay too much heed to the alternative charge of ' fanaticism ' brought against the *missionnaires* by the worldly and unbelieving, in whose eyes fanaticism and religious zeal are always convertible terms. On the other hand, it would appear that quiet, moderate-minded Catholics found their efforts less an inspiration than an embarrassment : while their aggressive and militant spirit inevitably made the hatred of their opponents for the Church and all its works more bitter than ever.

II

In attempting to estimate the part played by the Church in seconding the cause of reaction after 1815, we are confronted by the interesting but difficult problem of the alleged political activity of the famous ' Congregation of the Blessed Virgin '— usually called ' The Congregation ' *tout court*. On the one hand the enemies of the *parti prêtre* maintained at the time, and have never ceased to maintain since, that this organization was a hot-bed of ultra-Royalist intrigue, a reactionary secret society using the pretext of religious devotion to cloak a wide-spreading conspiracy to overthrow the work of the Revolution. The defenders of the clergy, on the other hand, assert no less vehemently that this charge is an absurd and malicious libel, and that the purpose of the Congregation was to assist the religious life of its members and nothing else. In defence of this view M. Geoffroy de Grandmaison has written an elaborate monograph in which the documents relating to the Congregation are for the first time made available to the public.

Which of these views are we to accept ? It seems at first hardly possible to dispute either that the motive which originally prompted the formation of the society in question was exclusively religious or that its religious character was maintained throughout the first years of its existence. In 1801, the year of the Concordat, a group of six young Catholics resident in Paris, students in medicine or in law, acting under the direction of a Jesuit priest, Father Delpuits, founded a ' Congregation ' under the title of *Sancta Maria Auxilium Christianorum.* Such a Congregation, it must be observed, was no new invention. It was only the revival of a mode of association which for more than two centuries had been part of the machinery devised by the Society of Jesus for fostering a spirit of devotion in the educated laity. As such, the system of ' Congregations ' had spread over the whole of Catholic Europe. In France, they were both numerous and influential. With the dissolution of the Jesuit order their existence naturally came to an end : indeed they were expressly forbidden by a decree of the Parlement of Paris. But if the Society of Jesus ceased to exist as an order, its traditions lived on in the hearts of its scattered members. Among these was Father Delpuits. Having taken his place in the ranks of the secular clergy he acquired considerable repute as a spiritual guide. Driven from France during the Revolution, he returned thither even before the advent of Napoleon to power. He now devoted himself specially to work among the students of Paris, for whose benefit he conceived the idea of founding a Congregation on the old lines.

To the original members were soon added fresh recruits. Of these the most notable were the two brothers, Mathieu and Eugène de Montmorency—the former destined to play a big part both in the Congregation and in Restoration politics. When Pius VII visited Paris in 1804 the members of the Congregation demonstrated their loyalty to the Head of the Church by kissing his feet in S. Sulpice:

and the Pope formally confirmed the young society, together with the similar organizations that had been, or were to be, formed in other parts of France. These provincial Congregations were affiliated to that of Paris as centre of the Congregationist organization.

The neighbourhood of Father Delpuits' abode to the *hôtels* of the Faubourg S. Germain provided him with an excellent opportunity of intercourse with their aristocratic occupants. There thus ensued a steady flow into the Congregation of scions of the old French noblesse. Such names as de Rohan, de Béthune, de Noailles, now begin to figure in its list of members. These young aristocrats took their full share in the charitable undertakings of the Congregation, which found their chief theatre in the great and neglected hospitals of Paris : though here no doubt the services of the less highly born but professionally qualified doctors who also belonged to it were more valuable still. Among these latter was Hyacinthe Laennec, one of the greatest names in modern French medicine and an original member of the Congregation.

The imprisonment of the Pope at Savona gave the Congregation a fresh opportunity of proving their loyalty to the Holy See. It was by the instrumentality of six of its members that the Bull of Excommunication against the Emperor reached Paris. Eugène de Montmorency brought it from Lyons to the capital concealed in his boot. Shortly afterwards it became known that the imperial police were meditating a spring on the Congregation. In order to prevent a dissolution by force, it was decided to suspend the meetings. But an imperial decree soon followed suppressing ' all the establishments known under the name of the " Congregation of the Holy Virgin." '

The Catholic loyalty of their members, however, remained unshaken. Mathieu de Montmorency organized the so-called *Oeuvre des Cardinaux Noirs,* to provide assistance for the members of the Sacred College who had opposed the imperial divorce and other victims of Napoleon's tyranny. It was members of the Congregation, too, who distributed the mysterious missives emanating from Savona over the length and breadth of France. Before long it was suggested that the Congregation should be re-established. M. Delpuits refused to comply, but was induced to surrender his function to the director of S. Sulpice, M. Duclaux, who authorized the revival of the meetings, though under stringent limitations. These meetings were transferred in 1812 to the house at the corner of the Rue du Bac, destined to become so notorious as the centre of Congreganist activities under the Restoration.

With the fall of Napoleon the meetings resumed their old form, and new members were admitted. The numbers increased rapidly, at least from 1815 onwards. Now, too, it became possible to place the Congregation once more under Jesuit direction. It is true that in France the return of the Jesuits was not yet officially permitted, in spite of the restoration of their order by a papal bull of 1814 ; but for the time being they were content to conceal themselves under the name of ' Society of Fathers of the Faith.' These two facts—the rapid growth of the Congregation and its Jesuit direction —quickly awakened the suspicion and alarm of the enemies of the *parti prêtre.* The wildest stories were current of a vast reactionary conspiracy with the Congregation as its centre and the Jesuits as its inspiring force. This idea survives in anti-clerical circles in France to this day. According to

Lacretelle, the anti-Royalist historian of the Restoration period,

> The Congregation succeeded to the heritage of the royalist secret societies and sanctified their turbulent designs. Its treasury was enriched by the offerings of opulent piety and by the still more abundant gifts which an ardent party spirit inspires. The whole movement was placed under the patronage of S. Ignatius Loyola. This club of devotees had its affiliated societies, its relations outside, exactly like the Club of the Jacobins. At Paris, the Maison des Missions Étrangères, restored to the Jesuits under the title of 'Fathers of the Faith,' was the principal rallying-point for pious exercises and political conferences.

This description is exaggerated, to say nothing of its inaccuracy in points of detail : and its exaggeration will be duly discounted by all who have not 'the Jesuits' on the brain. But had it any foundation in fact at all? The writers on the Royalist and clerical side maintain that the whole 'conspiracy' was a mare's nest : the Congregation was a religious fraternity pure and simple. Yet it is hard to believe that the popular impression connecting the Congegation with the secret activity of the ultra-Royalists rested on mere illusion. The impression was at least a very natural one. We know that under the Restoration the cause of the Church and the cause of Legitimate Monarchy were regarded as standing or falling together. 'It was impossible,' says M. de Grandmaison naively, 'that good Christians should be other than Royalist.' It is no less certain that the leading figures of the Congregation were also prominently identified with the ultra-Royalist party in politics. There were no more double-dyed Legitimists than Mathieu de Montmorency and Jules de Polignac. It may be conceded that the Congregation as such took no part in the political game. Nor is it possible to deny that if a number of well-known ultra-

Royalist politicians belonged to it, many others did not. Of the ultra-Royalist ministry which came into power in 1821 neither Villèle, the Prime Minister, nor any of his colleagues (with but one exception, Mathieu de Montmorency himself), was a member of the Congregation. It is clear, however, that, even though the actual meetings of the Congregation might be purely devotional in character, yet the habit of association and the personal relationships thus formed might well find expression in another and less spiritual field of action.

We have seen that, while the Congregation itself was never turned into a focus of resistance to Napoleon's anti-papal policy, yet its members found other means of taking joint action on the Pope's behalf. So, too, under the Restoration, there is some reason for believing that by the side of the Congregation there was an association, largely, though not entirely, composed of its members, which was identified with the cause of political reaction. In any case, whether this is so or not, the fact that the Congregation was exclusively religious by no means implies that all its members were actuated by religious motives.

The Congregation, like the Church under Constantine, was the victim of its own success. It included so many persons of rank and influence that an ambitious and not very scrupulous young man might well think it worth his while to join it for the sake of making acquaintances who might be useful to him in carving out a career. The situation is probably summed up fairly accurately by the historian Viel-Castel, himself a Royalist, though by no means of the extremer sort :

' Among those who composed the Congregation,' he says, ' some, especially in its early days, had been called to it by purely religious motives, others had mingled political con-

siderations with these motives, while others only entered later
with the hope of opening out for themselves a road to fortune.
. . . The disinterestedness of the first has always protested
with sincerity against the reproaches of ambition and intrigue
which are hurled against an association which for them was
never anything but a work of piety : while as for the political
Congreganists, who at the bottom of their hearts knew what
they were after, it was not from them that one could expect a
frank avowal of their secret intentions, especially at a time
when the evident exaggeration of the charges with which their
enemies sought to overwhelm them allowed them to defend
themselves by denials that were for the most part well-founded,
though too absolute.'

In any case the indignation of the enemies of the
Congregation against the jobbery of which it was
very probably the instrument (at any rate in the
later part of the Restoration period) must not be
taken too seriously. A political party is always
strangely jealous for the integrity of its opponents :
and the July Revolution was to prove that self-
seeking was not a fault of Royalists only. ' Do
you know, *messieurs les ministres*,' said the Duc de
Broglie to his colleagues of Louis Philippe's first
ministry, ' the definition of a Carlist ? A Carlist
is some one who occupies a position that somebody
else wants.'

III

The composition of the *Chambre Introuvable*
might have seemed to justify the rosiest hopes on
the part of the Church and its political supporters.
For reasons that have been already indicated, these
hopes were hardly to be realized. A certain measure of success was, however, achieved. The most
important victory secured by the champions of
the Church was the abolition of divorce. Its protagonist on this occasion was the Vicomte de
Bonald, whose learned and brilliant polemic against
the principles of the Revolution will be noticed

later. His vehement arguments carried the day :
and a law decreeing the substitution for divorce of
separation *a thoro et mensa* was passed by both
Chambers.

Attempts to improve the financial position of
the clergy were less successful. There were two
possible methods of effecting this improvement.
The first was to increase the sum paid by the State
for the maintenance of public worship. Such payment, in turn, might be made in either of two ways
—by an annual grant or by the permanent allocation of a sum, chargeable on the National Debt, on
which the clergy should receive the interest. Of
these two methods the Church's champions not unnaturally preferred the latter, as putting its revenues
beyond the reach of the fluctuations of the political
situation. With this object a Bill was introduced
assuring to the Church an income of eighty-two
million francs per annum, being the amount allotted
to it by the Constitution Civile and representing
a capital of two milliards. The condition of the
national exchequer not permitting so large a sum
to be disbursed at once, it was provided that two-
thirds only should be paid for the present, the full
amount becoming due in five or six years' time.

So generous an endowment of an institution that
was far from enjoying universal popularity or confidence was bound to be bitterly opposed, especially
in view of the known embarrassment of the
national finances. Its supporters pleaded that it
was no more than a fair compensation for the vast
wealth taken from the Church by the Revolution.
But their opponents replied that the State had a
perfect right to effect this confiscation, and, further,
that the clergy, being a public service, must be
paid in the same way as other public services—by
an allocation in the budget from year to year.

The proposal was eventually dropped : though a minor provision suppressing the pensions conferred on ecclesiastics who had married or resigned their orders was passed by a large majority.

A somewhat more successful attempt was made to render operative the alternative method of providing for the clergy, viz. by reconstituting the Church as a property-owning corporation. This was what the clergy themselves really desired. The system of a State-paid priesthood was obnoxious to them, not only as an innovation introduced at the time of the hated Revolution, but also on the higher ground that it made their spiritual activity unduly subordinate to the State. The conception of the clergy as (in Mirabeau's phrase) *une police morale salariée par l'État* is indeed revolting to any one who regards the Church as a divine society having a corporate life and witness of its own. It is true that under the restored Bourbons the clergy had good reason to anticipate that the civil power would be not their enemy but their friend—indeed, they were only too willing to lean on the secular arm. Yet the political possibilities of the future were incalculable : and it was only wise to secure themselves if they could against the inclinations of a less sympathetic régime to ' put on the screw.'

The experience of the Church under Napoleon had hardly been encouraging : and a similar experience in the future could only be guarded against by giving to the clerical order property of its own. Such re-endowment might be effected either through new donations or by restoring all or part of the property formerly held by the Church. The former method was the less sweeping and provocative, and was therefore essayed first. A Bill was introduced into the Chamber of Deputies which gave permission to the clergy ' to accept and possess such movable and immovable property as might be given them either by gift or by testamentary disposition.' At the same time an elaborate system of *bureaux* was to be set up to administer the property in question. The measure passed the Lower House, though only in the teeth of vehement opposition : but when it came before the Peers, these refused to concede more than the bare permission to receive gifts and legacies, and consigned the *bureaux diocesains* and the rest of the proposed machinery to limbo. In this mutilated form the Bill came back to the Deputies, who were compelled, with a very bad grace, to accept it.

There remained the further, and infinitely more perilous, question of the Church's right to receive back the property taken from it at the Revolution. That this property would be restored in its entirety even those who were blindest to the facts of the situation can scarcely have dared to hope. The restored monarchy could not have survived for an hour such an expropriation of the host of new proprietors, great and small, who had founded their fortunes by the purchase of *biens nationaux*. But there still remained unalienated in the hands of the Government a considerable portion of the Church's former property, consisting for the most part of forest lands, and estimated at an annual value of about ten million francs. The champions of ' legitimacy ' clamoured for its restitution to its rightful owners. This, they maintained, was all the more a debt of honour in view of the refusal of the legislature to put the Church in possession of the two milliards that had been avowedly intended as a compensation for its lost estates. The Government did not conceal its distaste for the proposal. But the majority persisted, and the measure was carried (April 24, 1816). As the only way of barring

further action in the matter, the King declared
the session closed : and the life of the *Chambre
Introuvable* came to an end.

With its disappearance from the scene, there
disappeared also the Church's best chance of realizing its aspirations.   The new House was of a much
less reactionary cast.   Neither the scheme for providing the clergy with a capital source of income
nor that for restoring to the Church what still
remained of its former property was revived.   A
Bill was, however, introduced into the Chamber
of Peers providing that ' any legally authorized
ecclesiastical establishment might accept, with the
King's permission, such movable or immovable
property and such *rentes* as might be given to it,
either by living donors or by will, and that such
property should be possessed by it in perpetuity
and should not be alienated without the King's
permission.'   This Bill, with the substitution for
the phrase ' legally authorized establishment ' of
' establishment recognized by the law,' was passed
by both Chambers (January 2, 1817).   The principle of endowment was thus recognized, though
the practical benefit to be derived from this source
was likely for a long time to be small.

CHAPTER X

THE CONCORDAT OF 1817
1817-20

IMMEDIATELY after the return of Louis XVIII in 1814 the question had been mooted of a new Concordat. The alternative of maintaining a settlement made by the usurper was bound to be offensive to Bourbon pride. Moreover, the Concordat of 1801 did little more than sanction formally the administrative provisions of the Civil Constitution of the clergy—a characteristic product of the Revolution that all good Royalists abhorred. Thus even on the part of the civil power there was a desire to put the relations between Church and State on a new basis. Much more was a change desirable in the eyes of the Church itself. Neither the Court of Rome nor the French clergy had ever regarded the settlement of 1801 as anything but a concession to bitter necessity. Nor had it even been universally accepted. All through Napoleon's régime the *Petite Église* had maintained its rather grotesque protest against what it regarded as a base surrender to the secular power. And with the return of the old dynasty that protest was to be powerfully reinforced. Of the bishops who had preferred to be deposed rather than recognize Napoleon's handiwork some had died in the meanwhile : but the remainder came back in the train of Louis XVIII.

Chief among them was Alexandre de Talleyrand-

Périgord, uncle and first patron of the former Bishop of Autun. Appointed Archbishop of Reims nearly forty years before, he was now, though nearly eighty, to become Archbishop of Paris and Grand Almoner of France. In the latter capacity he was the official head of ecclesiastical affairs. He was also high in favour with the Court. Such was his loathing for the Concordat of 1801 that, though Cardinal Consalvi was at this time in Paris, he found a pretext for declining to discuss the affairs of the Church with one who had been implicated in so nefarious a transaction. His nephew's memory was less inconveniently long. Writing in the spring of 1814 to Consalvi, the ex-bishop, now Foreign Minister to the Provisional Government of France, had thus gracefully delivered himself : ' It is a pleasure to me to resume at a happier time a long-standing correspondence with your Eminence.'

The first step was to send an emissary to Rome. The person chosen for the purpose was another *émigré* prelate, M. Courtois de Pressigny, formerly Bishop of St. Malo. His instructions were simple : to bring things back to where they were before the Revolution. The Concordat of 1516 was to be revived, with certain necessary modifications. The one hundred and thirty odd episcopal sees that existed before 1789 were to be restored as an assertion of principle—though it was admitted that certain of them might be suppressed later, if the full number was found excessive. So completely was the Concordat of 1801 to be abrogated that the bishops since appointed were to be compelled to receive the royal nomination afresh.

The Holy See declined to make so clean a sweep of what, after all, however grudgingly conceded, had been its own work. ' Take care,' said Consalvi to the Royalist bishop. ' If you are always talking to us about royal legitimacy, we shall have to remind you of papal infallibility.' The counter-suggestion was made that to the fifty dioceses retained in 1801 there should be added as many of the suppressed remainder as should be necessary. This proposal was sent to Paris to be considered by the ecclesiastical committee under the presidency of the Grand Almoner. But the committee decided against it : and the Government resolved to adhere to its original position.

The return of Napoleon put a stop to these negotiations for the time being. But after the Hundred Days they were resumed : the negotiator this time being the Comte de Blacas. His instructions were the same as those of his predecessor. But he was advised to be more tactful in carrying them out and to save the face of the Holy See by avoiding any demand for the explicit abrogation of the Concordat of 1801. These precautions were duly observed. In particular M. de Blacas showed the utmost possible deference to the omnipotent Consalvi. The result was that in a very short time a draft agreement was drawn up. The Concordat of 1516 was re-established, and that of 1801 declared in consequence to be no longer effective. The Organic Articles were abolished. Provision was made for a new delimitation of dioceses. The Pope and the King were given authority to transfer bishops as might be necessary.

It soon became clear, however, that the terms of the agreement were not really satisfactory to any of the parties concerned. The King demanded that the bishops appointed since 1801 should formally resign and receive a fresh nomination from him. The Pope, for his part, was suspicious of the attitude both of the former Constitutional bishops appointed by Napoleon and of the bishops who had declined to accept the Concordat of 1801, and was anxious for an explicit assurance from both groups of their loyalty to the Holy See. He also expressed misgivings as to the oath imposed on all Frenchmen to observe the Charte : the guarantee of religious liberty contained in that instrument seeming to him discordant with the laws of the Church. Finally, when the agreement was brought before the Council of State, objection was raised both to the abrogation of the Organic Articles and to the power given to the Pope and the King to remove bishops from their sees.

These difficulties, however, as the result of further negotiations, were overcome by concessions on both sides. Of the surviving ' non-Concordatist' bishops, six (including the Grand Almoner) made their peace with the Pope by a joint letter in which, while carefully avoiding any condemnation of their past conduct, they declared their submission to the wishes of the Holy See as now expressed. The other four, however, refused to concede even as much as this, preferring rather to return to the exile they had so recently quitted. The last of them, Thémines, formerly Bishop of Blois, continued to maintain till his dying day (1829) that he was the sole legitimate bishop in the Church of France !

At length, on June 11, 1817, a revised agreement received the signature of Consalvi and de Blacas. The chief articles were as follows : The Concordat of 1516 was re-established, and that of 1801 abrogated (1 and 2). The Organic Articles were abrogated ' in such of their provisions as are contrary to the laws and doctrines of the Church ' (3). The sees suppressed in 1801 were to be re-established up to a number to be agreed on (4).

The sees founded in 1801 were maintained—also their existing occupants except in cases ' founded on grave and legitimate causes ' (5 and 6). A suitable endowment *en bien-fonds et en rentes sur l'État* was assured to all episcopal sees ' as soon as circumstances should permit.' Meanwhile ' a revenue sufficient to improve their condition' was to be assigned them. The endowment of chapters, benefices, and seminaries was to be provided for (8). The Pope was to issue as soon as possible a bull creating, and defining the limits of, the additional dioceses (9). The King promised to do all he could to remove the ' obstacles which stand in the way of religion and the execution of the laws of the Church ' (10). The re-establishment of the Concordat in force prior to 1789 was not to involve that of the abbeys and priories existing at that date (12).

In order to allay the Pope's qualms as to the oath to observe the Charte, a declaration was annexed stating in the King's name that the toleration established by the Charte was ' purely civil.'

The revised agreement having been duly signed and forwarded to Paris, both parties assumed that the matter was at an end. Nothing now remained but to put the treaty into execution. The Pope issued the required bull within less than two months (August 6, 1817). By it the number of sees was raised from fifty to ninety-two : and the boundaries of the new dioceses were defined. The Pope also declared that ' he endowed the churches preserved or created by the new arrangement with a charge on the public debt,' and that ' pending such time as the bishops should be put in possession of their revenues he assigned to them such revenues as were necessary to improve their condition.'

Such language was no doubt gratifying to Roman pride. It says less for Roman prudence. The illusions of the Quirinal seem, however, to have been fully shared by Louis XVIII and his Prime Minister, the Duc de Richelieu. Accordingly the appointments both to the newly created sees and to those left vacant by Napoleon were speedily made : and the Pope accorded institution to most of the nominees. The Grand Almoner and two other French bishops received the Hat.

It was the Garde des Sceaux, M. de Pasquier, who first disturbed this blissful ignorance by pointing out the need of parliamentary sanction for the Concordat. Faced with the real facts of the situation, the Government could only acquiesce. The Pope was informed that the installation of the new bishops must be postponed until the consent of the Chambers had been obtained, and was also asked to defer his institution of the twenty-three (out of fifty-seven) who had not yet received it. A draft measure was then drawn up under M. Pasquier's direction.

Meanwhile a strong current of opposition to the terms of the Concordat was flowing throughout the country. The Government had intended to keep these terms a secret till they should actually be brought before the Chambers. But the Roman authorities had been less cautious and had communicated them to the foreign press. At once a loud clamour arose from Gallicans, Liberals, and free-thinkers alike. This assumed such proportions that the Government found it necessary to calm the public mind by a soothing article in the *Moniteur* promising that there should be no infringement of the liberties of the Gallican Church nor further charges for ecclesiastical purposes on the public purse.

The Government Bill, having received the Cabinet's approval, was introduced into the Chamber of Deputies on November 22, 1817.   It was obviously designed to mitigate the more objectionable features of the Concordat.   Its main provisions were as follows : (1) The King was to appoint to all archbishoprics and bishoprics in virtue of the prerogative inherent in the Crown.   (2) The bishops were to apply to the Pope for canonical institution according to ancient forms.   (3) The Concordat of 1801 was abrogated without prejudice to the effects which it had already produced, and especially to the clause ratifying the sale of ecclesiastical property.   (4) Forty-two sees were added to the fifty already existing.   The endowments of these was to be drawn from the funds provided for ecclesiastical purposes by the budget of 1817.   (5) Bulls, briefs, etc., emanating from the Court of Rome must not be published without first receiving the royal sanction.   Those which concerned ' the Universal Church, the interests of the State in general, or the State of France in particular ' must also be verified by the Chambers.   (6) *Appels comme d'abus* (i.e. appeals against alleged infringement by the Church of the rights of the State) must be brought before the Royal Courts, not, as previously, before the Council of State.   (7) The reception and publication of the Concordat of 1817, as well as of the bull re-establishing the new dioceses, must be understood to be without prejudice to ' the terms of the Charte, the laws of the kingdom, and the liberties of the Gallican Church.'

The committee to which the Bill was submitted included two pronounced Ultramontanes, MM. Marcellus and Trinquelaque.   These were loud in their criticism of a measure which, they maintained, practically annulled the Concordat it pro-

fessed to sanction. Their colleagues, on the other
hand, thought that the measure did not go far
enough. They desired more adequate guarantees
against papal encroachments : and, in particular,
considered the number of new dioceses excessive.
Their opposition was the more embarrassing because of the support it enjoyed in the Chambers and
the country generally. The so-called *Doctrinaires*,
with M. Royer-Collard at their head, demanded a
reopening of the negotiations with the Holy See
with a view to a new settlement. Even the Right
was not unanimous in supporting the Concordat.
Meanwhile the opposition outside the Chambers
grew apace and found expression in a hailstorm of
pamphlets, against which the Abbé Frayssinous
and other apologists of the Church sought, not very
successfully, to make head.

The Government persisted in its resolution :
but agreed to send an envoy to persuade the
Pope to assent to a reduction in the number of new
dioceses, and to give a general approval to the
terms of the measure. As there was good hope
that this attempt would prove successful, the way
seemed open to a settlement, when an incident
occurred which dashed all hopes of peace to the
ground. M. de Marcellus, conscience-stricken at the
discrepancies between the Concordat and the Bill
as amended by his committee, decided to consult
the Pope privately. He received a reply in which
the Holy Father expressed his grief at the terms
of the measure and exhorted him to oppose it in
the Chamber with might and main. At the same
time he hinted that, if the worst came to the worst,
he might accept it. The real intentions of the
Holy See were clear enough. But Marcellus could
not resist the temptation to make political capital
out of the Pope's distress. The result was to

stiffen the opposition to the Bill from both sides. The ultras declined to consent to a measure of which the Pope disapproved : the Liberals to lend themselves to an arrangement which (they said) this disapproval was bound to render nugatory. The Government thus found itself with no choice but to withdraw the Bill.

It being impossible to secure parliamentary sanction for the Concordat, the only thing to be done appeared to be to induce the Pope, if possible, to consent to its abrogation, and to the substitution of an alternative arrangement. But this solution of the difficulty the Pope flatly declined to accept. He had already unmade one Concordat : he was not going to unmake another. Besides, many of the bishops who were to fill the new sees were already appointed and instituted. The Cardinals were equally intractable. Consalvi alone showed any inclination to make allowance for the extremely difficult position of the Government : and even he declared that he could never consent to lower the prestige of the Holy Father by an explicit abrogation.

The French Government now suggested that as an interim arrangement the Pope should authorize the bishops of the sees established in 1802 to administer the territory assigned to those created in 1817. Consalvi agreed, though unwillingly, to accept this proposal on condition that the bishops concerned made no objection. Accordingly, on November 15, 1818, the Pope addressed to the Cardinal de Talleyrand-Périgord, and sent to the Prime Minister for transmission, a letter in which he outlined the proposed arrangement, and asked the Cardinal to ascertain the views of the bishops on the matter and to forward the result of his inquiry to Rome.

The Prime Minister, however, instead of sending
on the Pope's letter, merely indited to the Cardinal
a letter on his own account informing him of the
Pope's desire, and asking him to forward the
bishops' answer to the *Government*. Further, the
consultation was to be one not of the episcopate
as a whole, but of each bishop individually. It is
hardly surprising that the Cardinal declined to lend
himself to the course suggested. It was impossible, he said, to discover what the bishops really
thought unless they were given an opportunity of
conferring. Nor did he conceal his dislike for the
Government's plan. Rigid Gallican and aristo-
crat as he was, he revolted at the thought of appeas-
ing popular clamour by so plenary an exercise of
papal authority.

The situation thus appeared to have issued in a
deadlock when the crisis occurred which drove the
Richelieu ministry from power. The new Government (of which the leading figures were M. Dessolles, the Prime Minister, and M. Decazes) was by
no means anxious to tackle so thorny a problem :
and showed at first a desire to postpone further
action. It soon became clear, however, that delay
might be dangerous. The new ministry was far
more liberal than its predecessors : the ultra-
Royalists were assiduous in stigmatizing it as
the foe of religion and the Church. The Pope
was alarmed, and informed the French Government
that if he did not receive within two or three weeks
some grounds for anticipating a speedy settlement,
he would declare the bishops who had been instituted the lawful pastors of their dioceses and
instruct them to repair to them immediately.

Thus pressed, the Government at last tackled the
problem in earnest. An interview took place between Decazes, Minister of the Interior, on the one

hand, and Cardinal de Périgord with three other bishops on the other. At this the objections to an individual consultation of the bishops were admitted on both sides, and it was agreed that a better way would be to assemble the leading members of the episcopate, of all shades of opinion, to explain the situation, and to obtain from them a letter declaring their adhesion to the Pope's suggestion. In pursuance of this plan a meeting of thirteen bishops was held on May 11th, and Decazes made his explanation.

After he was gone, however, the bishops decided to ask permission to hold another meeting, to include all the bishops then in Paris. At this second meeting forty bishops were present, who asked that before writing to the Pope they should be allowed to see the correspondence between the Government and its representative at Rome. This the Government declined to accord, except for certain selected extracts it was thought safe to show. The bishops were informed of the Government's refusal on May 26th, when the majority of them were present at St. Denis for an important ceremony. At the same time a draft letter to the Pope, drawn up by M. de Quélen, coadjutor of Paris, was presented and discussed. The bishops gave it a general approval : but entrusted it to a committee for revision. It emerged very considerably altered, and in a sense decidedly hostile to the Government. The bishops had been asked for an explicit approval of the proposed arrangement with the Pope : the revised draft made them say no more than that 'they would accept and execute whatever the Pope might think fit to decide in the interests of religion.' The draft also contained a highly exaggerated picture of the oppressed state of the Church in France. In this form the letter was accepted (May 29th), and presented by Cardinal de Périgord to the King. Louis flatly declined to forward it to the Pope unless the most objectionable passages were removed. The Cardinal replied that he could give no undertaking to this effect. In fact a few days later thirty-seven bishops with three Cardinals at their head addressed to the King a letter more provocative still, in which they entreated him ' to reduce to impotence the enemies of Jesus Christ, who are also his own, and to restore to the Catholic religion, if not its ancient prerogatives, at least the deference that is its due.'

Nothing, then, was to be looked for from the bishops. The only hope of peace now lay in the moderation of the Holy See itself. The bishops' letter was unofficially shown to Consalvi with an intimation that the King had done his utmost and could do no more. Even Consalvi was in despair. At last the Government made an official declaration that seemed to furnish a glimmer of hope. This expressed its intention of ' curtailing as far as possible the duration of the provisory measures now contemplated, and of employing all the means in its power to put the Church of France in enjoyment of a stable and definitive position, as well as of realizing, according to constitutional forms and as soon as the resources of the State should permit, an increase in the number of sees.' The promise was vague enough : but at least it enabled the Holy See to rebut the charge that it had conceded much in return for nothing. After some hesitation the Pope, on August 23, 1819, announced in consistory his decision.

While careful to save appearances by describing the Concordat of 1817 not as abrogated but only as ' suspended,' ' owing to financial reasons and

other impediments,' he declared that pending the
erection of the new dioceses promised by the
Government the bishops who at the moment governed the churches of France were authorized to
administer their dioceses within the boundaries laid
down in 1801, and that in consequence the bishops
nominated in 1817 must for the meantime abstain
from exercising the powers which their canonical
institution had conferred upon them.   At the same
time he preconised the prelates whom the King had
just appointed to the vacant sees of 1801.   The
French episcopate was thus once more complete—
for the first time for ten years.

The Pope might describe the 1817 Concordat as
only suspended : but every one knew that it was
dead and buried.   The rage of the ultra-Royalists
was red-hot.   In vain the Government pleaded all
that had been done since the Restoration to better
the condition of the clergy.   The journals of the
extreme Right stigmatized it as an ' atheist government.'   Most formidable of all were the attacks of
Lamennais, now approaching the most reactionary
phase of his career.   When the Cour de Cassation
declined to uphold the action of a local tribunal in
fining a Protestant for refusing to decorate his
house for Corpus Christi, he asked ' whether it was
true that the law was atheist.'   To which M. Odilon
Barrot replied that in France 'the law *was* atheist,
and was bound to be '—a declaration which infuriated the extreme Right and was not much relished
even by the Government.

The situation of the ministry was certainly un-
enviable.   Denounced from one side as the enemy
of religion, it was at the same time denounced from
the other for its excessive partiality to clerical
claims.   The organ of the extreme Liberals, the
Minerve, even accused it of favouring the Jesuits

and intending to re-establish formally their order in France. The Government hotly repudiated the charge : but the *Minerve* stuck to its guns. It pointed to the fact that under the name of *Pères de la Foi* the Jesuits were already encamped upon the soil of France and were playing—with ministerial connivance, it was asserted—a rapidly increasing part in the education of the upper classes.

The clergy and the clerically-minded laity had never concealed their aversion for the national monopoly of education centred in the Université—a body instituted by Napoleon to embrace all grades of the teaching profession. No pains had been spared to extend the activities of the ' Brothers of Christian Doctrine ' as against the so-called *écoles lancastriennes,* with their secular tone and pupil-teacher system borrowed from Protestant England. For children of higher social position there were the *petits séminaires.* These were in theory intended for candidates for the priesthood only : but in practice Catholic parents were encouraged to send their children to them even though there might be no idea of their being ordained. In this way the child was not only given a strictly Catholic education, but was withdrawn from the State system of education altogether, the *petits séminaires* having been expressly exempted from the control of the Université. This method of eluding the State monopoly infuriated the Liberals, the more so that the *séminaires* were largely under Jesuit superintendence. When about this time M. Royer-Collard resigned the post of President of the Committee of Public Instruction, the *Minerve* declared that his resignation had been brought about by increasing clerical interference in educational affairs—interference which the Government had encouraged rather than opposed.

Anxious to disarm its critic, the Government appointed as his successor M. Cuvier, a Protestant. It was now the turn of the Catholics to be indignant.

Thus attacked from both sides, the ministry found its policy of moderation more and more difficult to enforce. The election as a deputy of the former Constitutional bishop and member of the Convention, Grégoire, produced a crisis. Not only were the ultra-Royalists outraged but the Powers were seriously alarmed. To quiet their apprehensions the King consented to an electoral law designed to make such a deplorable occurrence henceforth impossible. The Prime Minister, Dessolles, refused to identify himself with this policy and resigned. He was succeeded by Decazes, who managed to get a vote passed excluding Grégoire from the Chamber. But the extreme Right refused to be pacified. Their attacks on the 'royal favourite' became more and more virulent : and the assassination of the Duc de Berri outside the Opéra, on February 13, 1820, sealed his fate. He had of course no part whatever in the tragedy : but the ultras loudly proclaimed, if not his complicity, at least his responsibility, and he was forced to resign. 'He has slipped up in a pool of blood,' his enemies remarked with satisfaction.

CHAPTER XI

THE TRIUMPH OF REACTION
1820–30

THE fall of the Decazes ministry in 1820 marks
the beginning of the régime of political and
ecclesiastical reaction which maintained itself in
the teeth of ever-increasing opposition, until it
finally collapsed in 1830, dragging down Legitimate
Monarchy in its fall. In succession to Decazes, the
Duc de Richelieu returned to the uncongenial post
of Prime Minister. But he was getting an old
man : and the real control of affairs fell increasingly into the hands of M. de Villèle, a Royalist of far
deeper dye. Circumstances combined with Villèle's
influence to force the steps of Ministers more and
more into the paths of reaction.

An important part in this process was played by
a Bill introduced by the Government in 1821 and
designed to secure the creation of twelve new bishoprics. The complexion of the committee to which
the Government's *projet* was entrusted is sufficiently indicated by the fact that its *rapporteur* was
Bonald. In making his report to the Chamber
Bonald began by laying down in the most uncompromising terms the importance of religion as the
indispensable foundation and guarantee of all true
civilization. He went on to depict the existing
state of religion in France in the gloomiest colours,
and declared that the Government appeared to be
insufficiently alive to the gravity of the situation.

For this reason the committee had extended the scheme submitted to it and proposed that, instead of creating twelve new sees, power should be given to the Government (in concert with the Pope) to erect as many as it might think desirable without further recourse to the Chambers. The proposal was a direct challenge to the ministry, with which the extreme Right was itching to undertake a trial of strength. The challenge was taken up : and the Government insisted on its original proposal being maintained. A bitter and protracted discussion followed, the Right clamouring for the adoption of the committee's proposal, the Left finding even the Government's scheme excessive.

The ministry, unable to command the majority required for passing its own plan into law, was faced with the necessity of allying itself with one or the other of the opposing party. Villèle and his colleague Corbière, without consulting the rest of the ministry, entered into negotiations with the committee, and a compromise was made by which twelve sees were to be created immediately and eighteen others as soon as the necessary means were forthcoming. This arrangement was then brought before the Cabinet. The Chancellor, Pasquier, strongly opposed it : but Richelieu declared in its favour, and his adhesion determined that of his colleagues. Next day (May 18th) the new scheme was expounded in the Chamber of Deputies by Bonald on behalf of the committee. Corbière, on behalf of the Government, accepted it : and it was carried. The Liberals, of course, vehemently opposed it : and not all the ministerialists voted in its favour. The opposition of the Liberals was renewed in the House of Peers : but again without success. The measure was carried : and having received the Royal assent became law.

The effect of this capitulation to the Right was soon seen in divisions in the Cabinet. The more moderate ministers, Decazes' former colleagues, found themselves more and more out of harmony with the advanced Royalism of Villèle and Corbière, and resented their attempts to stampede them into a policy of which they disapproved. This section at first carried the day ; and Villèle and Corbière left the Government. But the ultra-Royalist element in the Chamber continued to grow in strength ; and now the Court was captured by the same interest.

Louis XVIII had hitherto exerted his influence steadily in favour of moderate counsels. The policy of the royal favourite, Decazes, was the King's policy too. The reactionary sentiments of Monsieur (the future Charles X) seemed to his royal brother not only unwise but ridiculous. But the King was fast declining towards dotage. All through his life the cold, cynical temperament of Louis had left him a prey to ennui : and as senile weakness increased, the need of distraction became more imperious. The friends of the Congregation were ready with an Abishag for this obese and valetudinarian David in the person of the charming and insidious Mme de Cayla.

The mainspring of this pleasant Court intrigue was Vicomte Sosthêne de la Rochefoucauld, a Clerical of the darkest hue. His partner in conspiracy, the Abbé Liautard, thus describes in his *Memoirs* the task entrusted to Mme de Cayla : ' One may easily imagine,' he writes, ' how much care and minute attention was required to despoil the King of his own ideas, to refashion in some sort his brain, his memory, his thought, all his faculties, all his affections.' The memory of Decazes was to be blotted out ; the King was to be reconciled with

Monsieur ; and the interests of divine right and sound religion thus secured. The plot achieved its object. Outvoted in the Chamber and unsupported at Court, Richelieu and his colleagues found their position intolerable and resigned. Villèle was entrusted with the formation of a new ministry (December, 1821).

Neither the new Prime Minister nor his chief colleague, Corbière, shared fully the extravagant sentiments of the extreme Right. But their position compelled them to court the support of men much more reactionary than themselves. The Duc Mathieu de Montmorency, a worthy man but an ultra of the ultras, and one of the earliest members of the Congregation, became Minister of Foreign Affairs ; and various minor offices were entrusted to persons of the same uncompromising type. ' It was from this moment especially,' thinks the historian Viel-Castel, ' that to be a member of the Congregation became a title of admission to political functions.'

In June, 1822, two royal ordinances were issued which showed unmistakably in what direction the tide was flowing. The one re-established the post of Grand-Master of the Université, suppressed in the early days of the Restoration. The other appointed as its first occupant M. Frayssinous, Bishop of Hermopolis. For an ecclesiastic Frayssinous was a person of distinctly moderate views. But he was a bishop and, as such, necessarily suspect to all who feared the growing political influence of the Church. Even Chateaubriand was strongly adverse to the appointment. Moreover, the personal moderation of the new Grand-Master was hardly likely to be proof against the pressure of his more intransigent brother bishops.

A circular issued by Frayssinous a few days after

his installation is significant. ' He who has the misfortune,' he writes, ' to live without religion or *not to be devoted to the reigning House* cannot but feel that he is in some measure unsuited to be an instructor of youth.' Unfortunately there were large sections of the population in which no love was felt for either the monarchy or the Church. This was specially the case among the *bourgeoisie*, from whose ranks the bulk of the subjects of higher education and of their instructors were drawn.

In the University of Paris the new régime was bitterly unpopular, both with teachers and students. At the prize-giving of the École de Médecine disorderly scenes arose because an ecclesiastic had been appointed to preside. The unfortunate abbé, on leaving the hall, was pursued by hisses and angry shouts. Four days later a royal ordinance suppressed the École (November) and ordered its reorganization. This proved to involve the deposition of eleven distinguished professors, known or suspected to be opponents of the ministry.

Another ordinance suppressed the famous École Normale at Paris. The lectures of M. Guizot on modern history at the Sorbonne were suspended : the equally celebrated course of M. Victor Cousin in philosophy had incurred the same fate the year before. Yet even so the extremists remained unsatisfied. In a letter published in the *Drapeau Blanc*, in 1823, Lamennais accused Frayssinous not only of irreligion but of immorality, and described the schools under his control as ' seminaries of atheism and antechambers of hell.'

The appointment of Frayssinous was by no means the only indication of the favour enjoyed by the Church and clergy in the highest circles. Several high-placed ecclesiastics were called to the Council of State : others received the honour of peerage. In the Chambers large sums were voted for the support of ecclesiastical establishments. A law was passed in 1822 to protect religion from the attacks of its enemies in the press. Some young men of Aix were fined and imprisoned for preferring a secular to an ecclesiastical procession on Ash Wednesday. The law of 1814 for the due observance of Sunday was strictly enforced.

The clergy themselves spared no pains to turn the situation to account. The zeal of the *mission-naires* was redoubled. Breathless crowds hung upon their lips : and the voice of opposition no longer ventured to make itself heard. The official *Moniteur* rehearsed in glowing accents the triumphs of the Church through their agency : nor did the Voltairian opinions of those who directed the *Journal des Débats* prevent that paper from indulging in similar doxologies.

The war with Spain, undertaken in 1823 with the object of restoring the bloody tyrant Ferdinand VII to the throne of which the Cortes had deprived him—' *my* war,' as Chateaubriand, at that time Foreign Secretary, proudly called it—aroused extraordinary enthusiasm in clerical hearts. The bishops loudly proclaimed it a crusade destined for the overthrow of a régime which had not only violated the sacred principle of Legitimacy and dared to promulgate a free constitution, but had confiscated the property and violated the privileges of the clergy, and had even broken off relations with the Holy See. The successful prosecution of the campaign by the Duc d'Angoulême gave the signal for a renewed outburst of fanaticism in the ultra-Royalist press. Lamennais sang the praises of the Inquisition and declared toleration ' a breach of the divine law.'

At the same time the exigencies of the *parti*

prêtre rose higher and higher. In a pastoral issued late in 1823, Cardinal de Clermont-Tonnerre, Archbishop of Toulouse, declared that the time was come to restore the ancient discipline of the Church. He demanded the restoration of the *état civil* to the clergy, the convoking of diocesan synods and of provincial councils, the re-establishment of the holidays abolished by the Concordat and of the religious orders, the absolute independence of the clergy, and finally the suppression of the Organic Articles. The Cardinal's claims created such alarm that the Government thought it necessary to intervene. The Council of State decreed that his letter involved *abus* and suppressed it. Soon afterwards the Minister of the Interior wrote a circular to the bishops recommending them to see that the Gallican Articles were taught in their seminaries. The suggestion, however, provoked much opposition and was by no means universally carried out.

The victory won over Liberalism in Spain meant the triumph of reaction in France as well. The Restoration had inscribed victory on its banners at last; and the Government was resolved to make full use of its laurels before they had time to fade. An ordinance dissolving the Chamber was obtained from the dying King (December 24, 1823); and the result of the new elections proved to be all that the most zealous ultra could have desired. At the Tuileries the new Chamber was nicknamed the *Chambre Retrouvée*: of four hundred and thirty deputies only thirteen were Liberals. Its first act was to decree for itself an existence of seven years.

In the course of 1824 a variety of measures were brought forward, two of which call for notice here as specially concerning the Church. The one sought to give the King the right, by a simple royal ordinance and without previous consultation with the Chambers, to authorize the existence of religious communities of women and to empower them to hold, receive, and administer gifts and legacies. The other had as its object to repress acts of robbery and theft in churches by assimilating them to the same offences when committed in private houses and rendering them liable to punishment by penal servitude for life or even by death.

To both the Lower House was ready to give the heartiest welcome : their only fault being that they did not go far enough. The Peers, however, into whose House they were first introduced, were less sympathetic. The first was rejected by a narrow majority. The second was carried : but an attempt made by the bishops and their lay supporters to make ' sacrilege ' (i.e. the profanation of holy things independently of theft or violence) a penal offence met with no success. As the majority of the Lower House was determined that this clause should be introduced, the Government thought it best to withdraw the measure from its consideration, feeling that, as passed by the Peers, it might be thrown out as inadequate. The ultras were thus balked for the moment. But their complete victory could not be long delayed. A few months or even weeks would see the dying King in his grave : and then, with the accession of Monsieur, the most fervid reactionary of them all, they would have things all their own way. Meanwhile the creation, on August 24th, of a new Ministry of Ecclesiastical Affairs, with M. Frayssinous as its first holder, was an earnest of the triumph that the new régime held in store for the Church.

Less than a month later the King was dead (September 16, 1824): and Charles X ascended the throne.

Though a worse king, he was a better man than his brother. Writing to Queen Victoria immediately after his death, Leopold I, King of the Belgians, an acute observer and well acquainted with both, thus compares the two monarchs : ' Louis XVIII was a clever, hard-hearted man, shackled by no principle, very proud and false. Charles X was an honest man, a kind friend, an honourable master, sincere in his opinions, and inclined to do everything that is right.' This estimate is largely just.

In nothing was the contrast between the brothers more marked than in their attitude towards religion. It is hard to say whether Louis XVIII really believed in anything : though of course the Most Christian King was bound to keep his scepticism to himself. In Charles X, on the other hand, belief assumed the proportions of fanaticism. In his youth he had taken his full share in the vices and follies of the old French Court : but the lapse of years had stilled his passions and endowed him with the austere and bigoted pietism that so often characterizes the reformed rake. That his devotion to the Church was sincere admits of no doubt : the misfortune was that, in this as in other things, he could never temper zeal with prudence.

The keynote of the new reign was clearly sounded from the start. At the opening of its first parliamentary session Charles intimated his intention of ' closing up the last wounds of the Revolution ' and of ' sealing the pact between the Altar and the Throne ' by a solemn coronation at Reims. Louis XVIII had never been crowned. There had been talk of it in 1818 : but the state of the king's health had caused the design to be postponed and, finally, abandoned. Probably, too, on second thoughts, neither he nor his advisers thought it wise to challenge in this way that attachment to the principles of the Revolution which was still so potent a force in France. Charles X was made of different stuff. Convinced that concession had been the ruin of Louis XVI, he would allow neither Liberal anger nor Liberal ridicule to divert him from his path. Moreover, the political situation of 1825 was very different from that of 1818. Whatever might be the strength of Liberal and anti-clerical ideas in the nation outside, within the walls of the Chamber of Deputies such ideas were a negligible quantity. In their reply to the royal address the deputies hailed with enthusiasm the announcement of the coming coronation : and the religious foundations of the political and social order were uncompromisingly proclaimed. True, the House of Peers still retained its incurable vice of moderation. Yet even here much could be done with the help of the King's personal influence and of the episcopal vote.

No time was lost in getting to work. The attempts to give legislative sanction to the claims of the hierarchy, largely foiled in 1824, were renewed in 1825 with a success which, if not quite complete, left little to be desired. The Garde des Sceaux, M. Peyronnet, had declared in the previous year that the criminal law could take no cognizance of ' sacrilege ' as such. Faced with the alternatives of changing his mind or resigning, he chose the former. In January, 1825, he brought before the Chambers a measure of truly mediaeval ferocity. Not only was *sacrilège simple,* or the profanation of the sacred vessels, declared a crime punishable with death : but if the profanation extended to the consecrated Host and wine, committed ' deliberately and through hatred and contempt of religion,' the punishment was to be the same as that reserved for parricides : i.e. the guilty person was to be led to execution barefoot, and before being decapitated, to have his right hand cut off. The penalty for *vol sacrilège* (i.e. sacrilege accompanied by theft) was to be either death or penal servitude for life, or a lesser term according to the circumstances of the offence.

This amazing proposal was first brought before the House of Peers, where it was eloquently opposed by some of the most eminent members of that assembly, notably the ex-Chancellor Pasquier and the Duc de Broglie. It was pointed out that it really contravened the religious freedom guaranteed by the Charte. ' Sacrilege ' by its very definition implied the Real Presence of Christ in the Mass : but it could be no part of the law's business to vindicate a dogma denied by many Frenchmen, both Protestants and free-thinkers. Such arguments naturally carried no weight with those whose whole object was to overthrow religious equality altogether and to make Catholicism once more the only religion recognized by the State. Foremost among the defenders of the measure was Bonald, who displayed sentiments not unworthy of Torquemada. In answer to the plea that Christianity is a religion that prefers to pardon rather than to punish, he declared, ' If the good owe their life to society in service, the wicked owe theirs in example. The Saviour asked pardon for His murderers : but the Father did not grant His prayer. As for him who commits sacrilege, *by a sentence of death you are sending him before his natural judge.*' The last sentence appeared so atrocious even to some of the speaker's own party that it was omitted in the official report of the debate. But the fact that the words were spoken is beyond question : for they were taken up by Pasquier, who compared them to the cry of the Inquisitors during the slaughter of the Albigenses : ' Kill, kill them *all* : God will recognize His own.'

To its credit the Upper House hesitated long before it accepted the measure ; and even then it was only passed by a small majority and with the help of the episcopal members of the assembly, who on this occasion formally decided to infringe their own resolution of the previous year to abstain from voting on laws involving capital punishment. Further, two amendments were carried, the one adding publicity to the conditions governing the offence, the other withdrawing the barbarous additions of mutilation to the death penalty. It is only fair to add that the credit of the latter belongs to Bonald.

In the Lower House the Bill encountered an opposition not less determined and still more eloquent. The leader of the attack was Royer-Collard, who for all his doctrinaire Liberal views was a devout practising Catholic, if of a Gallican and Jansenist cast. It was above all in the interests of religion that he opposed the measure. He spoke scornfully of the new crime of *lèse-majesté divine* ; and denounced ' a principle absurd, impious, and sanguinary, culled from the darkness of the Middle Ages—a principle which arms ignorance and human passions with the terrible sword of the divine authority.' ' Religion and the civil authority,' he said, ' move on different planes : the latter cannot legislate for the former. Are governments the successors of the Apostles ? They have not received from on high the mission to declare what is true and what is not.' The real inwardness of Bonald's theocratic doctrines is ruthlessly exposed. ' The theocracy of our time is not so much religious as political : it is part of that system of universal reaction which is carrying us away

The speech is accounted Royer-Collard's master-piece : and certainly it is a noble utterance. But it is hardly necessary to say that on the majority his arguments were entirely thrown away. For many, indeed, even the death penalty itself was insufficient to avenge the crime of *déicide*. One deputy declared that ' toleration is nothing more than atheism.' But despite its deplorable limitations from the ultra standpoint the Bill was passed by a majority of one hundred and fifteen : and on April 25th it was formally promulgated as law. It remained, however, virtually a dead letter, as the Courts did not dare to apply it.

Concurrently with the law of sacrilege, a second measure made its way through the Chambers in the early months of 1825. This (like the Bill rejected by the Peers in 1824) sought to give the Crown power to authorize religious communities of women by royal ordinance. A certain number of such communities already enjoyed recognition by a law of 1817 : but many more were still without legal status. It was now provided that they might acquire this if, after their statutes had been approved by the diocesan and the Council of State, a royal ordinance were issued to that effect. A community once authorized was to be able to acquire property either by gift or by legacy : nor could it be dissolved without the same formalities as were necessary for its foundation. A member of a community might, if she chose, endow her house or order with not more than a quarter of her property. This last provision was much criticized, the Liberals objecting to the permission, the Clericals to its limitation. But eventually it was carried with a Clerical amendment that the limitation should only apply to an estate of over ten thousand francs. On the main provision of the Bill, however, the Liberal opposition was so effectively maintained that the Government had to effect a compromise by which authorization by ' simple ordinance ' could be accorded only to communities existing prior to January 1, 1825. For all others the consent of the Chamber must be obtained. In this amended form the Bill passed both Houses, and was accepted by the King, though with a very ill grace.

None the less, it was with a cheerful sense of ground gained that Charlés X could now set out for Reims. The preparations for the coronation had been made on a magnificent scale. Nothing was left undone which could make it an exact replica of similar occasions in the glorious days of the old monarchy. The only anachronism was the royal oath to observe the Charte. For this the King felt an intense repugnance : and indeed it was hard to imagine Francis I or Louis XIV submitting to such an indignity. But at the moment there seemed no help for it : and no doubt the King and his friends had good hopes that by the time the next coronation arrived the disagreeable necessity would have passed away. In all else the precedents of the past were scrupulously followed.

Not even the historic *Sainte Ampoule* was lacking. This was a precious flask containing a holy oil traditionally brought to S. Remi by a dove from heaven for the baptism and hallowing of Clovis, and used ever since to anoint the Kings of France at their coronation. Unfortunately, during the Revolution it had been publicly smashed to pieces by a commissary of the Convention, so that the survival of its contents seemed improbable. However, not long before the coronation of Charles X, it was discovered that the Sainte Ampoule had not been utterly destroyed after all. Faithful hands had picked up the fragments, to one of which a little of the sacred chrism still adhered. This had been mixed with fresh oil and placed in another vessel. Thus, as the *Moniteur* officially declared, ' there can no longer remain any doubt that the holy oil which will flow on the brow of Charles X is the same as that which since Clovis has hallowed the monarchs of France.'

The King made a triumphal entry into Reims on May 28th, and went immediately to the cathedral, where he was solemnly received by the archbishop. Next day was the coronation. The Chambers had voted six million francs to meet its expenses: and part of this sum had been used to put the glorious old church in repair and to cover its walls with sumptuous hangings. Having taken the oath, the King received the sword of Charlemagne from the hands of the archbishop. Then, kneeling before the altar, he was anointed seven times with oil from the Sainte Ampoule. The regalia were handed to him : and finally the crown was placed upon his head. The cathedral echoed with shouts of ' *Vive le Roi !* ' while the *oiseleurs du Roi* let loose a flight of doves and other birds. The ceremony was concluded by a magnificent banquet in the *Salle du Tau* of the archiepiscopal palace. To make all complete Charles the next day, following the custom of his predecessors, touched for the ' King's Evil.'

The coronation may be called the high-water mark of Legitimate Monarchy under the Restoration. From this moment the tide of reaction begins to fall. It is difficult for one belonging to the English nation, with its jealous attachment to the pageantry that links the present to the historic past, to imagine the frenzy of fury and scurrility excited by the scene at Reims among the extreme Liberals of France. Béranger wrote a poem called *Le Sacre de Charles le Simple*, in which every feature of the coronation ceremony was burlesqued and turned into ridicule. For this performance the poet received nine months' imprisonment—but every one read his poem. Even among men of more moderate views a growing alarm began to be felt as to whither the ship of State was tending. Quite apart from the implications of its ceremonial, the coronation itself had been accompanied by circumstances that seemed ominous for the future. Not only had the sermon of Cardinal de la Fare directly attacked the Charte, but among the recipients of the Order of the Saint Esprit (the highest in France) at the time of the coronation was Cardinal de Clermont-Tonnerre, whose pastoral had been suppressed by the Government less than two years before.

The triumph of the *parti prêtre* seemed complete ; and its members made no attempt to dissimulate their sense of it. The *missionnaires* made their peregrinations with more *éclat* than ever. At Besançon the solemn ' planting of the cross ' was accompanied by salvoes of artillery and the strains of a military band. The presence of the Jesuits in the land was no longer denied : their educational work received a wider scope. An eminent mathematician, seventy-two years of age, was deprived of his pension for voting against the candidate of the Congregation in an election to the Academy of Sciences. Still more provocative of public indignation (though also much more defensible, if the Church is to retain the right to impose its own discipline) was the frequent refusal of Catholic burial to those considered to be of defective or unorthodox faith.

Yet, even so, the desires of the *hommes noirs*

remained unslaked. Lamennais denounced the laws concerning sacrilege and communities of women as ' not only heretical but atheistic,' and declared that France had no longer a Christian government but only ' a democratic government founded on atheism.' As the condition of her becoming a Christian land once more, he demanded the protection of Catholicism by the State to the exclusion of all other religions. A country curé in the Diocese of Blois went further still and gave the argument a personal turn by declaring that both Louis XVIII and Charles X were damned for their acceptance of the Charte. Such extravagances caused widespread misgivings even among members of the Royalist party. The opposition plucked up fresh heart. The Cour Royale no longer consented to protect the Congregation and the Jesuits from attacks in the Liberal press. When the *Constitutionnel* and the *Courrier* were arraigned before it for attacking ' religion and its ministers ' they were acquitted (December 3, 1825).

It was not, however, from the Liberal quarter that the culminating explosion of anti-Jesuit feeling came. Among the lesser champions of Royalism was a certain M. de Montlosier. The career of this eccentric and unbalanced individual had been varied. By turns member of the Constituante, *émigré*, official under the Empire, he had, after the Restoration, zealously espoused the cause of reaction on its political side. With its ecclesiastical aspect, however, he had no sympathy whatever. Profoundly imbued with the old Gallican spirit, he viewed the Jesuits with an abhorrence that amounted to obsession. In two letters published in the *Drapeau Blanc* in August, 1825, he had denounced their growing influence and accused the Government of being their tool. The letters made a great stir; and next year Montlosier followed up the attack with a work called *Mémoire à consulter sur un système réligieux tendant à renverser la religion, la société, et le trône.* The object of this strange performance was to reveal what its author called ' a vast conspiracy against religion, against the King, against society.' ' The situation being known to me,' he adds, ' my conscience bids me combat it : according to our laws I must reveal it.' The source of danger is found in four ' scourges ' : (1) the Congregation, (2) the Jesuits, (3) Ultramontanism, (4) the aggressive spirit of the clergy. Of the first he declares (and here the historian will certainly be disposed to agree with him) that ' its object is no less difficult to define than its nature.' ' When necessary it will consist of mere pious meetings— then its members are angels. It will also be when desired a Senate, a deliberative assembly—then they are sages. Finally it will be, when circum- stances demand, a focus of intrigue, of espionage, of delation—then they are demons.' The secret workings of the Congregation are traced not only in the conduct of public affairs and the distribution of Government offices but even in the most obscure and improbable quarters, such as the sale of cheap liquor to certain publicans, and the placing of domestics that they may act as spies upon their masters. And behind this dark labyrinth of in- trigue were the shadowy figures of Jesuit priests —at their head the Abbé Loeven . . . (the author does not complete the name). The book concludes by demanding the putting into execution of the already existing laws against the Jesuits and the inclusion in the curriculum of seminaries of the Gal- lican Articles.

The exaggerations and absurdities of this grotesque performance are obvious. Only the most fanatical anti-clerical would venture nowadays to take Montlosier's assertions at their face value. But in 1826 the public opinion of France was not disposed to be critical, any more than that of England during the ' No Popery ' agitation of 1850. And in any case there was a good deal of truth mixed up with his extravagances. The effect on the popular mind was therefore immense. Montlosier became a national hero. The *Constitutionnel* hailed him as the ' torch of France.'

The publication a month after that of Montlosier's book of the second part of Lamennais' *Religion considérée dans ses rapports avec l'ordre civil et social* added fuel to the flame. In this work the Ultramontane thesis was stated in its most extreme form. The royal power was declared to be subordinate to that of the Pope, who had the right, if necessary, to absolve subjects from their allegiance. The Gallican Articles were denounced as ' equally fatal to religion, to civilization, and to society.' Those who accepted them were ' schismatics.' Lamennais professed himself unable to find language adequate to stigmatize the Government, the deputies, even the bishops. He drew a dreadful picture of the state of mind of the Archbishop of Paris, who (he said) was the victim of an extraordinary malady which led him to get up frequently in the middle of the night calling for his doctor and confessor, and was understood to have its root in an unquiet conscience.

The Government took fright. Lamennais was again brought before the Courts. But the penalty imposed was a mere fine of thirty francs : and the culprit, after his condemnation, only showed himself more intransigent than ever. At the same time Montlosier was deprived of his pension.

The attitude of the bishops was somewhat equivocal. The majority were still mainly Gallican in ecclesiastical complexion, but Ultramontanism had made strides even in their ranks, and some of them were its avowed defenders. Several of the bishops publicly espoused the cause of the Jesuits : and under the auspices of Cardinal de Croy, Archbishop of Rouen and Grand Almoner of France, a ' Society for the Propagation of the Faith ' was inaugurated which, according to the Liberal press, was simply the revival of the sixteenth-century League in a still more formidable shape. The Government, feeling itself compromised by these proceedings, tried to extract from the episcopate a declaration in favour of the Articles of 1682. The bishops were in a dilemma. Even those who were Gallicans at heart shrank from offering a direct challenge to the Holy See, which had condemned the Articles. To have to offer such a challenge as a sop to anti-clerical feeling must have been more repugnant still. After much discussion fourteen archbishops and bishops consented to make a declaration of some kind : and most of the others were induced (though with some difficulty) to add their subscription later. But a number flatly refused, while others made qualifications which deprived their adhesion of most of its value. The declaration in any case did not go very far. No mention was made of the *Declaratio cleri Gallicani* of 1682 : the signatories were explicit only in regard to the substance of the first Article—i.e. the independence of the temporal and spiritual powers : and a protest was added against anything that might ' derogate from the primacy of S. Peter and the pontiff his successor.'

All this was little calculated to allay the inquietude of the public. The Liberal Opposition in the Chambers waxed more confident daily—the

more so that it could now rely on the co-operation
of a group among the Royalist deputies called the
défectionnaires. The leader of the group, M. Agier,
challenged Frayssinous for an explanation as to
the progress of Ultramontanism, and in particular
as to the activities of the Congregation and the
Jesuits. This explanation the Minister of Ecclesiastical Affairs felt compelled to make. The fact
that the Congregation existed was not denied :
though of course the usual plea was advanced that
it was a purely religious organization and had no
influence on public affairs. As to the Jesuits, the
Minister admitted their reappearance in France
and that they were tolerated, though not recognized. But their educational activity was represented as being on a very limited scale : and Frayssinous declared that, as head of the national system
of education, he felt no inquietude about them.
The Opposition rejected the Minister's assurances
and paid heed only to his admissions, which produced a very damaging effect. At the same time
Montlosier appeared once more in the field with a
formal denunciation addressed to the Courts of
Justice protesting against the Congregation and the
Jesuits and demanding that the clergy should be
compelled to accept the Gallican Articles. The
Cour Royale declared itself incompetent to deal
with the matter, but affirmed in unmistakable
terms that the presence of the Jesuits in France
was illegal (August 16, 1826).

Neither this decision, however, nor the popular
enthusiasm that greeted it could produce any effect
on the obstinacy of the King and his advisers. For
some time they had harboured designs on the
liberty of the Press : and in December a Bill was
introduced into the Chambers the provisions of
which virtually amounted to its extinction. Mean-

while Montlosier, still on the war-path, had presented to the Peers a petition demanding the execution of the existing laws against the Congregation and the Jesuits. The Upper House refused to sanction proceedings against the former : but they pronounced against the latter and asked the Government to take action accordingly. No attention being paid to their request, they retorted by so mutilating the Press Bill that the Government was forced to withdraw it (April 17, 1827). It found some consolation in imposing a rigid censorship on both books and newspapers.

As 1827 drew towards its end, the royal *camarilla* resolved on a bold stroke. On November 5th two ordinances appeared in the *Moniteur*, the one dissolving the Chambers, the other creating seventy-two new peers. But the elections that ensued proved a bitter disappointment. The Government found itself so weak in the Lower House that Villèle resigned. In his place the King would have liked to appoint Prince Jules de Polignac. But the time was not yet come for that stalwart Congreganist to effect the overthrow of the dynasty. The royal wishes were overruled : and Martignac, a representative of the moderate Royalists, became the new head of the Government. Of the former ministers only two remained at their posts, one of them being Frayssinous. Soon, however, the hostile attitude of the deputies compelled both to resign. In place of Frayssinous, Feutrier, Bishop of Beauvais, a strong Gallican, became Minister of Ecclesiastical Affairs.

With the knowledge of the Liberalizing sympathies of the new Chamber to back them up, the ministry now ventured on a series of steps intended to withdraw education from what was considered the excessive control of the clergy. On its accession to power, the post of Grand Master of the Université had been abolished : and a Ministry of Public Education set up instead. Its first act was to issue an ordinance submitting the ecclesiastical elementary schools to the control of local committees consisting of nine members, three only of whom were to be appointed by the bishop.

About the same time a commission of inquiry was set up to consider the question of secondary education. In pursuance of the commission's report two further ordinances were issued on June 16, 1828. The first declared that eight secondary schools belonging to an ' unrecognized congregation ' (i.e. the Jesuits) were henceforth subject to the control of the Université and, further, that in future no one might teach in any secondary ecclesiastical school without first making an affirmation that he did not belong to any such congregation. By the second, the number of pupils in the *petits séminaires* was limited, with a view to their being restricted to bona fide candidates for the sacred ministry.

The rage of the Clericals knew no bounds. An *Association for the defence of the Catholic Religion* was immediately formed. The bishops and the Catholic press loudly exclaimed that a new era of persecution had begun. The King received a fiery manifesto denouncing the ordinances signed by seventy-three bishops with Cardinal de Clermont-Tonnerre at their head. In the hope that Rome might prove more reasonable than the episcopate the Government requested the Pope to intervene. Its hope was not in vain : for the Cardinal Secretary of State issued a letter which reduced most of the protestants to silence. Clermont-Tonnerre and others, however, still held their ground. The former, in answer to a request from the Ministry of

Public Education to supply the information required by the ordinances, made a reply which has become famous : ' My Lord, the motto of my family, given it by Pope Calixtus in 1120, is this : *Etiamsi omnes, non ego.* It is also that of my conscience. I have the honour to be, etc.'

The execution of the ordinances followed, but in a manner that drew upon the Government the shafts of the more advanced members of both parties. The Liberals complained with reason that their execution was incomplete. The eight Jesuit schools were closed : but the regulations concerning the *petits séminaires* were very leniently applied. The Clericals, on the other hand, raised their usual cries of ' impiety ' and ' atheism.' Loved by neither side, the Martignac ministry gradually tottered towards its fall. At last the King found a reason for dismissing it : and appointed his bosom ally, Jules de Polignac, as Prime Minister (August 8, 1829). The ultra-Royalists believed that they were masters of the situation at last : the Church rejoiced because its hour was come. But the patience of the country was exhausted ; Charles and his friends heaped folly upon folly ; and in less than twelve months the July Revolution of 1830 sent the flimsy structure of absolutism crashing to the ground.

CHAPTER XII

THE PROPHETS OF THE COUNTER-
REVOLUTION—
DE MAISTRE : DE BONALD : LAMENNAIS

WHATEVER the intrinsic merits of the ' principles of 1789 ' may have been, the circumstances of their vindication were hardly such as to
recommend them to contemporary opinion. The
attitude of Burke is fairly representative of the
moral revulsion produced by the crimes of the
Revolution in high-principled and moderate men
outside France. When external observers felt thus,
we can hardly be surprised at the still greater
loathing experienced by those who were actually
the Revolution's victims. Foremost among these
were of course the members of the erstwhile privileged classes. But even those who were not (like
the *noblesse* and the Catholic Church) attacked
by it in their most vital interests might well wonder,
as its birth-pangs subsided, whether the Revolution had been such a blessing after all. Its evangelists had promised a Golden Age : but what had
been achieved was a Reign of Terror followed by a
Directory. Never even in Paris were politics more
corrupt or social morality more relaxed than during
the last five years of the eighteenth century. The
forces of disorder were inadequately controlled ; the
national finances were bankrupt ; the jobber and
the profiteer reigned supreme. It is hardly sur-

prising if a certain cynicism prevailed as to the virtues of the revolutionary principle. It was this cynicism which prepared the way for Napoleon's rise to power. It was the same feeling which—especially after the collapse of the Napoleonic experiment—procured at least a hearing for the remarkable school of political philosophers who represent the theory of the Counter-Revolution, the vindication of a rigid political and social order as against liberty issuing in perpetual flux.

It must be admitted that to the English reader of to-day there is something almost incredible in the theories of this school. It is hard to realize that able men living in the nineteenth century could seriously propound and recommend a system that seems to have been spun in the brain of some mediaeval dreamer. But that is only because during the last hundred years men's minds have (generally speaking) moved further and further away from the political ideas on which the old Europe was based. While the Revolution was still recent history, it was possible to regard it as a mere episode, a temporary and futile insurrection against the eternal laws governing human society. The idea that the clock could be put back and the Revolution made as though it had never been, was the delusion not of a few theorizing publicists only, but also of practical statesmen like Metternich. What else was the meaning of the Holy Alliance? It is true that the manufacturers of that egregious instrument would have been very unwilling to swallow de Maistre's theories whole. Indeed de Maistre sought to reconcile and unite two conceptions which historically have always been sharply antagonistic—autocratic monarchy and an autocratic Papacy. But the man of thought and the man of action were alike in being the

sworn foes of democratic liberty and in looking
for their political ideals to the past and not to the
future.

'The prophet of the past,' some one has called
de Maistre. For him and his school the theocracy
which the thirteenth-century Papacy attempted,
and the absolute monarchy which seventeenth-
century France achieved, were still living principles.
There, as Sainte Beuve has pointed out, was their
mistake. 'These principles,' he says, 'formerly and
indeed yesterday still living, when thus replanted
became as abstract and dead as those of the con-
stitution-mongers whom these champions of the
old order scoffed at.' None the less, the doctrines
of the school in question are far from having a
merely historical interest. Few indeed to-day—
except a small minority of thorough-going re-
actionaries of the type of M. Paul Bourget—would
care to admit sympathy with their views on secular
government. But in the ecclesiastical sphere, de
Maistre, at any rate, is the very opposite of a spent
or negligible force : for he is the true father of
modern Ultramontanism. The Ultramontane, indeed, approaches the question of papal authority
from a somewhat different standpoint : but it was
the hand of de Maistre that forged the chief
weapons of his armoury.

It is a curious and interesting fact, too, that the
doctrines of the 'Theocratic School,' as he called
them, exercised a powerful attraction upon the
mind of Auguste Comte. 'Too little justice has
been done,' says Comte, 'to the immortal school
which rose at the beginning of the nineteenth
century under the noble presidency of de Maistre,
worthily completed by Bonald.' Comte's own system of 'Positivism' shows clear traces of the influence thus brought to bear upon him.

I

The circumstances of de Maistre's life had so profound a bearing upon his philosophy that it is desirable to dwell upon them for a moment. Count Joseph Marie de Maistre was born at Chambéry in 1753 of a French family settled in Piedmont. He received his early education at the hands of the Jesuits, whose order he never ceased to revere. Entering the public service of Savoy in 1774, he held various offices in succession, while devoting his leisure hours to hard and unremitting study. Rather oddly, he showed in his youth a certain amount of sympathy for the new political ideas then in circulation. But the Revolution came : and for him it was to mean utter ruin and disaster.

In 1792, Savoy was invaded by the French : and de Maistre with his wife and children fled to Aosta. Towards the end of the same year the ' National Assembly of the Allobroges ' passed a law enjoining all citizens who had left Savoy to return thither within two months under pain of having their property confiscated. Madame de Maistre, in the hope of saving the family estates, returned to Savoy : and her husband soon joined her at Chambéry. But the persecutions to which they were subjected became intolerable. The de Maistres fled to Lausanne, whence after three years' stay they migrated to Turin (1797), and finally to Venice. Here they endured the direst poverty and misery. ' The student of de Maistre's philosophy,' says Lord Morley with reference to this period of his career, ' may see in what crushing personal anguish some of its most sinister growths had their roots.'

In 1800, his King, Charles IV, appointed him Grand Chancellor of Sardinia, the only part of his

dominions which the march of the Revolution had
left to him. Two years later he was appointed
Minister Plenipotentiary of Sardinia at the Court
of St. Petersburg—a post which he was to hold
for fourteen long years. The King whom he
served was himself so miserably poor that he could
do nothing for his representative : and de Maistre
had ' to keep up the appearance of an ambassador
on the salary of a clerk.' He had to face a Russian
winter without a pelisse. But even these hard-
ships were more tolerable than separation from
his beloved family.

Meanwhile he gave himself to study more assidu-
ously than ever. It was during these years that he
prepared the materials for his most important
works. Nor did his poverty prevent his gifts and
charm from winning him a footing in the highest
society of the Russian capital. His character was
certainly far from reflecting the harsh rigorism
of his doctrines : to the end of his life he maintained cordial relations with a number of ' heretics.' At length, in 1817, he returned to his native
land, again restored to the King of Sardinia. Here
he received the high office of First President :
but the King preferred other counsellors. It was
during these years that his most famous books
were written : *Du Pape, Les Soireés de St. Péters-
bourg, L'Église Gallicane.* He died February 26,
1821.

The starting point of all de Maistre's thought is
the necessity of order. In the agelong duel between authority and liberty he is all on the side of
the former. He detests freedom in all its forms—
political, intellectual, religious. For him the crime
of the Revolution lay precisely here—that it set
out to make men free. Man is not fit to be trusted
with liberty : he will only misuse it if he has it.

Original sin (conceived by de Maistre in its darkest colours) holds him tight in its clutch. His fallen nature is fundamentally perverse : and therefore his life and happiness depend on his being governed. All true authority, in de Maistre's view, comes from above—*omnis potestas a Deo.* Rousseau's doctrine of the sovereignty of the people fills him with horror. So does the idea of the Encyclopaedists that political and social arrangements can be progressively modified and improved in accordance with the dictates of human reason. The order of society is fixed and static. It exists by divine decree : and men must not impiously presume to meddle with the work of God's hands. To correspond with the two sides of human nature —body and soul—God has established two kinds of sovereignty, a temporal and a spiritual. The temporal authority is vested in the King, the spiritual in the Pope. In each case the sovereign is the representative and organ of the Deity : and in each case his authority is absolute. But as the spiritual is above the temporal, so (in case of disagreement) the temporal must give way to the spiritual power. The Pope is the apex of the social pyramid—arbiter of kings, supreme court of appeal for mankind, vicegerent of Jesus Christ, answerable to God alone. In this way mankind is to achieve that unity which is at once the germ-idea and the ultimate goal of all de Maistre's philosophy—a unity of the only kind considered by him to be worthy of the name—a unity effected and guaranteed by a single supreme authority.

The ideas of de Maistre as to temporal authority are contained in two works—*Considérations sur la France* and *Le Principe Générateur des Constitutions.* The nation is not a mere aggregate of individuals, but a living organism called into

existence (like all living things) by the will of God.
The vital principle of this organism resides in a
sovereign race which embodies for it the divine
authority and holds its power direct from God. If
a sovereign race become extinct, God intervenes to
inaugurate a new one. Thus true sovereignty is
hereditary. An elective monarchy is an anomaly.
Further, in order that the monarch's sovereignty
may be complete and perfect, it is necessary that it
shall receive consecration from the Pope. When
such consecration is lacking (e.g. in the case of
Protestant sovereigns) the sovereignty is not ille-
gitimate but inferior. The power of the monarch
is absolute. No resistance to him is permissible :
and if perchance the structure of sovereignty
should be overset, it will re-establish itself in lapse
of time by a natural process. The monarch is the
source of all legislation and of every kind of jurisdiction. He is bound only by fundamental laws
which are unwritten and have their origin in the
nature of things.

To de Maistre all written constitutions are
anathema. He will have nothing to do with
' parchments soiled with black ink.' For a
written constitution is a man-made invention,
whereas a true constitution is a divine creation.
The same objection rules out all amendment of
existing institutions. These amendments must
be man-made too. What is, is right.

But supposing the monarch abuses his power :
what then ? De Maistre himself would be quite
willing, however great the evil, to wait until the
inevitable operation of natural laws sets things to
rights. He sees, however, that such a solution will
not satisfy every one. Assuredly, in no case can
any right to resist be recognized in the monarch's
subjects themselves. If there is resistance it must

be in the name of a higher authority. This
authority de Maistre finds in the Pope, who pos-
sesses the power, in case of intolerable and obstinate wrongdoing, to absolve the monarch's
subjects from their allegiance.

II

The political philosophy of de Maistre has been
dealt with here at some length, not only because he
is the most distinguished figure in a remarkable
school of thought, but still more because of the
influence of his writings upon the ecclesiastical
politics of the nineteenth century. Of Bonald it
is necessary to say less. His views as to secular government were virtually identical with those of de
Maistre. But they arrived at the same conclusions by
independent routes. Bonald himself says, ' I was
neither [de Maistre's] disciple nor master.' Moreover, the ecclesiastical element occupies a less prominent place in his system than in de Maistre's.

The antecedents and circumstances of the two
men were not dissimilar. Both came of noble French
families ; both were forced into exile by the Revolution ; and both were, not cloistered and visionary
recluses, but men immersed in practical affairs.

The Vicomte Louis Gabriel Ambroise de Bonald
was born in 1754, and served as a young man in the
mousquetaires. Disgusted by the turn taken by
the Revolution (to which in its opening phases he
had not been unsympathetic) he left France in
1791 and, after a brief period of service in Flanders
with the *émigré* ' army of Coblentz,' settled at
Heidelberg. Here he wrote his first book, the
Théorie du Pouvoir, in which he sought to combat
the revolutionary doctrines. He returned to France
in 1797 ; and for two years lay in hiding in Paris.
During this time he wrote three other important

works : *Le Divorce* (published 1800), *Essai Analytique sur l'Ordre Sociale* (1801), and *La Législation Primitive* (1802). In 1802 he left Paris and retired to his birthplace, Millau, in the Rouergue.

Bonald's doctrines were by no means unpalatable to Napoleon, who sought to enlist him in his service. But the ardent partisan of the old régime did not respond very cordially to these advances. It was only after repeated refusals that he consented to be a Counsellor of the Université (1810) : and he declined to act as preceptor to the son of Louis Bonaparte, King of Holland. The Restoration was naturally much more to his taste. He was a deputy from 1815 to 1822 : and took a prominent part in the discussions of his Chamber on the extreme reactionary side. He collaborated with Chateaubriand in the *Conservateur* : but their political views were wide apart and the rupture between them was resounding. Louis XVIII made him in turn Minister (1822) and Peer of France (1823). In 1822 he was (very appropriately) appointed to preside over the commission for the censorship of the press. He retired from public life in 1829 : and the events of 1830 precluded all possibility of a return. In his eyes Louis Philippe was a usurper.

For the rest of his days he remained in seclusion. He died in 1840, aged 86. Jules Simon said of him : ' There is not to be found in his long career one action which is not consistent with his principles, one expression which belies them.' His fourth son, as Archbishop of Lyons (1839) and Cardinal (1841), was one of the most notable figures in the French Church of his time.

Bonald was a voluminous author. But his writings are almost entirely unread nowadays, partly because of the fantastic nature of the matter and arguments, partly because of their often difficult and technical style. For him, as for de Maistre, the spirit of the eighteenth century and of the Revolution is ' Satanic.' He is never weary of declaiming against assertions of men's ' rights.' ' The Revolution,' he says, ' began with the declaration of the rights of man : it will only end with the declaration of the rights of God.' The individual is nothing : society is everything.

On the question of resistance to a tyrannical exercise of the sovereign's power Bonald is even more uncompromising than de Maistre. He will not admit the right of deposition under any circumstances. No *deus ex machina* is introduced in the person of the Pope. The Pope, indeed, plays but a small part in Bonald's scheme of things. When de Maistre published his *Du Pape* Bonald told him that the position it took up was his own. But actually one cannot help doubting whether such full-blooded Ultramontanism was entirely to his taste. If in some ways even de Maistre, as M. Emile Ollivier says, was '*gallican sans le savoir*,' this was still truer of Bonald. Louis XIV is much more his ideal than Innocent III. On the other hand, he is bigotedly Catholic because Catholicism means order, whereas Protestantism spells individualism and anarchy. But whether Catholicism or Protestantism hold sway, his view demands that all the subjects of a State shall have but one religion : otherwise the unity of the national life is broken up. Thus the Revocation of the Edict of Nantes by Louis XIV was a necessary act. Religion is for Bonald chiefly important as a guarantee of order. It makes men believe in a moral order of the universe : and it helps to keep the poor content by giving them the hope of the balance being redressed in the next world.

III

De Maistre and Bonald both died in the faith in which they had lived.   The case was very different with the third and by far the most celebrated of the prophets of the Counter-Revolution—the brilliant, wayward, unhappy genius Lamennais, that ' pilgrim of eternity ' who sought truth at the bottom of every well in turn, yet seemed doomed never to find it.

Félicité Robert de Lamennais was born at St. Malo (which, it may be recalled, was Chateaubriand's birthplace also) on June 29, 1782.   He was the youngest son of Pierre de la Mennais, a wealthy Breton *armateur* or naval stores contractor.   The student of heredity will not fail to notice that his maternal grandmother was an Irishwoman.   Unfortunately for him his mother died when he was five.   In consequence his inborn love of solitude was far too freely indulged : and his stormy, moody, irritable nature grew more and more fixed, to be the burden and curse of his later years.   He never knew what home life meant.   ' Ennui,' he once said, ' was born in the family circle on a winter's evening.'   Though quiet and intelligent, he obstinately resisted all attempts to instruct him.   At last, in despair, his father handed him over to the care of his uncle, Robert des Saudrais, a charming man and a good scholar, who took his rebellious subject to his small property of La Chesnaie and set him to work.   But the uncle was no more successful than his predecessors.   One day as a punishment he shut the boy up in his library, at the same time forbidding him to look into a collection of the works of eighteenth-century *philosophes* that reposed in a separate bookcase nicknamed by its owner ' Hell.'   Féli rushed on the forbidden fruit :

and the taste for knowledge at once sprung into being. Without assistance from his uncle, who thought it best to leave him to himself, he got on so fast that he was soon able to read the Latin classics without difficulty.

On reaching the age of fifteen Féli entered his father's business—an occupation which proved to be entirely against the grain. The effect of his browsings among the anti-Christian writers of his uncle's library now made itself felt. A priest undertook to prepare him for his first communion : but the young neophyte was so argumentative that his instructor thought it best to postpone the event. From the mental and spiritual distresses of this time Féli sought relief in a passionate devotion to study, reading omnivorously in six languages.

So life went on until, in 1804, a crisis occurred in his spiritual development. An unfortunate love affair (so it is alleged) was followed by a period of deepest depression. At this moment his brother Jean Marie, a priest, arrived upon the scene. Jean Marie was of a temperament singularly different from that of his brother. He was as much a man of affairs as Féli was the reverse. His eager enthusiasm was unmarred by subtlety or introspective moodiness. Such a personality at such a crisis was bound to exercise a profound influence. Under its sway, Féli first consented to make his first communion—then went on to lend himself to his brother's ardent schemes for restoring Catholicism in France. The prospect of a mission to fulfil, a cause to serve, gave to life a significance hitherto sought in vain. He left the counting house : and at La Chesnaie he and his brother gave themselves to the study of theology and ecclesiastical history.

The result of their joint labours appeared in a work called *Réflexions sur l'état de l'Église en France au XVIIIme siècle et sur sa situation présente.* The only remedy for a disillusioned and disorganized society was shown to lie in a revived Catholicism. For this an efficient and highly organized body of clergy was indispensable : and the writers suggested a whole programme of reforms with the object of bringing it into existence. The book was published anonymously in 1808, and was promptly suppressed by the imperial police. Napoleon had no liking for programmes that were not his own. After a stay of something over two years as Professor of Mathematics at the College of St. Malo (during which time, under pressure from his brother, he took minor orders) Lamennais returned to La Chesnaie. Here his solitary existence soon produced a return of his old black melancholy. Scanning the future with gloomy eyes, he saw more and more in the priesthood (despite an intense personal distaste for it) the stout bark which alone might convey him across the storm-tossed and uncharted seas of life. At least the step would be definite and final. ' What pleases me in it,' he wrote, ' is that it would end all. . . . But even that,' he went on, is ' perhaps only an illusion. . . . The cross that one bears is always that which one would not wish to bear.'

From such perplexities Lamennais once more sought relief in work. He was engaged in a treatise, *De la tradition de l'Église sur l'institution des Évêques.* Betaking himself to Paris to see it through the press (July, 1814), he found the capital in the hands of the Allies, and Napoleon on his way to Elba. The turn of events rather blunted the point of a book designed to controvert Napoleon's plan of transferring the institution of bishops from the Pope to the metropolitan. ' Everybody praises it,' he complained, ' but nobody buys it.'

At Paris, Lamennais beguiled his leisure with certain journalistic experiments in the Royalist press, and also produced a pamphlet denouncing the Imperial Université as ' of all the conceptions of Bonaparte . . . the most profoundly anti-social ; in a word, the most worthy of its author.' To the writer of such sentiments Napoleon's return from exile threatened danger : and Lamennais fled to England, obtaining a post in a school in Kensington Gore.

In London he became intimate with a Breton *émigré* priest, the Abbé Carron, to whom he confided his difficulties. At last, by a fatal resolution, he placed himself unreservedly in the abbé's hands. The good priest leaped on his opportunity. To him Lamennais' misgivings were nothing but the outcome of a morbid scrupulosity. Unhesitatingly he decided that his friend must become a priest : and Lamennais accepted his decision. In November, 1815, he returned to Paris, where his old friend the Abbé Teysserre was overjoyed to hear of his resolve. He himself was less serenely confident. ' It is certainly not my own inclination to which I have listened,' he wrote, ' in deciding to enter the ecclesiastical state : *mais enfin*—one must try to turn this short life to account for heaven.' Some weeks after his return he was ordained subdeacon. His unallayed misgivings now betrayed themselves in a terrible and prolonged fit of depression. But the incurably optimistic M. Teysserre declined to pay attention to these signals of distress. In his eyes the wrong road was the ' way of the Cross,' the traveller's gloomy forebodings the 'Dark Night ' of the elect soul. Lamennais was ordained deacon in the first week of Lent, 1816, and priest a fortnight later at Vannes.

He returned at once to Paris, where he celebrated his first mass in the Chapel of the Feuillantines. One who was present recalled later that the celebrant's face was deathly pale and ' covered with a cold sweat.' His melancholy persisted unabated. It was only under pressure that he would say his daily mass. His health began to give way. ' I am ill,' he wrote. ' Henceforth I can only be extraordinarily unhappy.'

When at length the cloud lifted a little, his first thought was to go back to La Chesnaie. But his friends resisted this ; and urged him to seek distraction in literary work. Thus pressed he embarked, very unwillingly, on what was to be his first great work. At the end of 1817 appeared the first volume of the famous *Essai sur l'indifférence dans les matières réligieuses*—described by its author as ' extraordinarily mediocre,' but by the enthusiastic Teysserre (who for this once at any rate was not far from the mark) as ' uniting the style of Rousseau, the reasoning of Pascal, the eloquence of Bossuet.'

The ' religious indifference ' with which the book deals is not what the author calls ' practical indifference '—i.e. the state of mind of those who, while outwardly professing religious belief, refuse to allow it to affect their manner of life. It is ' systematic ' or ' dogmatic ' indifference—i.e. the formal denial of religious (by which Lamennais always means Catholic) truth.

The subjects of such 'indifference ' he divides into three classes. The first comprises those who, seeing in religion nothing but a political institution, believe it necessary only for the populace. The second embraces those who admit the necessity of a religion for all men but reject revelation. The third is composed of those *indifférents mitigés* who recognize the necessity of a revealed religion but allow themselves to deny the truths that it teaches with the exception of certain fundamental articles. These three classes he sets himself to refute in turn.

As against the first he appeals to history to prove that the use of religion as a mere instrument of government issues inevitably in national disintegration and decay. He then proceeds to expose the intellectual confusion which believes that religion is false and yet necessary for morality, and the practical absurdity which expects that the ' populace ' will allow itself to be hoodwinked in this way. As against the second class—the Deists, the followers of Rousseau—he maintains that so-called ' natural religion ' is a pure abstraction. Its professors can never agree as to what are the doctrines in which it is supposed to consist : and its logical result is atheism. The same may be said of the third type of indifference—Protestantism : for ' every religious system founded on the exclusion of authority contains within itself the germ of atheism and is bound to produce it in the long run.' At best the principle of private judgement can only issue in doctrinal anarchy.

This concludes the first part of the volume. The purpose of the second is to vindicate the importance of religion to ' those who do not reason and are indifferent only through carelessness and laziness.' Most men are indifferent because they want to be. They think to save themselves the trouble of carrying out the duties of religion, and so to achieve happiness. But actually, the further a man gets from religion, the further he gets from happiness too.

The success of the *Essai* was immediate and enormous. ' A clap of thunder under a leaden sky,' de Maistre called it. ' In a single day,' says Lacordaire, ' M. de Lamennais found himself invested with the authority of Bossuet.' His modest lodging in the Feuillantines was besieged with visitors. But such attentions were little to Lamennais' taste. ' They want to see me,' he writes, ' as a sort of monkey at a fair ' ; and he sighs *Omnia vanitas!* and thinks with longing of the woods of La Chesnaie.

Not peace, however, but a sword was always his portion. The *Essai* appeared in the closing days of 1817. Just before this the Richelieu ministry had fallen : and the ultra-Royalists, from being omnipotent in the Chamber, sank to a feeble minority. With the object of making merciless war on the new ministry they founded a journal, the *Conservateur*. The co-operation of Lamennais was obtained : and for ten years, in the *Conservateur* and elsewhere, he was to be the *enfant terrible* of the reactionary press.

And yet, actually, there was little real sympathy between him and the party on behalf of which he wielded his formidable pen. In his eyes the cause of Legitimate Monarchy, as such, was a small thing. To the political ultra-Royalists it was all in all : to Lamennais it was, at best, no more than a means to an end. Thus it is easy (as it is usual) to exaggerate the gulf between the Lamennais of the *Drapeau Blanc* and the Lamennais of the *Avenir*. In both cases he was seeking the same end—the triumph of religion : the differences lay chiefly in the choice of the means of securing it. The Liberalism against which he fought was not Liberalism in the political sense, but Liberalism as Newman understood it—the setting up in the

sphere of religion of free thought and free discussion
in the place of revealed truth. In the first stage
of his career, the cause of religion seemed to him,
as to most of his contemporaries, to be bound up
with that of monarchy. The ' principles of the
Revolution ' were equally opposed to both. Co-
operation therefore between their respective champions was natural and inevitable. But in truth the
two lines of attack were only parallel and never
really coincided. This became increasingly clear
as time went on. Even as early as 1820, Lamennais confided to a friend his intention of retiring
from an opposition ' founded on principles opposed
to my own.' The intention was not executed :
but the instinct was just. The bulk of the Royalists of the Restoration had inherited the Gallican
tradition of the *ancien régime*. Their object was not
to exalt the Holy See but to use it for their own
purposes. The claim of the spiritual power to
direct and dominate the temporal was not less
monstrous in their eyes than in those of the
Liberals. For Lamennais, on the other hand,
Ultramontanism was nothing less than the cause
of God Himself. Any claim on the part of the
secular power to intervene in spiritual matters
seemed to him intolerable : and to defend such
interference by the specious plea of ' protection '
was to add insult to injury. ' Let men protect
religion less and tolerate it more,' he cried. Once
give the Church its freedom, and it might safely be
left to do its work in its own way.

For the present, however, the ultra-Royalists
had no cause to complain of either the zeal or the
courage of their recruit. Meanwhile he was fever-
ishly pushing on with the second volume of the
Essai, which appeared about the middle of 1820.
In this he vehemently attacked the Cartesian

philosophy which, by its exaltation of the individual reason, had, he maintained, ' destroyed at a single blow every kind of authority, both temporal and religious.' In its place he sought to establish a system of his own, based on what he called *sensus communis*, i.e. the universal testimony of the human race. The ' reason of all ' was thus set up in opposition to the individual reason as the sole criterion of truth : and this universal reason it was the function of authority to interpret. The line of argument is summed up by the author himself in the following words : ' There exists one true religion and one only which is absolutely necessary to salvation ; neither feeling nor reason is the general means appointed to men to discern the true religion ; that means is authority ; so that the true religion is incontestedly that which reposes on the greatest visible authority.' That is to say (in Lamennais's view) it is the Catholic religion, reposing on the authority of the Pope : though it is not easy to see (and Lamennais is not very successful in showing) how this conclusion emerges from the definition.

The success of the second volume of the *Essai* was by no means equal to that of the first. The sceptical world was unable to take the apologist's argument seriously, while the Catholics resented, and felt compromised by, so radical an overturning of the approved apologetic. Not only were a number of refutations forthcoming, but the *Essai* itself was delated to Rome.

The issue between Lamennais and his adversaries was not one of philosophic method only. His outspoken denunciations of Gallicanism—described by him as a ' system which consists in believing as little as possible without being a heretic, in order to obey as little as possible without being a rebel '—

had raised up against him a host of enemies among the French clergy. These enemies hoped, by inducing the Pope to condemn Lamennais's ' theory of certitude,' to destroy his prestige and so to discredit his anti-Gallican opinions, which the Holy Father was little likely to condemn directly.

Their action, however, merely anticipated that of Lamennais himself, who submitted his book to the Holy Father and declared himself ready to abide by his judgement. Meanwhile he attempted to strengthen his position by writing a *Défense de l'Essai* (1821). The Pope, in truth, would gladly have avoided the necessity of pronouncing on the matter at all. To condemn so valiant a champion of Rome was highly distasteful. On the other hand, the opponents were insistent and very influentially supported. The decision was postponed as long as possible : and when it came it was in the indirect and unobtrusive form of an *imprimatur* granted by the Master of the Sacred Palace to an Italian translation of the *Défense*. So far as it went, however, it was a verdict in Lamennais's favour : and the author felt justified in completing his work by the production of a third and fourth volume (1824).

It is generally agreed that both in manner and substance they are very inferior to their predecessors. In them Lamennais sets himself to prove the strange thesis that Christianity has always been the religion of the human race : ' seeing that the truths of religion being mutually independent and presupposing one another, they are all implicit in the primal revelation, just as the truths that God reveals to the elect in heaven are implicit in those which are the objects of faith in this present life.' Here is the ' Doctrine of Development ' with a vengeance !

The two last volumes of the *Essai* were written at La Chesnaie. Here Lamennais lived in extreme solitude and retirement, and (it must be added) in a poverty no less extreme. In addition to his main enterprise he continued to contribute numerous articles to the Royalist press. From this monotonous and laborious existence he was called in 1824 by an unexpected opportunity of paying a visit to Rome. He arrived there on June 27, 1824. His reception at first was flattering enough : but after the first curiosity was abated, he was chagrined to find himself in great measure ignored. The Pope, too, at his first interview, was kind but reserved. The rather suspicious attitude of the Curia was probably due to the insinuations of the French Government, which feared that Lamennais might establish himself in Rome as the secret agent of the French Ultramontanes. Leo XII, however, seems to have quickly convinced himself of Lamennais's entire good faith. His second interview with the pilgrim was both intimate and prolonged. He spoke afterwards in high terms of his talents and character : though he described him (truly enough) as an *esaltato* and ' one of those lovers of perfection who, if they were allowed, would turn the world upside down.'

The papal favour was so marked that a rumour reached France that he was to be created a Cardinal. The rumour was false at the time : but there are good grounds for believing that Lamennais was the Cardinal reserved *in petto* of whom (according to Cardinal Wiseman) Leo XII spoke at a consistory in 1827 or 1828. ' He is a man whom it is necessary to lead with one's hand on his heart,' the Pope is reported to have said of him. If Leo had been still Pope in 1831 the *Avenir* episode might have had a different issue.

Early in September Lamennais was back again in Paris. He prepared to take up his abode as usual at the Grande Aumônerie. But the Grand Almoner, the Archbishop-Prince de Croy, sent a curt message to him to 'leave promptly.' Lamennais wrote back : ' Three weeks ago the Sovereign Pontiff pressed me to accept an apartment at the Vatican. I thank you for so soon giving me an opportunity of appreciating the difference between men and countries.'

The incident was significant. The alliance between Lamennais and the ultra-Royalists was by this time attenuated to vanishing point. The more that party grew in power, the more visible its Gallican bias became. Thus the Ultramontane champion now found himself as much excluded from the Royalist press as from the Liberal. If he was to make his voice heard, it could only be by means of a book. In 1825, therefore, he published the first part of his work : *De la réligion considérée dans ses rapports avec l'ordre politique et civile.*

The purpose of this first part is to denounce what the author calls ' the atheist State.' The old Christian monarchy is a thing of the past : France has become a democracy. Now Catholicism and Democracy are mutually exclusive, ' because an authority supreme and invariable in the religious order is incompatible with an authority which varies incessantly in the political order.' The aim of the democratic idea is the secularization of the State : and this aim is progressively realized as religion is more and more excluded from every form of political privilege and influence. On one condition only can the Church attain to anything more than a bare toleration : that condition is its complete subordination to the State. ' The annihilation of Christianity in France by the establishment of a National Church—this is what the Revolution really desires.'

A second and concluding part of the same work appeared in the following year. Its argument is thus summed up in the words of the author himself : ' Without the Pope no Church : without the Church no Christianity : without Christianity no religion for any people which would be Christian, and in consequence no society : so that the very life of nations has its source in the papal power.' This power is essentially monarchical. ' To deny the Pope either infallibility or the plenitude of power or a sovereignty truly monarchical is to deny the Church its own existence, to destroy it entirely.'

The Gallican claim, therefore, to reserve to the Church certain liberties is absurd and intolerable. The Four Articles of 1682 are reduced to two : (1) political Gallicanism—that the civil power is absolutely independent of the spiritual ; (2) religious Gallicanism—that a General Council is above the Pope. As against the first, Lamennais (like de Maistre) claims for the Pope not an absolute supremacy over the civil power, but a ' directive and ordinative power ' to remind kings and peoples of their reciprocal duties and to mediate between them in case of a conflict. As against the second he holds that to set a Council above the Pope is not only to change the monarchical government given to the Church by Christ Himself, but to compromise its unity and to subordinate it to the civil power. Only when the Church and its Head attain to that full independence and sovereignty which represent the divine order of its being will the process of dissolution under which modern society is sinking be stayed.

It is hard to say which of the parties attacked—

Gallicans, Royalists, or Liberals—was the most infuriated by a work in which the principles both of the *ancien régime* and of the Revolution were equally defied. The crisis produced by its appearance and the resulting trial of Lamennais have been already narrated. Henceforth the breach between him and the Royalist party was complete. His thesis was hotly attacked from the Gallican side, one clerical writer describing his Ultramontanism as ' a gangrene, a cruel, poisonous ulcer.'

Lamennais of course cared for none of these things. Of his opponents he spoke in private, though not in public, with angry scorn. One hope still remained to him—that Rome would speak. Again and again in his letters he utters his longing for ' a word, a single word of authority.' But the word was not forthcoming : and for the moment despair gripped his heart. ' She is the seat of fear and of feebleness,' he cries. ' Yet,' he adds, ' that shall not prevent me from fighting to the end. I will hold fast in my Thermopylae.' The Throne had failed him. He was now to turn to the People.

CHAPTER XIII

THE STORY OF THE 'AVENIR'
1830-34

TO any one less dominated by the sense of the truth and power of his own ideas than Lamennais, the outlook in 1828 might well have appeared desperate. Never for a moment had he faltered in his initial purpose—the enthroning of religion as the ruling principle of human society. But in the existing situation, neither the present nor the future seemed to hold out any prospect of his purpose being fulfilled. The monarchy had proved a broken reed. Its Gallicanism was incurable: what it sought was not the triumph of the Church but its subservience to the ends of the secular power. And in any case (as Lamennais saw at least as early as the end of 1827) its days were numbered—so much greater therefore the folly of those who, by associating the Church with its fortunes, could only make it the partner of its fall.

But if the monarchy fell, what then? Its fall must mean the triumph of the revolutionary principle, which sought not the mere subjection of the Church but its ruin. So at least the bulk of the clergy firmly believed. For this reason, as the flood tide of Liberalism rose, they huddled more and more under the shadow of the Throne.

The policy of the Martignac ministry only strengthened this belief. Though by no means a 'Liberal' Government, it was far more tinged with

Liberal ideas than its predecessor. But if the Villèle
ministry (in clerical eyes) had scourged the Church
with whips, the Martignac ministry chastised it
with scorpions. By the ordinances of April and
June, 1828, even such freedom of education as it
possessed was taken away. To contemplate, therefore, an abandonment of the age-long alliance between the Altar and the Throne in favour of an
alliance with a Liberalism not partial but full-blown
must have seemed the policy of a madman. Yet
this was what Lamennais dared to propose. 'If you
are afraid of Liberalism, then Catholicize it.' So, in
a few words, he summed up the programme of the
second phase of his career.

Lamennais's optimistic view of the situation is
largely to be explained by the presence within the
Liberal ranks of a group represented by such men
as Guizot, Cousin, and Jouffroy. This group—
usually called the 'Doctrinaires'—had its organ of
expression in the *Globe* newspaper. At that time,
as throughout the nineteenth century, the vague
term ' Liberalism ' was made to cover a wide divergence of opinion. This divergence the course of
events between 1830 and 1848 was to bring clearly
into view. But for the moment it was kept in the
background by a common opposition to the abso-
lutist designs of the royal *camarilla*. From the men
of the extreme Left, of course, the Church had nothing whatever to hope for. They had inherited the
bitter hatred and contempt for Catholicism of their
Jacobin forebears, and, like them, would easily turn
to persecution if once they had the power. With
such, however, the 'Doctrinaires' had little in common. Though not Catholic but rationalist in their
intellectual attitude, they viewed Catholicism with
sympathy as a great historical embodiment of that
spiritual interpretation of the universe which

formed the core of their own creed. They dreaded the anarchy that the unrestrained triumph of the revolutionary spirit was bound to entail. Above all they had—what the Jacobins had not—a sincere belief in liberty for its own sake.

Here, then, was a common ground between them and Lamennais. Convinced as the latter had ever been that the Church had only to become free to make its triumph a certainty, he now boldly made appeal to the one school of thought which, he believed, was prepared to make it free. It was with this object that he wrote the work in which the new orientation of his ideas first becomes explicit— *Du progrès de la Révolution et de la guerre contre l'Église* (1828).

Once again it is the *social* value of Christianity as a cementing agent that is the starting-point of his thought. If the religious society be weakened, the political society is weakened too. It is precisely here, he holds, that the Liberals go astray. They desire an ordered society : yet, by their substitution of the individual reason for authority in the religious sphere, they are doing their best to bring about that *anarchie des esprits* which can only issue in social anarchy. Such individualism is the enemy of order and of liberty alike: and men will in the long run realize that this is so, if only in the bitter school of suffering, ' more potent than reason itself.' ' Then they will be astonished to find that they have sought so long and so vainly, with such weariness and pain, what Christianity offers them, what they can find in it alone : the union of order and liberty.' In the meantime, however, the Church must strain every nerve to save society from itself. It must ' raise above the ruins of Christian civilization the torch of truth ' and compel men to see that ' outside of Catholicism there is and there can be nothing but error, disorder, calamities, and irremediable disorder.' But this it can only do under a régime of *freedom*—freedom for itself, freedom for those to whom it addresses its appeal. Let the Church therefore abandon its association with outworn institutions (he means, of course, the monarchy) ; and let it abstain from all part in the political conflict. ' Be bishops, be priests, and nothing more '—he cries to the clergy. ' Envelope men,' he cries, ' with your love, and let love penetrate where truth could never find a way.'

The success of the book was enormous : and the rage of the Royalists knew no bounds. A formal episcopal condemnation was at once forthcoming from the lips of M. de Quélen, Archbishop of Paris. In a pastoral letter he denounced ' the temerity which sought to shake society itself by doctrines that sow discord and hatred between the sovereign and his subjects.' To this attack Lamennais replied by a *First* and *Second Letter to the Archbishop*, in which the prelate was not too respectfully handled. The opinion of the clergy as a whole was invincibly hostile to his ideas : and even the writers of the *Globe* maintained a rigid silence in regard to an appeal which, intending to win, had perhaps only embarrassed, them. Most discouraging of all was the continued silence of Rome. She did not indeed condemn, though sufficiently pressed to do so : yet neither did she approve. To attack Gallicanism was well enough : but Lamennais's remedy might well prove worse than the disease. *Non tali auxilio.* Once again, the bitterness of her disappointed champion overflows in his private correspondence. ' A humid and sombre cloud covers the head of the sacred mount, and within this cloud a silence of death.'

All this time, Lamennais was at La Chesnaie.

But now he was no longer solitary. Round him had gathered a little community of his most talented disciples, forming a sort of ' Third Order ' of a teaching congregation at Malestroit of which Lamennais was the nominal head. Of the members of this ' Breton Port-Royal ' the best beloved and the most ardent was the Abbé Gerbet, in later years Bishop of Perpignan and sometimes described by his admirers as ' the Fénelon of the nineteenth century.' Not less distinguished was the young poet, Maurice de Guérin, to whose memory Matthew Arnold has consecrated one of the most delicate of his essays.

But a more renowned recruit than either of these arrived at La Chesnaie in the early summer of 1830. This was the Abbé Lacordaire, previously a rising ornament of the Paris Bar, but now a priest twenty-eight years of age and contemplating missionary work in the United States. In pursuit of this plan he decided to ask leave to join Lamennais's congregation, regarding him as ' the one great man of the Church of France.' This was the reason of his coming to La Chesnaie. He had already a slight acquaintance with Lamennais, whose personal appearance at the time of their first meeting he had thus described : ' He is a little dried-up man with a thin yellow face, simple in his manner, sharp in speech, full of his book. If he were placed in a company of ecclesiastics, with his brown frock coat, his knee breeches, and his black silk stockings, he would be taken for the sacristan.' His second evening at La Chesnaie, however, showed how absolute was the sway that this unimpressive-looking person exercised over his twelve companions. Writing many years later, Lacordaire thus portrays the scene : ' The company assembled in an old *salon* devoid of adornment. M. de la

Mennais half reclined on a couch with M. Gerbet sitting at the end of it and the young men gathered round in a circle. The conversation and deportment breathed a sort of idolatry such as I have never witnessed before.'

The sub-acid flavour of the last sentence betrays (we may surmise) a certain 'wisdom after the event.' For the moment, at any rate, Lacordaire himself would appear to have fallen an easy victim to the spell. He describes Lamennais in a letter of this time as 'a Druid risen again in Armorica, who sings of liberty with *une voix un peu sauvage.*'

At the same time, the members of the prophet's circle were by no means permitted to lapse into a passive hero-worship. They were expected to work very hard. Lamennais had designed a vast encyclopaedic work of which he himself had sketched out the plan in a *Sommaire d'une synthèse des connaissances humaines.* In one or other section of this enterprise each of his disciples was expected to take a part under the general supervision of the Master. In addition they had the privilege of receiving instruction in the 'Mennaisian philosophy' from the author's own lips—instruction given partly by means of formal lectures, but even more effectively in the freer play of conversational discourse : for Lamennais was a wonderful talker. Besides guiding the minds he also directed the consciences of his disciples, hearing their confessions and preaching them sermons. Yet with all this there was no trace of superiority in his manner. He joined readily in the recreations of his companions and was always kind, simple, and gay, except when now and again a black fit took him. For 'the barometer of his humour,' as one of them said, 'was subject to many variations.'

This quiet studious existence was interrupted by

the outbreak of the July Revolution (1830). The event which Lamennais had prophesied for nearly three years had come to pass. Legitimate Monarchy collapsed, and Liberalism sat enthroned in its place. Now was the opportunity to put into practice the policy already elaborated by the great writer in view of the inevitable crisis. But how was it to be realized ? What was to be its organ ? The suggestion of a Paris journalist to the Abbé Gerbet that a newspaper should be founded was passed on to Lamennais. Nothing could have been more congenial : for journalism was the breath of his nostrils. The only difficulty was one of ways and means. The floating of a ' daily ' is a big undertaking. The devoted Gerbet made himself responsible for this side of the business. A company was formed, funds were collected, and a prospectus issued. Lamennais left La Chesnaie for Paris in September, 1830, and on October 16th the first number of the new journal appeared. Its name was *l'Avenir* : its motto, ' God and Liberty.'

The editor in chief was of course Lamennais himself, and many of the leading articles were written by him. His talent, however, being of the sort that requires a ' good subject,' the bulk of the work fell on Lacordaire, from whose prolific pen there poured an incessant stream of articles. With him was associated, after the first few weeks of the paper's existence, Charles de Montalembert, the third and youngest of the great trio whose names are imperishably linked with the story of the *Avenir*.

This charming and gifted youth (he was only twenty), the son of a French peer of crusading lineage and a Scots mother, was travelling in Ireland when Gerbet's prospectus fell into his hands. His ardent nature at once burst into flame.

Already ' God and Liberty ' were the twin passions
of his soul, and the opportunity of serving both
together seemed to him a direct call from heaven.
' If I am wanted for the *Avenir,*' he wrote, ' I will
give everything else up.'   He hurried to Paris,
where he was introduced to Lamennais and fell at
once under his spell.   Lamennais on his side was
not less attracted. ' What happiness ! ' he wrote in
his diary. ' My fairest hopes are fulfilled. This is
perhaps the happiest day of my life.'   He had
indeed made the truest friend he ever had.

The name of the new journal fitly expressed the
boundless confidence with which its promoters en-
visaged the age now beginning. Mankind stands on
the brink of a new era. *Tout renaît, tout change,
tout se transforme.* The people are clamouring for
two things—liberty and equality.   But just as the
desire for both springs ultimately from Christianity, so apart from Christianity neither can properly
exist.   A society without religion must oscillate
perpetually between despotism and anarchy. Here,
then, is the Church's opportunity.   Amid the
crash of earthly thrones, a single authority still remains unshaken—that of the Pope.   Let Catholics
therefore rally round the common Father of mankind and so save the world.

But in order that the Church may discharge
its mission, it must win the confidence of the
masses. This confidence it has forfeited at present
as the result of its fatal alliance with the monarchy.   Its first step, then, must be to renounce
this alliance for good and all.   The priest must
no longer condescend to be the ' gendarme of
royalty.'   But this alone is not enough. The
Church must also become *free*.   Such freedom can
only be had in one way—by the rupture of the
Concordat, the complete separation of the Church

and the State. Ideally (as Lamennais had never ceased to believe and teach) Church and State ' ought to be inseparable as soul and body.' But this is impossible so long as unity of belief is lacking. As things are, the functions of the State are wielded by ministers of any belief or of no belief at all. Yet these men actually claim the right of appointing the chief ministers of the Church and even, to a large extent, of dictating what it may or may not do. At such a price does the Church purchase the poor pittance provided by the State for its ministers. Here is the crux of the matter. Let the Church boldly refuse the ' salary ' which is the badge and instrument of its servitude : and let it cast itself without reserve on the free-will offerings of the faithful. Let it renounce every kind of political privilege, and let its ministers be content with the liberty that is the birthright of every Frenchman. Yet even so (writes Lamennais) ' there will still remain to the Christian priest a great and magnificent privilege—the privilege of devotion and sacrifice—a privilege which cannot be taken away from him, for he holds it from God. It is God Who has established him to be the man of the people : . . . to suffer with them, to die with them—there is the privilege of the priest.'

Thus possessed at last of the power to work out its own destiny, the Church is to fling itself fearlessly into the mighty tide of democracy to direct and control it. It must not be content with the ambulance-work of charity : it must co-operate actively in the building up of a social order founded on justice. Modern political economy sacrifices the man to the wealth he produces. The new order must embody the principle that the well-being of the worker takes precedence of all else and must rescue him from the tyranny of the capitalist who exploits him. To achieve this object, the workers must be allowed the right of association.

So much for the social programme of the *Avenir* —a programme on which all its contributors were agreed. With regard to its political programme there was less unanimity. Lamennais boldly declared for a Republic, believing it to be the only form of government possible for France in the future: Lacordaire was a democrat, while Montalembert championed the aristocratic principle on lines similar to those laid down by the ' Young England ' party in our own country at a rather later date. On the main point of ' liberty,' however, all were agreed. The excessive centralization which is the bane of French life must be restricted. The right of association must be conceded in the political as in the economic sphere, and provincial and communal self-government restored so far as purely local matters are concerned.

In four directions especially should the principle of liberty be applied. Education must be free : the monopoly of the Université must go. The Press must be free : the censorship must be abolished. Association must be free : the right to form religious communities must be fully conceded by the repeal of the restrictive legislation of the Restoration period. Above all, there must be complete freedom of worship : and every religious body must be allowed to exercise its own discipline over its own members. Nor should liberty be regarded as the privilege of Frenchmen only. The nations now in bondage must be set free from their despots as the prelude to the setting up of a vast Christian republic in which all nations shall live in peace and liberty under the fatherly guidance of Christ's Vicar.

It was as the champion of ' oppressed nationali-

ties ' that Montalembert, in particular, distinguished himself. In passionate language he pleads
the cause of Belgium, of Ireland, of Poland most
of all. He calls upon the Government of his own
country to give at least its moral support to the
Poles in their desperate fight for freedom against
their Russian masters : and when his entreaties
have proved vain and the Polish insurrection has
been wiped out in blood, his soul is filled with a
great bitterness. ' The governments,' he cries,
' are become even as those brazen statues which the
nations sprinkled with blood in order to melt their
hearts, but which had no heart and only uttered
their oracles in the victor's behalf.'

Outspoken criticism of this sort was little to the
taste of the French Government. The relations
between the writers of the *Avenir* and the new
régime were indeed at no time really cordial on
either side. On behalf of the former, Montalembert frankly declared that their ' obedience and
love ' was strictly conditioned by the fidelity of
the Government to the principle of religious liberty.
Any violation of this was vehemently denounced.

When the old ex-Bishop Grégoire died unrecon-
ciled to the Church because of his obstinate refusal
to deny his ' Constitutional ' past, the Archbishop
of Paris refused him Catholic burial. But the
church was forced by the police, and in their
presence some obscure, inhibited priest performed
the Catholic rites. Lamennais had little cause to
love Archbishop de Quélen. But this did not prevent the *Avenir* from passionately defending his assertion of the Church's right to exercise its own
discipline. Again, when the Garde Nationale stood
calmly by while on February 14, 1831, the Paris
mob profaned and sacked the Church of S. Germain
l'Auxerrois, pulling down the great cross adorned

with golden fleur-de-lis which crowned it and
trampling it underfoot, Montalembert's indignation overflowed in his famous article, ' The Cross.'
' There has actually been found,' he wrote, ' a
people which has proclaimed itself the high priest
of civilization, the liberator of the nations, the
master of the future : and this people has broken
in pieces the Cross ! That people is the people of
Paris. Yes, the people of Paris *as a whole*. For
if we deny the name to the group of criminals who
have committed this outrage, we cannot refuse it
to those who have tolerated it.' And the article
concludes : ' We lovingly pick up the fragments
of Christ's Cross and swear an eternal worship of
them. If it has been broken in our churches, we
enthrone it in our hearts.'

If the attitude of the *Avenir* towards the Government was thus at best one of guarded acquiescence,
the Government on its side watched the unfolding
of the new programme with profound mistrust.
The July Revolution meant the triumph not of the
People, but of the *bourgeoisie*. Now the *bourgeoisie* was at that time the least Catholic section
of the French nation. It was deeply penetrated
with Voltairian ideas : and desired nothing less
than such a regeneration of the Church as Lamennais and his friends had in view. So far from
wishing the Church's action extended, it was
anxious rather to restrain it within the narrowest
possible limits. As for making the Holy See the
arbiter of the destinies of mankind, the idea must
have appeared to it at once intolerable and grotesque.

The same lack of sympathy was not less evident
in the political sphere. Two words were constantly
on the lips of the *Avenir* writers—' the People '
and ' Liberty.' But the new rulers of France were

just as afraid of the People as they were of the Royalists : while the sole liberty they desired was liberty for themselves. In the hands of the classes below them, liberty, they believed, was bound to become license. Thus when Lamennais and his friends hailed the triumph of ' democracy,' they shivered uneasily in their seats and wrote them down as dangerous revolutionaries.

To Louis Philippe himself, Lamennais's frank declaration for a Republic must have seemed a deliberate challenge. Having become king he intended to remain so, and to be no puppet-king either. Neither he nor his friends desired in the least a change in the system of government, but only the shifting of its control to their own hands. Lamennais himself saw this clearly and said so with his usual directness. ' They have brought back by one door,' he wrote, ' what had gone out by the other.'

Quite apart, too, from the nature of its ideas, the very fact that the *Avenir* had ideas at all was an offence. Ideas were disturbing and therefore dangerous in the eyes of the wealthy, materially-minded business men for whose benefit the Revolution of 1830 had been made.

Nor could Lamennais console himself for this official coolness—a coolness which (as we shall see) could on occasion go to the length of actual repression—by the thought that he had the mass of Catholic opinion behind him. Among a certain number of the younger men, both clergy and laity, the *Avenir* programme awakened genuine enthusiasm. But the older clergy, and the bishops above all, regarded it as nothing less than high treason to all they held most dear. The plight of these men after the revolution of 1830 was almost pitiful. They had been accustomed so long to lean upon the Throne that when this support was removed they were as though dazed and helpless. Their one desire and prayer was for the return of the old order of things. And as the situation developed their dismay and forebodings increased.

No doubt Lamennais exaggerated when he spoke of the Liberal triumph as giving the signal for a violent persecution. Yet the clergy were certainly made to feel as uncomfortable as possible. The authorities were suspicious of a body known to be attached by such close ties to the fallen dynasty, and lent a ready ear to charges of ' conspiracy.' When the rabble of some town gratified its lawless instincts by attacking a church or seminary, no serious attempt was made either to repress or punish the outbreak. The *croix de mission* were thrown down, the clergy insulted in the streets, and held up to scorn and calumny in the gutter-press and on the stage.

So menacing was the situation that Archbishop de Quélen had to go into hiding for a while. The Cardinal Archbishops of Reims and Besançon left the country. It was in Paris that the violence of the mob assumed the most serious proportions. On the same day (February 14, 1831) on which S. Germain l'Auxerrois was profaned, the mob also attacked the archiepiscopal palace under the shadow of Notre Dame. The splendid building orginally erected by Bishop Maurice de Sully in the thirteenth century was razed to the ground in five hours. The contents of the library with its precious manuscripts, the pictures and works of art, were burned, stolen, or thrown into the river : while Montalembert, on duty as a member of the National Guard, watched with rage in his heart the débris floating down the Seine. It is hardly surprising that the victims of such ebullitions of democratic feeling found the invitation to make an alliance with ' the People ' provoking rather than alluring.

And what of the Pope ? How did *he* regard the alliance with Democracy so urgently pressed upon him, with such golden evocations of a supremacy far surpassing anything that his mightiest predecessors had known ? At the moment when the *Avenir* first appeared Pius VIII lay on his deathbed. He died in November, 1830 : and three months later Cardinal Capellari was elected to succeed him as Gregory XVI. The new Pope was an ecclesiastic of the narrowest type, whose name has become almost a by-word for blind and stubborn reaction. A Camaldolese monk, and sixty-six years of age, he had a mind constitutionally averse from new ideas of every kind, without anything in his training or career to counteract this defect. Having had little experience of administration, he was intensely distrustful both of himself and others. Yet this timid and reactionary individual was no sooner on the pontifical throne than he was confronted with a situation which would have taxed a Hildebrand or a Julius II. For years the Carbonari and similar secret societies had been diligently fomenting disaffection towards the inefficient and oppressive government of the Popes : and now, under the stimulus provided by the successful revolutions of the preceding year in other countries, the whole of the papal dominions burst into revolt. Gregory, at his wits' end, turned for help to Austria, who was only too anxious to oblige him. The insurrection was quickly stamped out. But it had given the Pope's nerves a bad shaking : and made him less disposed than ever to make terms with those ' Liberal principles ' which he (quite rightly) regarded as incompatible with the governmental system he was pledged to uphold.

With the Government, the French episcopate, the Pope, thus ranged against them, the enterprise of Lamennais and his friends was doomed from the start. One by one the opposing forces were to come into action and to make each its contribution to the final catastrophe. It was the Government which first made its hand felt. Within the first five weeks of the *Avenir's* existence two of its numbers were confiscated by the police. Lacordaire and Lamennais, as the respective writers of the impugned articles, were cited before the courts. The mere fact of a prosecution was of little account to either. But the expenses involved threatened a further serious drain on funds never really adequate. For this and other reasons it was thought advisable to organize a wider basis of support.

The foundation of the *Agence générale pour la défense de la liberté réligieuse* was the result. Already in the *Avenir* of October 30, 1830, Lamennais had adumbrated a ' great confederation, a vast society of mutual assurance ' to maintain the rights of the individual against the possible tyranny of the central power. The association was to be open to all ' men of goodwill ' without respect to their political or religious convictions, and was to be provided with elected committees for each commune and department. This ambitious project was at once seen to be impracticable : but in founding the *Agence Générale* the promoters sought to direct the same principle towards a more limited objective. Its aims are thus summed up in the Prospectus : (1) to redress all acts contrary to the freedom of the Church's ministry by proceedings before the Chambers and in the law-courts, (2) to support every grade of school against breaches of educational freedom, (3) to maintain the right of forming religious associations, (4) to co-ordinate the activities of all existing organizations for the maintenance of religious liberty. At the head of the *Agence* was a council of seven, with Lamennais as chairman and Lacordaire, Montalembert, and the Comte de Coux as its most active members.

An organization was formed embracing the whole of France. Lacordaire was responsible for the north and west, Montalembert for the south, de Coux for the centre and east. Meetings were held, associations and committees formed. Meanwhile the new organization bravely set itself to justify the terms of its prospectus. The right of religious congregations to settle on French soil was vindicated in the case of the Capuchins of Aix and the Trappists of Meilleray. In the former town a certain General Delort, who had ordered the arrest of all Capuchins and friars as ' beggars and vagabonds,' was removed from his command.

More notable still were the efforts made on behalf of freedom of education. It was in this connection that the famous episode of the *École Libre* occurred. As a protest against the refusal of the Government to abate the State monopoly of education in the interest of Catholic parents, the following placard was posted up on all the walls of Paris :

The *Agence Générale* . . . is founding a free day-school without the authorization of the Université at 5 Rue des Beaux Arts. It will teach the elements of religion, French, Latin, Greek, arithmetic, etc. The instruction will be given by members of the *Agence*, M. de Coux, the Abbé Lacordaire, the Vicomte de Montalembert, who take upon themselves the legal responsibility for this school. The school will open on Monday, May 9th [1831].

At this opening twelve children were present, together with a certain number of spectators. Before the teaching began Lacordaire made a short

speech describing the object of the experiment.
Nothing happened the first day : but on the next
a commissioner of police arrived and declared the
school closed.   Lacordaire merely told the children
to come again next day.   They did so : and in the
afternoon the commissioner repeated his visit wearing a tricolour scarf.   A delightfully French scene
followed.   ' In the name of the law,' said the commissioner, ' I call upon the children here present
to withdraw.'   ' In the name of the parents whose
authorization I possess,' said Lacordaire, ' I order
you to remain.'   The commissioner's summons
and Lacordaire's reply were repeated three times.
The children then shouted, ' We will remain ' :
whereupon they and their teachers were bundled
out into the street.

Summoned to appear before a police court,
Lacordaire and his colleagues refused to recognize
the competence of such a tribunal.   They demanded that the case should be tried before the
Court of Assizes as a political offence.   The police-
court accepted this view and declined jurisdiction.
At the instance of the Government, the Cour Royale
now intervened: and declared its intention of try-
ing the case itself.   But before it could come on,
Montalembert's father died.   The young man
found himself a Peer of France.   At once he demanded that he should be allowed his privilege and
have his case tried before the House of Peers.   The
House accepted the claim, though by no means
willingly : and as the case of Montalembert could
not be separated from that of the others, all three
appeared before it on September 29, 1831.

When Montalembert was asked by the President
for his name he replied, ' Charles de Montalembert,
schoolmaster and Peer of France.'   His youth, his
recent bereavement, and his astonishing eloquence

won for his speech a regular ovation : and this success was followed up by a masterly improvised speech from Lacordaire in reply to the case for the Government. The Government, however, had told the House that it expected the condemnation of the accused : and it obtained it. The minimum penalty was imposed—a fine of one hundred francs.

Despite its result, the trial forms a landmark in the struggle for educational freedom in France, and undoubtedly prepared the way for the successful issue of that struggle in 1850. On the other hand, it did little to restore the waning fortunes of the movement with which its chief figures were associated. The hostility of the Government was now undisguised : and its supporters shared its attitude. As for the Catholics, their initial mistrust had by this time turned to undisguised dislike and opposition.

Their anger was raised to boiling point by a singularly wild and ill-judged article from Lamennais's pen that appeared in the *Avenir* after the outbreak of February 14, 1831. In this he actually charged the Royalists with deliberately inciting the mob to deeds of sacrilege, and went on to urge the Catholics of France to ' break for ever with the men whose incorrigible blindness puts the cause of religion in peril, who sacrifice God to their king.'

Lamennais himself realized afterwards that he had gone too far : but the mischief was done. From this moment the Legitimists sought his destruction. The bishops readily lent their aid. Quite apart from the nature of his ideas, the presumptuous claim of a mere unbeneficed priest to give a lead to the Church of France, independently, and even in spite of, the hierarchy, had grievously offended them. The propaganda of the *Agence Générale*, again, caused intense resentment. Many of the bishops publicly condemned the doctrines of the *Avenir*: others forbade their clergy to read it.

Gradually the frowns of the episcopate and the virulent and calumnious attacks of the Carlist press produced their effect.   Even those who had at first sympathized began to fall away.   Some feared the wrath of the ecclesiastical authorities : others felt that Lamennais and his friends were going too far or too fast.   The number of subscribers sank and sank.   The funds of the movement began to run out.

To crown all, Lamennais was slowly forced to realize that the Holy See disapproved of his enterprise and was even preparing to break its long silence by an overt condemnation.   The exiled ecclesiastics in Rome, with Cardinal de Rohan, Archbishop of Besançon, at their head, were working hand in hand with the Jesuits to this end : even his friends there condemned his ' temerity.' Thus pressed on all sides, he came to the conclusion that only one course remained—to suspend the *Avenir*.   His colleagues concurred : and the suspension was decided.

Next day, very early, Lacordaire came into Lamennais's room and said : ' I have been thinking.   We cannot end like this.   We must go to Rome to justify our intention and submit our thoughts to the Holy See.   Whatever happens, this striking step will be a benediction for us and a weapon snatched from the hand of our enemies.' It would have been far better, no doubt, if Lamennais had refused.   But the suggestion accorded too well with his own wishes for this.   Montalembert was wiser.   ' But if we are condemned . . . ? ' he objected.   ' It is impossible ! ' replied Lamennais quickly, ' we *can't* be condemned.'

The *Avenir* made its last appearance on Novem-

ber 15, 1831.   It contained the following words :
' If we withdraw for a moment, it is not from
weariness, still less from discouragement : it is to
go, even as of old times the warriors of Israel, to
consult the Lord in Shiloh. . . . Prostrate at the
feet of the Pontiff whom Jesus Christ has set as
guide and minister of His disciples we shall say,
" O Father, let fall your eyes on some of the least of
your children, who are accused of rebellion to your
infallible and mild authority.   They are before
you ; read in their hearts ; there is nothing they
wish to hide.   If one only of these thoughts differs
from yours, they disavow and abjure it." ' Just
a week later (November 22nd) Lamennais and
Lacordaire left Paris.   Montalembert joined them
at Lyons : and together the three friends journeyed
to Rome, ' the pilgrims of God and Liberty.'

As evening fell on December 30th they entered
the Eternal City.   It was the depth of winter :
and snow covered the Campagna.   ' We suffer
much from the cold and damp,' writes Lamennais.
Their reception was as chilly as the weather.   No
offer of apartments in the Vatican was made to
Lamennais this time.   The pilgrims took up their
abode in modest lodgings, where Lamennais remained in strict retreat writing a *Mémoire* to explain and justify his conduct to the Pope.   The
Cardinals, with a few exceptions, received them
with marked coldness : two even refused to receive
them at all.   The Pope for a long time gave no
reply to their request for an audience.   The
Mémoire was handed to Cardinal Pacca early in
February.   On February 25th the Cardinal brought
a note in reply which said that ' the Holy Father,
while giving full credit to their good intentions and
their talent, saw with displeasure that they had
broached certain controversies that were at least

dangerous: that their doctrines would be examined, but that, as their examination would be protracted, the Pope recommended them to return to France, where he would inform them in his own time of his decision.' ' It is the ruin of our hopes,' said Montalembert. But despite the Pope's hint Lamennais insisted on remaining at Rome. When at length Gregory XVI consented to receive them (March 15, 1832), the audience lasted but a quarter of an hour. The Pope made no allusion to their mission. He merely called his visitors' attention to the beauties of a statuette and gave them some gilt medals.

This treatment was of course calculated. The Pope utterly disapproved of the doctrines of the *Avenir* and of the way in which they had been expressed. He was being urged to crush the movement for good and all, not only by the French bishops and the Jesuits, but also by the reactionary governments of Austria, Prussia, and Russia. On the other hand, in view of Lamennais's past services to the Ultramontane cause, he was unwilling to impose on him the stigma of an open condemnation. He wished, therefore, by a policy of silence and delay to give Lamennais a tacit intimation of his disapproval in the hope that he would quietly go back to France and hold his tongue in future.

Lamennais's companions quickly perceived this. Seeing no good in remaining in Rome any longer, Lacordaire started on his return home immediately after the papal audience. Montalembert, a few weeks later, went on to Naples. But Lamennais held his ground. To quit Rome leaving a single stone unturned would have seemed to him a base desertion of his cause. He would go no further afield than to Frascati, where he settled in a little hermitage and began to write a new work. In this quiet solitude he heard the news of the papal brief of January 9, 1832, condemning the authors of the Polish insurrection. It was a blow at his heart. At once he left Frascati and returned to Rome, intending to quit it for ever. Before his departure he told all he met that, ' receiving no reply from the Catholic authority and having henceforth no other guide than his personal conviction,' he was returning to France to start the *Avenir* afresh. He left Rome on a fine evening in July, accompanied by the faithful Montalembert, who had rejoined him. From the carriage he turned a last look on the city and watched the sunset glow die on the dome of S. Peter's and fade into the gloom of night.

Hardly was Lamennais out of Rome when there arrived a letter addressed to the Pope and bearing the signature of a number of archbishops and bishops of the south of France. It was a formal indictment of Lamennais's errors, philosophical, theological, and political : and the signatories prayed the Pope to confirm the condemnation already passed upon these by themselves. Its effect in itself would possibly have been small : but a few days later came the news that while at Florence Lamennais had committed the extraordinary imprudence of personally informing the Papal Nuncio there of his intention to revive the *Avenir*. This was the last straw. An encyclical containing the official condemnation of Lamennais's doctrines was quickly put in hand.

Lamennais, meanwhile, was making his way across the Tyrol into Germany. He dared not return to France at once : for he knew that a warrant for debt was out against him. At Munich, then the great centre of the Catholic revival in Germany, he met, by a strange coincidence,

Lacordaire.   The question of reviving the *Avenir* was discussed between them.   Lamennais wished to do this at all costs.   Lacordaire was convinced that it was out of the question.   Eventually a compromise was made.   The *Avenir* was to disappear : but a review was to take its place as the organ of the Mennaisian ideas.   A few days later a banquet with music was given in Lamennais's honour by certain distinguished Catholic thinkers who were then teaching at the Munich University.   The guests were still at table when a message was brought to Lamennais that he was wanted outside.   Leaving the room, he found waiting for him a messenger from the Nuncio, who handed to him a sealed envelope.   He opened this and ran his eye over the contents.   It was a copy of the Encyclical *Mirari vos* (dated August 15, 1832), accompanied by a covering letter from Cardinal Pacca.   At once he returned to the dinner-table, no trace of the mortal wound visible on his face.   But when the guests rose he whispered to Lacordaire, ' There is an encyclical of the Pope against us : we have nothing to do but submit.' After the fête was over and he and his friends were back in their lodgings he read them the encyclical.

Its terms were indeed final and irrevocable.   It condemned (*a*) the idea that the Church has need of a regeneration and that it is necessary to separate it from the State ; (*b*) the alliance with the Liberal revolutionaries, even under the pretext of obtaining greater liberty for Catholics ; (*c*) the approval given to the revolt of peoples against their princes; (*d*) the ' imprudent and immoderate ' claim for the freedom of the Press and of opinion.   The repudiation of all for which Lamennais had fought and suffered could not have been more total or

more absolute.   At the end he said, ' It is the condemnation of freedom and the abandonment of
Polish nationality.'   After a moment's silence he
added, ' God has spoken : nothing remains for me
to say but *Fiat voluntas tua* and to serve these two
causes by my prayers, seeing that He forbids me
by the lips of His Vicar to serve them by my pen.'

His friends sat by in awed silence while with long
strides he paced the room.   After a while he sat
down and penned a document declaring in the
name of the editors of the *Avenir* and the Council
of the *Agence* that, ' respectfully submitting to the
supreme authority of Christ's Vicar, they retire
from the struggle in which they have loyally
engaged for two years and urgently counsel their
friends to do the same.   In consequence, the
Avenir . . . will not appear again and the *Agence
Générale* . . . is dissolved.'

Next day, after a night chiefly spent in prayer,
Lamennais proposed to his companions that they
should return at once to France.   They set out on
September 2nd, and after a few days' stay in Paris
Lamennais found himself once more among the
yellowing woods of La Chesnaie.   A number of his
old disciples gathered round him, the faithful
Gerbet at their head.   The old manner of life was
resumed.   Presently Lacordaire joined him too.
But at the end of three months it had become clear
to him that Lamennais's submissive mood was
passing and he determined to be gone.   He slipped
away secretly, leaving a note behind.   ' I leave La
Chesnaie this evening,' he wrote. ' I leave it from a
motive of honour, being convinced that henceforth
my life would be useless to you because of the
difference of our views on the Church and on
society, a difference which only increases daily.'

Was this the *only* motive ?   Or was there mingled

the desire to cut himself adrift from an association
that had become compromising ? It is hard to
say. Lamennais at least never forgave what he
regarded as an underhand desertion, and even
Montalembert condemned the action of his friend.
His own fidelity was of tougher fibre. Lacordaire
spared no pains to detach him, foreseeing what he
regarded as the inevitable issue. Yet Montalembert, now far away in Germany, still clung to his
beloved father, ' his best friend.' His exquisite
chivalry could not endure the thought of abandon-
ing that great unhappy soul until it had become
clear beyond all doubt that he must choose between
his master and his Church.

For indeed Lamennais's faith was fast slipping
away. His Ultramontanism had been always at
bottom rather political than religious. The Church
for him was, primarily if not exclusively, an instrument of social regeneration. Yet the Head of the
Church had definitely refused to assume the function
with which he had sought to invest him. If, then,
the new order of which he dreamed was not to come
through the Church, must it not come apart from
the Church ? Such were the thoughts that filled
his soul as he paced beneath the leafless oaks of his
Brittany home.

The final stage of this poignant spiritual drama
was precipitated by the publication of a brief
from the Pope to the Archbishop of Toulouse
(dated May 8, 1833), in which the sincerity of the
Avenir declaration was called in question. Montalembert besought his friend to keep silence, but
Lamennais would not listen. He wrote to the Pope
a letter in which, while renewing his promise to
abstain from discussing religious matters, he reserved to himself the right to think and act as he
thought fit ' in the purely temporal order.' About

the same time he dismissed his companions : and
the school of La Chesnaie came to an end.

Lamennais's letter to the Pope made the worst
possible impression at Rome. The Pope replied
by another brief addressed to the Bishop of
Rennes. He expressed his conviction that Lamennais still adhered to the condemned views, and
demanded that he should give an engagement to
' follow absolutely the doctrines set forth in the
last encyclical, and neither to write nor approve
anything contrary to them.' For a long time
Lamennais refused thus to disown his past. His
conscience forbade, he said. In vain he tried to
soften the Pope, who merely repeated his demand.
At last, yielding to the entreaties of Montalembert,
he signed the declaration required. By this time
he had left La Chesnaie himself and was living in
Paris.

The final rupture was postponed, but not for
long. Lamennais's soul was seething with revolt.
He wrote to Montalembert declaring that he intended ' though late in the day to begin a new life.'
' We shall see one another in heaven, I hope,' he
added, ' but henceforth we shall pursue different
ways on earth.' Montalembert was profoundly
alarmed. What did his friend mean ? he asked.
Lamennais's reply was terrible. If he had signed
the declaration, it was only as a means to peace at
any price. He would have signed anything—even
that the Pope is God Himself. Already he had
ceased to believe in Catholicism : and henceforth
he would exercise his priestly functions no more.

Yet still no overt act was forthcoming. Lamennais continued to reside in Paris, though its febrile
atmosphere was the worst possible *milieu* for a
neuropath beset with such spiritual anguish as his.
He proposed a visit to the East with Montalem-

bert : but the plan fell through. At length, in March, he determined on an irrevocable step. For a long time he had had in his possession the manuscript of his *Paroles d'un Croyant.* This strange, apocalyptic book is perhaps the only work of its author which is still read nowadays. It is inspired by the enthusiasm of humanity in its most ardent form : but there is nothing in it which reveals the writer as a Catholic. Moreover, it dealt with all the topics on which the Pope had bound Lamennais to silence. Yet he decided to publish it, handing it to Sainte Beuve for the purpose.

Such an act of defiance could not be passed over at Rome. The Pope put forth another encyclical, *Singulari nos,* dated July 7, 1834. In this, though still without mentioning the author's name, he ' in the plenitude of his apostolic power ' condemned the book (which he described as ' small in bulk but immense in perversity '), as 'containing propositions false, calumnious, rash, conducive to anarchy, contrary to the Word of God, impious, scandalous, erroneous, and already condemned by the Church.' Once again Montalembert urged Lamennais to submit. But he refused : he had gone too far. His friend realized that all was over. He made his own submission, and the two never met again. For a time letters were exchanged between them : but after July, 1836, even correspondence ceased.

The subsequent history of Lamennais lies outside the scope of this work. His career without the Church brought him no more happiness or satisfaction than his career within it. Once more he plunged into the muddy sea of journalism, but now on behalf of views strangely different from those he had previously espoused. He could indeed no more shed his idealism, nor the profound religious instinct which was ever the bottom of his thought, than he could shed his skin.   His sense, too, of a ' mission ' never left him.   ' Woe is me if I preach not the Gospel' was throughout as much his motto as S. Paul's.   But it was no longer now the Christian Gospel in any recognizable sense.   The final term of his intellectual evolution was a cloudy socialism.   He had lost faith in the Church : he never lost faith in the People.   *Vox populi vox Dei.* A theist he remained, but of the vaguest type.   The Revolution of 1848 seemed to promise the realization of his dreams : and in the National Assembly that followed it he took his place as a representative of the extreme Left on the benches of the Palais Bourbon.   A few yards away sat Lacordaire.   But subsequent events belied the fond consummation. On February 27, 1854, in a shabby Paris lodging, the tormented soul of the ' heresiarch ' found rest.   He had refused to see a priest : and by his own injunction he was buried without religious rites of any kind.

CHAPTER XIV

THE RELIGIOUS REVIVAL UNDER THE JULY MONARCHY : LACORDAIRE
1834-48

REPUDIATED by the Head of the Church and discredited by the tragic apostasy of its inspiring genius, the *Avenir* movement seemed to have ended in utter collapse. Yet actually it marks the beginning of one of the most notable revivals even in the history of that obstinately resurgent institution, the Catholic Church. It was the great fault of Lamennais's character that he could never bend the knee to circumstance. Having sought to achieve a certain end by certain means, when the means proved impracticable, he abandoned not the means but the end. His friends were wiser. Like him, they sought the triumph of a regenerated Catholicism. But unlike him, when one road proved barred, they were willing to try another. The reward of their mingled courage and discretion is written large in the history of nineteenth-century France.

It is easy to decry Ultramontanism. Yet in so far as it represents the claim of the Church to have a life of its own and to legislate for its own members, it embodies a principle that is vital to the health of any Christian body. In this matter French Ultramontanism and the Oxford Movement in England moved on parallel lines. Both were protests against a system tending to confound the Church with the State.

No doubt the alliance with the civil power was originally accepted by the Church with the object of bringing its influence to bear more effectively on the national life. But in the long run, it has usually tended to prove as much a hindrance as a help. And this for two reasons. In the first place, the State as the price of its assistance claims to intervene in matters that are the province of the spiritual authority. And further, the tone and temper of the ecclesiastical organism are gradually assimilated to those of the civil through the official encouragement of its more worldly in preference to its more spiritual elements. This has been the history of ' Establishments ' in most ages. It is true that there is nothing to prevent a spiritual revival from taking place within the Church even when it is bound by the most rigid bonds to the State. But such a revival must either compel the State to give the Church a greater measure of independence or else be itself doomed to extinction.

The former case was that of the Church revival in England during the nineteenth century : the latter that of the Church revival in France during the seventeenth. The age of Louis XIV was the classic age of French Catholicism. But the Church of S. Vincent de Paul and of Bossuet allowed itself to become the tool of Bourbon autocracy and became, as its punishment, the Church of Loménie de Brienne and of Talleyrand. The persecutions of the revolutionary epoch revived the spiritual principle within it : but the Napoleonic tyranny and the strict alliance between the Altar and the Throne under the Restoration once more depressed it. Despite his exaggerations and perversities, Lamennais was right in the main when he alleged

the Gallicanism of the episcopate under Charles X
as the great hindrance to the progress of Catholicism.

Yet, of course, it would be grossly unfair to
represent the clergy of the Restoration period as
given over to a complacent worldliness or indifferent to the interests of religion as such. Beyond
question, they relied too much on the arm of the
flesh. The bishops, too, were prone to regard
themselves rather as dignified persons of rank and
importance than as ministers of Christ and Fathers
in God. Yet the majority of the clergy were, if
not ardent apostles and evangelists, at least men
of blameless life and a real, though not perhaps
always very fervent, pastoral zeal. If ambition
and party spirit too often disfigured the clerical
character, was there ever a time in the history of
the Church when they did not ?

The best of the clergy were very good indeed.
It must not be forgotten that both the good Bishop
Myriel in *Les Misérables*, and the equally admirable
Abbé in *Les Courbezon*, are represented as exercising their ministry under the Restoration. We
are not expected, of course, to regard them as
typical : yet clearly their creators saw nothing
inherently impossible in such exquisitely Christian
types being found among the ecclesiastics of the
time.

Again (to pass from fiction to history), we have
the witness of Renan in his *Souvenirs d'enfance et
de jeunesse*. It is true that his experience (he
was born in 1825) belongs to a period slightly subsequent to that of the Restoration. But the old
priests whom in his Breton childhood he knew
and loved were men whose best work must have
been done before 1830. ' A clergy serious, disinterested, and honest,' he calls them : and adds,

' I have had the happiness of knowing absolute
virtue.' Later in the same work he thus sums up
his experience : ' The fact is that what is said of
clerical morals is, according to my experience,
destitute of any foundation. I have passed thirteen
years of my life in the hands of priests and I have
never seen the shadow of a scandal : I have never
known any but good priests.'

Such words, coming from such a quarter, are
incontrovertible : and they may fairly be set
against Stendhal's calumnious picture of clerical
life and manners under the Restoration in *Le Rouge
et le Noir*. Then, as now, it was the fashion of
anti-clerical writers to denounce the seminaries.
Stendhal's picture of that at Besançon to which he
sends the detestable Julien Storel is horrifying.
But it is unlikely that Stendhal had ever been inside
a seminary in his life, whereas Renan passed the
whole of his youth in one. The great critic, indeed,
does not conceal his opinion that the ecclesiastical
' tone ' of the vanished time was infinitely prefer-
able to that which succeeded it under the influence
of Ultramontanists like Lacordaire and Dupanloup. ' Everything in those old priests,' he writes,
' was honest, sensible, imbued with a profound
sense of professional honour. If they were entirely
untouched by the currents of modern speculation
and discovery, they had none of the Ultramontane
taste for the irrational, which has developed since
their time.' ' The old school knew how to be
extravagant in a sober way (*délirer avec sobriété*):
it carried even into the absurd the rules of good
sense.'

Here no doubt speaks the *odium theologicum*.
And perhaps the whole of Renan's picture is not
uncoloured by his intense dislike of the temper and
methods of the Roman Church as he knew it in

later life. It is unnecessary, however, to sym-
pathize entirely with the developments of modern
Roman Catholicism to see where, with all its
admirable qualities, the old Gallican type of priesthood failed. The clergy of the Restoration, taking
them as a whole, were grave, kindly, pious, conscientious. But they had lost touch with the age.
As pastors of the faithful remnant who, among the
surging tides of nineteenth-century materialism
and unbelief, clung with simple faith to the beliefs
of their forefathers, they were admirable. But the
expansive force that recovers lost ground and wins
new was lacking. Their attitude towards the
world outside their own little circles of *dévots* and
Legitimists was one of pained bewilderment.
Society seemed to them to have abandoned the old
standards and bulwarks altogether : between it
and them there was no common standing-ground.
They could only wring their hands and sigh for the
return of an order of things that had vanished for
ever. Their theology was that of the seventeenth
century, their preaching earnest but flat, their
apologetic timid and conventional.

But already, outside France, a more valiant
school of thought was arising within the Church to
challenge the new age. In Catholic Germany, no
less than in France, an undue subservience to the
secular power had lowered the tone and crippled the
energies of the Church. Whatever might be the
intrinsic value of the doctrines known as ' Febro-
nianism,' their adoption by the worldly ecclesiastical princes of South Germany merely as a pretext
for making themselves independent of the Holy
See had fatally compromised them. Again, the
ecclesiastical policy of the Emperor Joseph II in
his dominions no doubt included many needful and
perfectly justifiable reforms : but, being inspired

not so much by zeal for religion as by *l'esprit philosophique* and the doctrine of the omnipotent State, it had the effect of increasing rather than diminishing the spiritual torpor from which the Church was suffering. The inclusion of South Germany within the zone of the Napoleonic Caesarism did nothing to improve the situation.

But in the twenties of the nineteenth century a notable revival of Catholic life and thought took place under the inspiration of such men as Görres, Baader, the brothers Schlegel, and the young Döllinger. This school, which had its centre at Munich, was Ultramontane in its desire to set the Church free from State control. When the Prussian Government, in 1837, imprisoned Archbishop Droste zu Vischering of Cologne for ignoring its edicts concerning mixed marriages, Görres wrote his *Athanasius* in the archbishop's defence.

At the same time, the Munich writers were eager to effect a reconciliation between the traditional teaching of the Church and the discoveries of modern historical and scientific research. It was probably in this sense that Lamennais spoke of the German clergy as having an ' almost Protestant spirit.' They themselves would have hotly repudiated the charge. It was only as time brought changes in the character of Ultramontanism that what they understood to be the claims of historical truth drove such men as Döllinger and Hefele into the anti-Ultramontane camp.

That goodwill and intellectual sympathy existed between this group and the leaders of the *Avenir* movement is clear from the reception given to the latter at Munich in 1831. And it was on lines similar to those of their German friends that Lamennais's colleagues after their leader's defection set themselves to inaugurate a forward movement on behalf of Catholicism in France. Both groups represented—though in rather different ways—the type of thought usually described as ' Liberal Catholicism.' Instead of turning their back, in scorn or grief, on the forces and ideas prevailing in the modern world, they sought to enlist them, so far as might be, in the service of Catholic truth. The Germans laid stress mainly on freedom of scientific and historical inquiry, the Frenchmen on political freedom and a bold acceptance of the principles of 1789. But in either case the result was to provide a new and more fruitful line of apologetic.

It was not long before Lacordaire had an opportunity of proving his mettle in this direction. After his final breach with Lamennais he passed through a time of painful perplexity. Conscious as he could not help being of his great gifts, he asked himself how he could best make them effective in the Church's service. Perhaps, too, there mingled with this feeling the remains of that ' vague torment of ambition ' which (as he tells us) had so devoured him at an earlier period of his life. In his uncertainty he turned to the woman whom years afterwards he called his ' Providence '— Madame Swetchine.

This remarkable person was of Russian extraction, had been converted to Catholicism as the result of her own study and reflection, and was already becoming, at her *salon* in the Rue St. Dominique, the Egeria of the rising generation of French Catholics. Lacordaire was introduced to her by Montalembert in 1830. ' From that day,' he writes, ' I took no resolution without discussing it with her.'

For some time he thought of writing a great apologetic work to be called *The Church and the*

World in the Nineteenth Century. But the project came to nothing. Something told him that it was as a preacher rather than as a writer that he would best serve the Church. Yet his first experience as a preacher was not encouraging. Before making a public appearance, he wished to test his powers before a small company of Madame Swetchine's friends. This he did one Sunday in May, 1833, in the Church of S. Roch. ' He will never make a preacher,' was the verdict. He himself was of the same opinion. The engagements he had already made to preach were cancelled.

An opportunity of a rather different kind soon presented itself. He was asked to give a course of conferences on religious subjects to the pupils of the Collège Stanislas. Almost unwillingly he accepted the invitation. The first conference was given on January 19, 1834. From the first moment it was clear that he had found his rôle at last. His previous failure had been due to the attempt to force his genius within the mould of the ' classic tradition ' bequeathed by the great pulpit orators of the seventeenth century. In these conferences, however, Lacordaire employed a form which was neither precisely sermon nor lecture, but a brilliant improvised discourse on the great fundamental truths of religion, in which all the resources of his eloquence and personal magnetism were flung forth with a magnificent spontaneity. ' It was not merely the priest who spoke but the poet, the citizen, the philosopher.'

His success was extraordinary. Such men as Chateaubriand, Victor Hugo, and Lamartine were there, together with all the ' thinking youth of Paris.' The eminent lawyer, M. Berryer, had once even to climb through a window to get in. But the past connection of the preacher with the

' traitor ' Lamennais was not forgotten by his enemies. To them, both the manner and the matter of his discourse were ' revolutionary,' and therefore odious. They repeated with horror such phrases as the ' Christian Republic,' or the assertion that ' the first tree of liberty was planted in Paradise by the hand of God Himself.'

Lacordaire was denounced at the same time to the Government, the Holy See, and the Archbishop of Paris. The Government declared that it viewed the conferences ' without distrust ' ; the Holy See referred the matter to the archbishop ; the archbishop suspended the conferences. When Lacordaire remonstrated, the prelate declared that he might resume them on condition that he wrote them out beforehand and submitted them for approval. But Lacordaire replied that the effect would be to paralyse his powers, and preferred to abandon the conferences altogether (December, 1834).

The check, however, was only temporary. A far wider and more imposing theatre than a college chapel was about to be opened to his powers. Already, at the beginning of 1834, one of his most fervent admirers, Frederic Ozanam, a young law-student who, though still only twenty years of age, had founded the now famous and world-wide Society of S. Vincent de Paul, had approached Archbishop de Quélen with a view to his asking Lacordaire to transfer his gifts to the celebrated pulpit of Notre Dame. The archbishop first expressed misgiving as to a project which he described as a ' novelty,' then announced that he had decided to have a course of sermons preached in his cathedral, not by Lacordaire but by the ' best preachers of the day.' Ozanam replied that the people whom it was desired to reach would not come to 'sermons.' What was wanted was a series of 'conferences' with Lacordaire to give them. The archbishop, however, clung to his plan : and on February 16, 1834, a series of sermons by seven different preachers was opened at Notre Dame. Ozanam proved to be perfectly right. The general public stayed away. Meanwhile the chapel at the Collège Stanislas was crowded to suffocation.

In the following December came the news that Lacordaire's conferences were finally abandoned. Ozanam was broken-hearted. But the Abbé Liautard, the Superior of the Collège Stanislas, was on his side. He wrote an expostulation on the subject which was circulated in manuscript among the clergy of Paris. This produced its effect. In January, 1835, Lacordaire was walking in the Luxembourg garden when he met an ecclesiastic of his acquaintance. The friend asked, ' Why don't you go and see the archbishop and have an explanation with him ? ' A few yards on he met another friend who asked the same question. ' Being somewhat superstitious in regard to Providence,' wrote Lacordaire in later years, ' I took my way towards S. Michael's convent where the archbishop then lived. I found him walking up and down the room with a melancholy preoccupied air. He gave me a slight sign of welcome, and I turned and walked up and down with him without his uttering a word. After a long silence he stopped suddenly and, looking at me with a scrutinizing glance, said, " I have an idea of entrusting to you the pulpit of Notre Dame : would you accept it ? " ' Lacordaire expressed his misgivings as to his fitness for the task : and asked for twenty-four hours to reflect. At the end of that time he said he would accept.

So began what was unquestionably to be the

most important factor in the revival of Catholicism in France under the July Monarchy—the famous *Conférences de Notre Dame*. The first of these was given at the beginning of the Lent of 1835. The vast nave was crowded—and crowded with men. Lacordaire has described his feelings on the occasion : ' I mounted the pulpit not without emotion but with firmness. I began my discourse with my eyes fixed on the archbishop. He listened with his head a little lowered in a state of absolute impassibility like a man who . . . ran personal risks in this solemn adventure. When I had embarked on my subject and my breast expanded with the necessity of gaining hold on so vast an assembly, there escaped me one of those cries the accent of which, when it is sincere and deep, never fails to move. The archbishop visibly trembled. A paleness covered his face : he raised his hand and darted an astonished glance at me. I understood that the battle was won in his mind. It was won, too, in the congregation.'

The ' cry ' of which Lacordaire speaks is no doubt, as M. d'Haussonville suggests, the famous apostrophe ' Assembly, assembly, what do you ask of me ? The truth. Then you yourselves have it not. You wish to receive it. You come here to be taught.' The subject of this first series of conferences was ' The Church ' : that of the first conference, ' The necessity of a teaching Church and its definite character.' Man, insists the preacher, is a being who must be taught (*un être enseigné*). This is as true of enlightened men as of the young and ignorant. ' Either truth is but a name and man the miserable sport of opinions which succeed one another without end, or indeed there must be on the earth a divine authority to teach men. The Church alone among human institutions constitutes a universal authority. Fallen humanity may conspire for its overthrow : but *mole sua stat,* and its very immobility is a victory.' ' The struggle is, then, within the very entrails of humanity—between the humanity of the senses and the humanity of the spirit. The humanity of the senses manifested itself in antiquity for four hundred years : the humanity of the spirit has manifested itself in modern times for eighteen hundred years. Which do you prefer ? The Church is the new humanity. Whoever attacks it invokes the past : whoever defends it appeals to the future.'

Mere curiosity, no doubt, had played a large part in drawing together the huge congregation which listened to that first conference : for his connection with Lamennais and the success and then the abrupt suspension of the Collège Stanislas Conferences had made the preacher the talk of the town. The same cause, too, must have helped largely to swell the numbers on subsequent occasions. The saying that ' Nothing succeeds like success ' is never truer than in the case of a popular preacher. But an audience of the type that filled the nave of the vast cathedral Sunday after Sunday could not be maintained by curiosity alone. Many who came for the first time from curiosity continued to come because they felt that the preacher had really something to say.

It has been said that the conferences ' converted nobody.' Even if this were true (which it almost certainly is not), the criticism is beside the mark. Lacordaire did not seek or expect to ' convert,' but (as he himself said) to ' prepare the way for faith.' Those for whom the conferences were designed were the ' clever young men' of Paris— doctors, lawyers, students, soldiers, etc. This was the class that, more than any other, was penetrated by Voltairian ideas and inclined to regard Christianity as a worn-out and even pernicious superstition. Lacordaire's aim was to make them see that, whether it were true or not, at least it had something to say for itself.

He was the better able to fulfil this task because he himself had known ' the anguish and the charm of unbelief.' All through the years that he spent at the university and during his first years as a lawyer at Paris he had been a sceptic. But slowly a conviction of the truth of Christianity forced itself upon him until at last, early in 1824, what he calls ' the last ray of light ' entered his soul. It was to assist some such gradual illumination in others that he now addressed himself. He spoke not as the priest and pastor admonishing his flock but ' as an equal to equals.' He did not say Brethren, but *Messieurs*. He claimed to be all that they were, nothing they were not. ' You are Frenchmen. I am one like you. Philosophers. I am one like you. Free and proud. I am more so than you.' Instead of decrying the new age like most preachers of the time, he exulted in its achievements and was proud to call it his own.

It is true that his sermons, as the Duc de Broglie says, were bold generalizations more calculated to open out great vistas than susceptible of rigorous proof. But this was accordant with their purpose. What he sought was less to provide proofs than to create a sympathetic attitude of mind in which the proofs might be approached. He sought to show that Catholicism corresponds to, and can alone satisfy, the deepest needs both of the individual and of society. He himself tells us that ' he reached his Catholic belief through his social beliefs ' : and he was addressing an age that was intensely interested in social theory—the age of

Saint-Simon and Fourier. It is therefore especially on the social action of Christianity that he, like Lamennais, lays stress. In vain, he urges again and again, do men look for a regeneration of human society apart from religion, for a society without God is doomed to destruction.

So great was the success of the first series of conferences that the archbishop asked Lacordaire to resume them in the Lent of 1836. The subject of this second series was ' The Doctrine of the Church in General : its nature and its sources.' Crowds still continued to flock to Notre Dame. The young priest with the dark eyes and the worn face became the hero of a sort of cult. A new shade of green was even called ' Lacordaire green ' after him. But if M. de Quélen had (for the moment at least) laid aside his former suspicions, Lacordaire's old enemies were still unpropitiated. Twenty-seven propositions extracted from his sermons had been delated to Rome : and the sermons themselves were described as ' the greatest degradation of speech and the completest anarchy not only of theological but of philosophical thought.'

M. de Quélen was again approached : and again the amiable, weak prelate listened to the serpent's voice. Personally he liked and admired Lacordaire : he had even spoken of him as ' the new prophet.' But he mistrusted both the Liberalism of his political and the Ultramontanism of his religious views. There seems no reason to believe that the archbishop recommended Lacordaire to discontinue his conferences. But Lacordaire knew of the intrigues and detractions of his adversaries and that M. de Quélen was not unheedful of them. Nor was he himself entirely satisfied with his efforts or confident of his qualifications. ' I understood,' he says in his *Memoirs*, ' that I was not yet ripe for the task.' For these reasons he decided to interrupt his conferences, at least for a time, and go to Rome. The decision was announced to the congregation at the end of the last conference of 1836. ' I leave,' he said, ' in the hands of my bishop this pulpit of Notre Dame henceforth established—established by him and by you—by the pastor and the people. For a moment this double commission has adorned my brow. Permit me to lay it down of myself, and for a time retire into solitude in the presence of my weakness and my God.'

In attributing his journey to Rome to the desire for solitude Lacordaire seems to have expressed truly enough the thought uppermost in his mind. ' Nothing can be done without solitude,' he wrote from Rome. ' A man is made from within himself, not from without.' But as Rome is neither the only, nor even the most obvious, place for a solitary's existence, we may surmise that other motives contributed to his decision.

One such motive, as Father Chocarne suggests, was the desire to justify himself against the attacks of his enemies and to prove his entire devotion to the Holy See by taking up his abode on the very threshold of the Apostles. But besides this there seems to have been already working in his mind an impulse which, obscure at the moment, was gradually to become clearer. ' My retirement to Rome,' he writes in his *Memoirs*, ' had a hidden end which was only to be revealed later on.' This ' end ' was the embracing of the religious life.

The development of his vocation was influenced considerably, if very indirectly, by an incident that occurred early in his stay at Rome. Lamennais had recently published his *Affaires de Rome*, giving a decidedly one-sided account of his treatment by the Holy See. Lacordaire on reading it at once sat down and penned a reply entitled *A Letter on the Holy See*, and addressed to the young men who had attended his conferences at Paris. His outspoken defence of the papal claims was a triumphant retort to his enemies in France and mightily pleased the Pope. Unfortunately it caused profound offence in another quarter. The manuscript was submitted by Mme Swetchine, at Lacordaire's request, to the Archbishop of Paris. The archbishop's Gallicanism took fright. He tried to prevent its publication. There ensued a correspondence between him and Lacordaire in which the priest was not too respectful to the prelate. The result was, for the time, a complete rupture.

In the circumstances it was impossible for Lacordaire to resume his preaching at Notre Dame. Moreover, the famous Jesuit, Père Ravignan, had been appointed to take his place. He prepared therefore for a long stay at Rome, taking up his residence at a house of the Jesuits. It was during his stay there that he seems to have formed his final resolve to become a religious—not without a struggle. ' The sacrifice was bitter,' he wrote later.

What order should he embrace ? His choice, he has told us, lay between the Jesuits and the Dominicans. But the Jesuits already existed in France : and it was Lacordaire's wish to re-establish an order as yet unrepresented there. Preacher as he was, the Order of Friars Preachers, with its tradition as the great preaching and teaching order of the later Middle Ages, appealed inevitably to his imagination. Its very unpopularity, due to its association with the Inquisition, was an additional attraction. To reintroduce it into France would be all the more a challenge.

Lacordaire, as one of his biographers admits, had a taste for the 'resounding'—an Englishman might call it the sensational.

The plan was not, however, carried into execution immediately. In September, 1837, he returned to France in response to an invitation to preach in Metz Cathedral. Here, and during a stay at Paris that followed, he announced his project to his more intimate friends. Their attitude was not very enthusiastic at first. M. de Quélen, too, was distinctly frigid. Lacordaire, however, refused to be discouraged. With the object of winning the support of public opinion for his scheme, he wrote a *Memoir on the Re-establishment of the Friars Preachers*. Then in July, 1838, he set out again for Rome with one companion, Hippolyte Réquedat. The two friends received the Dominican habit at the convent of La Minerva on April 9, 1839. They then retired to the convent of La Quercia for their year's novitiate. The Master General offered to shorten its duration to six months : but Lacordaire declined the offer. During this time he wrote his *Life of S. Dominic*, which Chateaubriand described as 'immense, like beauty itself,' and Mme Swetchine as 'a miracle.' It is certainly a charming piece of work, but uncritical to a degree.

On April 12, 1840, he and his companion took their final vows : and on Easter Day he preached at S. Louis des Français in Rome. His sermon opened with the words 'We have conquered! we have conquered!' He was given the convent of Santa Sabina to occupy : and here he was joined by his friends—first the architect Piel (a pioneer of the 'Gothic revival' in France), and soon afterwards Hernheim a converted Jew, the young painter Jean Baptiste Besson (the 'Dominican artist' of

Mrs. Sidney Lear's charming book), and a single priest, the Abbé Jandel. These, with Lacordaire and Réquedat, were the first French Dominicans of the revived order. Their surroundings were full of memories of the past and inspiration for the future—the church ' a primitive basilica in all the glory of its simplicity,' the convent hallowed by the residence of S. Dominic himself, and containing his cell and in its garden an ancient orange-tree planted by his own hand. The only cloud on their happiness was the illness of Réquedat, who died on September 3, 1840—*et primitiae et numen.*

At the end of eight months, Lacordaire concluded that it was time for him to go back to France and seek new recruits for his order. He left Rome on November 30th, and travelled through France wearing his religious habit. He took with him an old soutane to put on in case of necessity : but after a few days he decided that he would not want it and gave it away. The black and white habit of the Dominicans had not been seen in France for fifty years : and its reappearance caused some astonishment and amusement. But its wearer was not insulted.

By this time M. de Quélen was dead : and Mgr Affre was Archbishop of Paris. Lacordaire asked him to be allowed to preach again in Notre Dame. The archbishop consented. He also asked if he might wear his habit in the pulpit. Again the prelate made no objection. The congregation which welcomed the famous preacher (February 12, 1841) was naturally immense, though the discourse was not one of his best efforts and its length caused some weariness in a section of the audience. The next day the Garde des Sceaux, who had been one of his hearers, asked him to a big dinner party. During the meal M. Bourdian, a former Minister of

Justice under Charles X, leaned towards one of his neighbours and said, 'What a strange turn of events! If when I was Garde des Sceaux I had invited a Dominican to my table, my house would have been burned down next day.' 'However,' says Lacordaire, 'the house was not burnt and no newspaper even invoked the secular arm for my *auto-da-fé.*'

In addition to his single appearance at Notre Dame, Lacordaire's stay in Paris was also marked by the publication of the *Life of S. Dominic.* After two months he returned to Rome, taking with him five new brethren. The little group of his associates had just been transferred from Santa Sabina to San Clemente, where they were to make their novitiate.

Hitherto all had gone smoothly enough. But Lacordaire's enemies were at work again. His sermon at Notre Dame (the subject of which was 'The vocation of the French nation') had caused deep resentment among the Legitimists, who branded it as the utterance of a 'revolutionary' and a 'demagogue.' Letters were sent to Rome alleging that the plan for re-establishing the Dominican Order was nothing but a conspiracy to realize the ideas of the *Avenir* in another way. The effect was soon seen. Hardly had the novitiate begun when one evening there came a letter from the Cardinal Secretary of State ordering Lacordaire to remain in Rome alone, while his companions were sent to complete their novitiate elsewhere. Lacordaire was thunderstruck: but told his brethren to obey without reserve. He himself retired to the convent of La Minerva.

In the later part of the same year Lacordaire obtained permission to return to France to resume his preaching. He left Rome in September, and

went to Bordeaux, where he preached a ' station '
lasting from December, 1841, to March, 1842.
Galleries were erected in the nave to accommodate
the vast audience, which included all the official
bodies of the city.   The enthusiasm was so great
that the preacher had several times to restrain
the applause of his hearers.   From Bordeaux he
returned to Italy, spending the summer of 1842 at
Bosco in Piedmont, the place where half of his
companions had fulfilled their novitiate.   The
other half, having finished their own probationary
period elsewhere, came to Bosco too.   Lacordaire's
family—seven professed and three novices—were
once more re-united in what till 1845 was to be the
novice-house of the French Dominicans.

Lacordaire left Bosco in November, 1842, and
went to Nancy.   Here he preached a ' station '
lasting from December, 1842, to May, 1843. ' This
city,' he says, ' was far from showing the same
ardour as Bordeaux : nevertheless providence
had chosen it as the site of our first foundation.'   Among his hearers was M. Thierry de
St. Beaussant, who confided to Lacordaire his
desire to establish the Dominicans at Nancy.   The
bishop having given his consent, M. de St. Beaussant provided a small house for the purpose and
became himself a novice in the order. ' Brother
Réquedat,' says Lacordaire, ' gave me the first
soul of the edifice and Brother de St. Beaussant the
first stone.'

At Nancy, Lacordaire remained throughout the
greater part of 1843 supervising the setting up of
this first foundation, with Père Jandel, summoned
from Bosco, as the first superior.   The task was
not an easy one.   The Minister of Public Worship
and the Prefect of Nancy did their best to nip the
project in the bud.   The anti-clerical papers of

Nancy joined in the outcry : and Lacordaire had again to defend his reputation in the courts. But these difficulties were at last compromised. When Lacordaire quitted Nancy in the late autumn, he left the young community firmly established.

The golden period of the great preacher's life was about to begin. For a long time the public had been demanding his return to the Notre Dame pulpit. It was not that the ministry of Père Ravignan had failed to attract. But it was felt that room should be found for Lacordaire as well. After Archbishop Affre had already asked him several times to return, he consented to give the Advent course of 1843. Ravignan was to continue to give the Lent Conferences. The archbishop made one stipulation only—that Lacordaire should wear a soutane instead of his habit. But his conscience forbade. ' I have no *right*,' he told Mme Swetchine, ' to put off my habit.' The archbishop then wrote to the Pope. A few days later there came from the Master General of the Dominican Order a letter authorizing Lacordaire to preach as a secular priest. It was then settled that while preaching he should wear the canon's lace rochet and mozetta over his habit. In this guise he made his reappearance in the Notre Dame pulpit on December 3, 1843. The authorities had feared a disturbance : but by the time he had reached his third sentence he had won the hearts of his hearers. Next day even the Liberal *Siècle* was complimentary.

From this time onward, till 1851 (with the exception of the year 1847), Lacordaire continued to preach at Notre Dame. There were seventy-three sermons in all. The most famous are the course of 1846 on ' Jesus Christ ' and that of 1848 on ' God.' The interest of the vast audience was maintained to the end : and the attendance showed no signs of falling off. An eye-witness, M. Caro, has thus described the scene :

In those unquiet years . . . the young men, more avid than ever of emotions and ideas, came in crowds to seek them at the foot of that pulpit. These young men pointed out to one another among the assembly some illustrious personage or celebrated philosopher ; some writer of the highest order : Berryer, Cousin, Lamartine, Tocqueville, or the greatest of all, Chateaubriand. The preacher appeared : the novelty of his costume, the white robe from which emerged an ascetic's head, the sculpturesque beauty of the face made pale by fasting and toil, the flash of the glance, the ringing vibration of the voice, prepared the way for the triumph of his eloquence by the seductions of look and of imagination. At the height of the nineteenth century we were confronted with a monk, a real monk. This monk, however, if by his dress he belonged to the Middle Ages, belonged no less to our own country and century by his education, his ideas, his soul, his language, a language that was novel and picturesque, free, bold, adventurous in its very candour. It was, under the old vaulting of Notre Dame, the inauguration of romantic art in preaching.

Such preaching was indeed an entirely new thing. ' Victor Hugo,' says M. d'Haussonville, ' had broken the mould of tragic drama : Lacordaire broke the mould of the sermon.' He threw overboard all the time-honoured apparatus of exordium, ' heads,' and peroration, inherited from the classic preachers of the *Grand Siècle*, to follow freely the flight of his own inspiration. The classic preachers had learned their carefully written sermons by heart. Lacordaire, on the other hand, was ' essentially an improvisator.' Of course he did not preach without preparation. But his preparation was one of thought, not of language. Having settled beforehand the broad lines of his argument, he trusted for their expression to his incomparable resources of vocabulary and the inspiration of the moment. Thus he was able to respond fully to that strange effluence from his audience that every great orator knows so well.

Ravignan's eloquence was of a different sort— more restrained in its passion, more austere in its phrasing. The mission of Lacordaire was primarily to the doubting and unconverted. Ravignan, though an effective apologist, was at his best when helping the faithful towards higher levels of spiritual life. It was as a conductor of retreats that he specially shone. To him belongs the distinction of having originated the famous Holy Week Retreat at Notre Dame which has persisted to this day. This retreat is no tiny gathering of the exceptionally devout assembled in a side chapel, but a vast multitude filling a great cathedral.

It was in 1841 that Ravignan first obtained permission to follow up his Lent Conferences with a retreat in preparation for Easter. The church of the Abbaye-aux-bois, accommodating about a thousand persons, was put at his disposal. But when the preacher arrived, on the Monday evening in Holy Week, he found that the church had been full for two hours. There were no women : the congregation was entirely of men, mostly young. Ravignan proposed that the following evening the retreat should be transferred to the huge church of S. Eustache. This was done : and again the church was crowded. The preacher has recorded the overwhelming effect of the *Miserere* and *Stabat Mater* sung by three to four thousand men's voices. The following year the experiment was repeated : and this time it was followed by a general Communion on Easter Day at Notre Dame at which three thousand men received the Blessed Sacrament. Ravignan continued to conduct his conferences and retreats until 1846, when failure of health forced him into retirement. From that

time until he finally abandoned the pulpit of Notre
Dame in 1854 Lacordaire took his place.

It is sufficient to compare these imposing demonstrations with the far from crowded audiences that
followed the rather timid apologetic of M. Frayssinous at S. Sulpice under the Restoration to
realize the immense strides made by the Catholic
cause in the not very congenial atmosphere of the
monarchy of July. The Church had carried its
arms boldly into the enemy's camp, and had
returned laden with spoils as the reward of its
courage and enterprise. Nor was its success confined to the metropolis. There was a steady
growth of Catholic feeling all over France. The
number of ordinations has been well described as
' the barometer of the Church's progress.' From
1800 to 1815 priests were so few that only town
parishes could be provided with pastors. The
country districts were almost entirely abandoned.
In 1820, M. Frayssinous reported that ' in the
bosom of this very Christian kingdom fifteen
thousand cures remain vacant, in default of priests
to fill them.' The number of priests gradually
increased after 1830. The seminaries began to
fill up. The fact is the more remarkable in that the
inducements to ambition presented under the Restoration were no longer operative. It is clear,
therefore, that if vocations multiplied it was because a new spirit stirred the dry bones of the
Church. And of course in proportion as shepherds
were found to tend them, the numbers and devotion of the flocks increased. Some of the most
beautiful examples of the priestly character that the
French Church at this time produced were content
to toil as simple *curés de campagne*. At their head
stands the famous Curé d'Ars, Jean Baptiste
Vianney (1786–1859), canonized by Pius XI in 1924.

The restoration of the French Dominicans by Lacordaire is only one example of the revival of old and the foundation of new religious orders which mark this period. The Benedictines had preceded them in 1832. The Franciscans returned about the same time as the Dominicans. The Carmelites, the Marists, and the Eudists followed. Even more notable was the multiplication of religious communities of women. Among the laity the Society of S. Vincent de Paul, for personal service to the poor, grew in twenty years from the ' eight poor young fellows ' who started it to two thousand members in Paris alone, where they visited five thousand families. Their *confréries* in France numbered five hundred : and others had been established in England, Belgium, Spain, America, and even at Jerusalem. A great development of missionary activity in foreign lands attended the religious revival in France itself. It extended to Syria, India, Siam, China, and many other countries. Most heroic of all is the story of the French Mission in Indo-China. In 1830, an infamous king declared a war of extermination on the native Christians. The French missionaries clung to their posts : and a number of them fell victims to the most fiendish torments. The French Catholic missions in China had their martyrs too.

This revival of Catholic zeal was accompanied by the introduction of new devotions to maintain and stimulate personal zeal. The old Gallican piety had had an austere quasi-Jansenist flavour. The new piety was popular, full-blooded, even flamboyant. To finer souls it seemed bizarre and perhaps a little vulgar, like the devotional extravagances of Faber to Newman. But the rank and file of Catholics welcomed it : and it carried all before it. The two favourite weapons of modern Ultramontanism—the cults of the Sacred Heart and of the Immaculate Conception—made rapid progress. The former, which originated in the revelations of Marguerite Marie Alacoque under Louis XIV, had almost died out since the Revolution : but now it awoke to new life.   The cult of *Marie Immaculée* was greatly stimulated by the alleged appearances of the Virgin in the years following 1830.   First came the appearances at Paris to Cathérine Lebouré at various intervals between 1830 and 1838, resulting in the foundation of the Archi-confrérie of Notre Dame des Victoires with its symbol of the *Medaille Miraculeuse*.   In 1842 a young Alsatian Jew, Alphonse Ratisbonne—after-wards a celebrated preacher—was converted to Christianity by an appearance of the Virgin in a church at Rome.   But the most resounding of all these appearances was that to two children at La Salette in Dauphiné, in 1846.   The Virgin mani-fested herself clad in white and with tears in her eyes and uttered the words (in reference to the sins of the time), ' I can no longer restrain the arm of my Son.'   The place, in spite of its terrible bleakness and remoteness, quickly became an ob-ject of pilgrimage, and so continues in a measure to this day, though the glories of Lourdes have almost entirely eclipsed it.   It was under the sway of the emotions produced by these events that the French episcopate petitioned for the defini-tion of the dogma of the Immaculate Conception, which was finally proclaimed by Pius IX on Decem-ber 8, 1854.

It is no part of the plan of this work to pass judgement on these various developments or to assess how far they may or may not have included elements that were better away.   It is sufficient to register the fact that they were the accompaniment of a genuine religious revival, and the further fact that this revival was associated with a progressive exaltation of the claims of the Holy See. The new centralizing tendency found notable expression in the liturgical sphere. In 1832 a small company of priests had taken possession of the deserted priory of Solesmes with the intention of reviving the Benedictine discipline : and in 1836 a pontifical brief reconstituted the ancient order in their favour. The brief assigned to them as a special duty the work of 'restoring the sound traditions of pontifical jurisprudence and of the sacred liturgies.' For this task their abbot, the famous Dom Guéranger, was admirably fitted both by zeal and by learning. Under his direction a movement was initiated for abolishing the historic diocesan liturgies of France in favour of the Roman rite. The battle was long and closely fought. The dioceses naturally clung to their ancient Uses. The Gallican complexion of the episcopate ensured the opposition of the majority of its members. But a number of bishops favoured the movement and prescribed the Roman Use in their dioceses. The first to do so was Mgr Parisis, Bishop of Langres, in 1839. In 1842 Gregory XVI, while declining for the present to issue any injunction, deplored the 'variety of Uses' and praised those who had adopted the 'universal liturgy.' Under Pius IX the pressure from Rome became still more open and pronounced. More and more diocesans accepted the Roman rite—in 1856 even the strongly Gallican Archbishop Sibour of Paris.

CHAPTER XV

THE FIGHT FOR CATHOLIC EDUCATION: MONTALEMBERT
1833–48

ONE of the most formidable difficulties confronting the leaders of the Catholic forward movement in France (as those of the Tractarian revival in England) was the lack of sympathy with their ideas and methods displayed by the bulk of the hierarchy. In the years immediately succeeding 1830, the bishops, with certain notable exceptions, took up the pronouncedly Gallican attitude represented by such a prelate as M. de Quélen. This indeed was only natural. Appointed for the most part under the Restoration, they remained faithful to the principles that had dominated the ecclesiastical policy of that period. Secretly they longed to see Charles X back again : and it was only under pressure from the Holy See that they consented to take the oath of allegiance to his successor.

From this point of view the Government of Louis Philippe could scarcely view them with friendly eyes. But with their theological attitude it had little fault to find. As the older generation of bishops died off, the Government was careful to appoint in their place men of the same Gallican stamp. The official view of the episcopal function is not unfairly represented by the following definition culled from the *Manuel du droit ecclésiastique* of M. Dupin : ' Episcopate : a function of the Church exercised in the name and under the control of the State.' In its episcopal appointments the Government sought to choose men who, as far as possible, would lend themselves to this view of their office. It is true that they were not always able to carry their nominations through. For instance, when the priest who had given the last sacraments to the former Constitutional Bishop Grégoire, the Abbé Guillon, was designated to the See of Beauvais, the outcry was so great that the Pope refused to accept the nomination. Two others of the Government's nominees received the papal confirmation, but no prelates could be found to consecrate them. Extreme cases, however, apart, the civil power was able to have its own way.

The influence of the two chief feminine bishop-makers of the period worked in the same direction. The one—the Queen, Marie Amélie—was herself a decided Gallican : the other—the King's sister, Madame Adelaide—as became a former pupil of Mme de Genlis, was an *esprit fort*.

A Gallican priest, however, does not always make a permanently Gallican bishop. Without ascribing to the bishops of the time the deliberate hypocrisy of Ferdinand Fabre's terrible *Abbé Tigrane*, we may discern two potent influences that combined to push some, if not all, of them in an Ultramontane direction. Supervised and hampered in their functions by the Government, they inevitably turned to the Holy See as to the champion of their spiritual independence : though (as we shall see) the papal authority in the timid hands of Gregory XVI by no means always rose to the occasion. Again, they could not be altogether indifferent to the movements that were taking place in the flocks they governed. The process known in ecclesiastical circles in England as ' giving the bishops a lead ' was actively at work among the clergy and laity alike. Left to themselves, the bishops would probably have acquiesced tamely in the existing situation. But stalwarts like Lacordaire and Montalembert were crying out for a more independent and militant attitude on the part of the Church. The same temper had its representatives in the ranks of the hierarchy itself, notably in Mgr Parisis, the Bishop of Langres. Thus on at least one occasion—in 1844—the episcopal body submitted to a sort of *levée en masse* and, willingly or unwillingly, buckled on its armour for the fray.

Foremost among the demands of the younger and bolder spirits in the Catholic army was that for freedom of education. The efforts of Lacordaire and Montalembert in this direction in 1831 have already been described. For the time they had been unsuccessful ; but at least the intentions of their authors had been well advertised and there was no idea of turning back. From the Government little was to be hoped for. The Liberals might have seen drawbacks to the monopoly of the Université so long as it was administered by a bishop : but when the control of the machine had passed into their own hands it was much too valuable an asset to be let go. The chief exception to this attitude was M. Guizot. In 1833 he, as Minister of Public Instruction, secured the passing of a law allowing voluntary primary schools to be set up side by side with the communal schools. Again, in 1836, he introduced a measure conceding a similar permission in the case of secondary schools. But a member of the opposition contrived to pass an amendment by which

every principal of an *établissement libre* must declare on oath that he did not belong to an unauthorized congregation : and the Government
fell before the measure, even as amended, could
become law. Henceforth it was clear that if
ministers yielded at all they would yield only to
force.

From 1840 to 1850, therefore, the stronghold of
the Université monopoly was the object of a sus-
tained and at last successful siege. The hero of
the struggle was Montalembert, who in this way
rendered what was perhaps the most signal of his
many services to the Catholic cause. A letter
addressed by him in August, 1839, to M.Villemain,
then Minister of Public Instruction, was a kind of
declaration of war. The substitution of M. Cousin
for M. Villemain in 1840 seemed indeed for the
moment to hold out a hope that a trial of strength
might be averted. The new minister declared that
‘ the Charte ’ (of 1830) ‘ promises freedom of education ’ and ‘ that the monopoly of the Université
must be destroyed ’—an attitude in which the
Prime Minister seemed to concur. Cousin also
introduced a measure designed to give at least a
partial expression to this view. But in October
the ministry fell ; and M. Villemain was back
again in the saddle.

Early in the following year the new minister
introduced the Bill, called after its author’s name,
la loi Villemain. While conceding liberty of
education in principle, it permitted the opening
of voluntary schools only on certain stringent conditions. The principal and his assistants must
possess (1) certain degrees, (2) a certificate of morality, (3) a brevet of capacity distinct from
degrees—all of which could only be furnished by
the State. The same conditions were exacted in

the case of *petits séminaires* : though the restriction on the numbers of their pupils imposed in 1828 was removed.

It was this subjection of the *petits séminaires* to the yoke of the Université that most roused the ire of the Catholics. Fifty-six of the bishops protested vehemently, and M. Guizot, the new President of the Council, expressed his disapproval. The measure was withdrawn without even having been discussed by the Chambers.

The more militant of the bishops followed up this success by ardent attacks on the teaching given in the Université. The old Clerical warhoise, M. Clausel de Montals, Bishop of Chartres, especially distinguished himself by his trenchant, if not particularly temperate or well-informed, diatribes against the fashionable philosophy of MM. Cousin and Jouffroy. These attacks were seconded by the Ultramontane organ, the *Univers*, of which that most formidable of religious journalists, M. Louis Veuillot, had just been appointed editor. Between Montalembert and Veuillot there was to be little love lost in future years : but on the point at issue the two were at one and their co-operation was for the moment complete.

Montalembert published a pamphlet entitled *The Duty of Catholics in the matter of Freedom of Education*, in which he outlined a project for the formation of a ' Catholic party.' ' Liberty,' he wrote, ' is never received : it must be conquered.' This able and dignified presentment of the Catholic cause stands in welcome contrast to certain other productions emanating from the same side—notably the *Monopole Universitaire* of the Abbé Desgarets, Canon of Lyons, in which all the most disagreeable features of Catholic fanaticism found a vent.

Would Montalembert's suggestion be acted on ?

The bishops were divided.   The strongly Gallican Archbishop of Paris, Mgr Affre, and the majority, were strongly averse from any decided action.   But Clausel de Montals, Parisis, Cardinal de Bonald (Archbishop of Lyons), and a number of others were anxious for a fight :   and by their influence at last succeeded in bringing their brethren into line.   The introduction on February 2, 1844, of a new Education Bill gave the signal for the storm to burst.

The terms of this measure were in some ways more, in others less, generous to the Catholics than those of its predecessor.   The *petits séminaires* were allowed to retain their old position : but the number of their pupils was again restricted, while to the other conditions required of teachers in voluntary schools was added an oath that the teacher was not a member of an unauthorized religious order.   This last provision—aimed of course especially at the Jesuits—apart from anything else, effectively damned the project in Catholic eyes. The bishops—no longer a section of them only, but the episcopate as a whole—at once arose in their wrath and rained down petitions on the Government.   This unwonted exhibition of episcopal independence amazed even the Catholics themselves. ' What an imposing manifestation ! ' a priest wrote to Montalembert.   ' We have seen the renewal of the miracle of the statue of Memnon.   The truth that you have caused to arise in such splendour on the heads of our bishops has brought forth harmonious and eloquent sounds from those whom we were accustomed to think of as statues.'

In the Liberals of the Chamber surprise was mingled with fury.   M. Dupin mounted the tribune and adjured the Government to arraign the whole episcopal body before the Council of State.   Montalembert undertook the bishops' defence in the

House of Peers in a fiery speech which closed with
the famous defiance : ' We are the sons of the Cru-
saders and we will never give way before the sons
of Voltaire.'

The passage of the Bill through the Legislature
began in the same House a few days later (April 22,
1844).   Cousin, De Broglie, and Guizot declared
in its favour, though on somewhat different grounds.
Montalembert essayed the task of meeting their
arguments, as well as of replying to a bitter attack
made by Cousin on the Jesuits at a later stage
of the debate.   The great Catholic orator fought
every inch of the ground : and although the Bill
was carried by eighty-five votes to fifty-one (May
24th) it was with a number of amendments favourable to the Catholic party.   The measure was at
once brought before the Lower House.

On July 13, 1844, M. Thiers, as chairman of the
committee appointed to examine the Bill, declared
himself in favour of tests far more stringent than
those it imposed.   No doubt he scented an opportunity of overthrowing the Government.   Guizot
saw the threat beneath the words of his life-long
rival. His enthusiasm for the Bill promptly cooled.
Louis Philippe supported him : he had no wish
to have his throne overturned for a quarrel of
cuistres et bédeaux (pedants and beadles).   An
extraordinary incident provided a line of retreat.
At the close of the year the author of the Bill, M.
Villemain, was seized with insanity.   The poor
man had got the Jesuits ' on the brain ' in a literal
sense. He saw them everywhere, believed that
they were pursuing him and that they had taken
away his wife, pretending that he had murdered
her.   One day, crossing the Place de la Concorde
with a friend, he stopped suddenly, and pointing
to a heap of paving-stones exclaimed, ' Don't you

see them ? The Jesuits ! The Jesuits ! Let us run away ! ' The unfortunate minister resigned his portfolio : and Guizot at once seized the opportunity to withdraw the Bill.

The Catholics employed the respite in effecting a more complete organization of their forces. It is true that the majority of the bishops, exhausted by their effort of the preceding year, were content to stand aside. Montalembert did his best to convert Mgr Affre, but without success. The laity, however, now took the law into their own hands. Mgr Parisis and a few other bishops came forward to bless their efforts. A Central Catholic Committee was founded with Montalembert as its president and *Dieu et mon droit* as its motto. Subordinate committees were set up in the departments : and numerous Catholic journals sprang into existence all over France. The Legitimists showed themselves at first coy and suspicious : but Montalembert succeeded in winning them over. A petition of *pères de famille* in favour of liberty of teaching was extensively signed.

Meanwhile the ' sons of Voltaire ' were equally active. A charge by Cardinal de Bonald (dated February 4, 1845), condemning the *Manuel du droit ecclésiastique* of M. Dupin as ' full of false and heretical propositions calculated to destroy the true liberties of the Church,' was brought before the Council of State, which declared that it involved *abus* and ordered its suppression. Thereupon, sixty bishops publicly associated themselves with the cardinal's action, and Montalembert had the charge printed and distributed broadcast. The anti-clericals took their revenge by making what they called a *sortie* against the Jesuits. Michelet and Edgar Quinet described the history and character of the famous order in blood-curdling terms in their

lectures at the Collège de France. The less educated classes were stirred to the depths by the
dreadful portrait of the Jesuit Rodin in Eugène
Sue's *Wandering Jew*, at this time running as a
serial in the *Constitutionnel*. In the House of Peers
Cousin renewed his denunciation.

When the ground had thus been sufficiently prepared, M. Thiers, on May 2, 1845, demanded in the
Peers that the laws of the State against unauthorized congregations should be put in force. Guizot
did not dare to defend a cause so unpopular as
that of the Jesuits. He absented himself from the
debate. Next day the Chamber by an overwhelming majority voted their expulsion.

The Jesuits accepted the challenge and prepared
to resist. Their cause was taken up by Montalembert—all the more chivalrously in that he by no
means saw eye to eye with them on every point—
and by a certain number of the bishops. Mgr
Parisis wrote to urge them not to yield an inch.
Mgr Affre, on the other hand, declared himself
flatly opposed to resistance. It was even said that
he would be glad to see them go. Montalembert
again did his best to win him over, but without
success.

Meanwhile the Government was tacking. The
Prime Minister, Guizot, was strongly averse from
the proposed step. Yet he did not dare to fly
in the face of public opinion. He now conceived
the idea of approaching the Pope with a view to
effecting the dispersal of the Jesuits by an act of
the Holy See. Count Rossi, an Italian of consummate diplomatic ability, who was then in the
service of the French Government and was afterwards to be Pius IX's assassinated Prime Minister
in the Days of '48, was chosen to negotiate the
affair. His task was not an easy one : for Gregory

XVI had always been a friend of the Jesuits.   But
a number of the Cardinals were favourable.   Mgr
Affre wrote secretly to the Pope to urge him to
yield : and Louis Philippe mingled entreaties and
threats to the same end.   Early in July the following announcement appeared in the *Moniteur* :
' The King's Government has received news from
Rome.   The negotiations entrusted to M. Rossi
have been successful.   The Congregation of Jesuits
will cease to exist in France and will disperse of its
own accord.   Its houses will be closed and its
novitiate dissolved.'

The blow to Montalembert was terrible.   At
first he declined to believe his ears.   But the thing
was done : and he made the best of it.   ' Whatever
happens,' he wrote to the Jesuit Father Rozaven,
' in good as in evil fortune, nothing will ever shake
my inviolable attachment to the Church.'   The
' dispersal,' too, of the Jesuits did not in the end
prove—nor was it intended—to be a very serious
matter.   Cardinal Lambruschini, the Papal Secretary of State, told the French Jesuits that ' they
were to confine themselves to what the General
ordered them to do.'   The General, naturally, was
not very exacting.   Only three houses of professed
and two novitiates were closed, their members
being accommodated in the remaining houses.
With the staff of one of them two new houses were
founded in the very heart of Paris itself.   The
Government made a show of demanding more :
but nothing further was done.

The attack on the Jesuits had thus proved harm-
less enough.   Yet the sting of the Pope's surrender
remained and constituted a grave addition to the
difficulties under which Montalembert was already
labouring.   The *parti catholique* was indeed proving a somewhat difficult team to drive.   At the

one extreme there were what Ozanam called the *enfants perdus* of the *Univers*. The advanced Ultramontanism of this notorious organ, under the direction of Veuillot, always so much more Catholic than Christian, had already assumed the reckless and contemptuous tone for which the paper has become almost proverbial. At the other end were the faint-hearted Catholics, who were ready for peace at almost any price. The bishops were most of them of little use : they frankly disliked the ' laicism ' of the new movement. And now the Pope himself seemed inclined to make terms with the enemy.

At Rome, Rossi continued his efforts against the Catholic party. He tried to get the *Univers* suppressed in the papal states and drew up a draft Education Bill for France which he submitted to Cardinal Lambruschini. In a letter to the Nuncio at Paris, Montalembert, while admitting its 'numerous faults,' undertook the defence of the *Univers* and at the same time justified the political action taken by the Catholics. ' Does Rome,' he asked, ' want to break our weapons in our hands ? ' His intervention was not much relished at Rome : but it produced an impression, and Rossi's plans were foiled.

Lambruschini wrote to assure Montalembert that there was no idea of suppressing the *Univers* and that the Holy See left the members of the French Chambers perfectly free to act as they thought fit. At the same time he made a pointed reference to the attempts made to ' direct and judge the Church ' by those who had ' no mission to do so.' Montalembert in a second letter to the Nuncio hastened to disclaim any such intention. There the matter ended, except for a good-natured thrust at Montalembert by the Pope in conversation with the Catholic leader's wife's brother, Xavier de Mérode. ' Your brother-in-law,' said His Holiness, ' is a great orator. He talks really well—but he talks too much.'

Meanwhile a General Election loomed ahead : and the *parti catholique* were preparing to test their strength. In a circular issued by the Central Committee Montalembert exhorted his followers to concentrate their efforts on the one issue of educational freedom. Those candidates were to be supported who would give the most ample guarantees in this matter.

The Government became uncomfortable : and made a bid. Quinet's lectures at the Collège de France were suspended : and the Council of the Université, the focus of the opposition to the Catholic propaganda, was suppressed. In the Chamber, Guizot spoke with unction of the ' inviolable right of families in regard to education.' M. Thiers on his side made advances too. It was clear that the Catholics had begun to count for something. Montalembert redoubled his efforts, became ubiquitous, launched a rousing pamphlet on *The Duty of Catholics in the Elections.* These took place in August, 1846. The result surpassed all expectations—one hundred and forty deputies were returned who were pledged to support the cause of liberty of education.

A new protagonist in the struggle now appeared on the scene by the side of Montalembert in the Abbé Dupanloup, afterwards the famous Bishop of Orléans. Among the educationists of the time no name stood higher than his. After achieving immense success by his work among children at the famous ' Catechism of Saint Sulpice ' he had been called in 1837 by Archbishop de Quélen to the charge of the *petit séminaire* of the Paris diocese

called S. Nicholas du Chardonnet.   He found it in
rather low water, its membership almost entirely
confined to candidates for the priesthood.   In a
short time he had made it the most fashionable
school in the country.   The greatest of the noble
families of France vied with one another in seeking
admission to it for their sons.

Dupanloup's delightful manners had already
made him the pet of the Faubourg St. Germain :
and his reputation in this quarter was greatly
increased by his successful conduct of the delicate
negotiations (1838) resulting in the return of the
dying Talleyrand to the fold from which time and
circumstance had made that fascinating, if rather
sinister, personality so very wandering a sheep.
The genuineness of this ' conversion ' was at the
time, and remains to this day, the subject of much
controversy.   The anti-clericals openly scoffed.
' *Toute sa vie,*' some one said, ' *il a trompé les
hommes : et maintenant il pense à tromper le bon
Dieu.*'   But (as Renan maliciously says) ' There
was joy, if not in heaven, at least in the Catholic
world of the Faubourg St. Germain and the Faubourg St. Honoré.'

Renan himself was a pupil of Dupanloup's at
S. Nicholas—not as one of the youthful aristocrats,
of course, but as one of the 'clever boys' of humbler
origin whom Dupanloup prudently collected from
all over France to provide an intellectual element
in the academy that might conceivably have been
lacking otherwise.   Renan's account of his old
' director ' is not perhaps very charitable : Dupanloup was never a favourite of his.   But he does not
conceal either the ' adoration ' with which his
pupils regarded him or the admirable qualities of
his teaching.   ' The *fond des idées* which formed the
basis of this teaching was weak : but the form was

brilliant and a noble sentiment dominated and inspired (*entrainait*) everything.'

The support that such a man brought to Montalembert in his campaign was invaluable. At first, however, it proved somewhat of a bone of contention. The Catholic camp was, as usual, divided. One section desired to make terms with the Government, which was believed to be friendly to its aspirations. The other objected to a transaction of any sort. Dupanloup espoused the former view and gave it expression in a pamphlet called *The Present State of the Question*. At once the partisans of the opposite opinion—headed of course by the irrepressible Veuillot—fell on him tooth and nail. Montalembert undertook his defence, though he told Dupanloup privately that he was opposed himself to any transaction. By his efforts the controversy was for the moment allayed, in time for the introduction of the Government's long promised Education Bill (April 12, 1847).

The author of this, M. Salvandy, the Minister of Public Instruction, had made an honest attempt to meet the wishes of the Catholics. In his *Exposé des motifs* he proclaimed the ' sacred rights of families ' and admitted also the right of the Church to concern itself with education. The Bill itself made considerable concessions. The certificate of morality, the brevet of capacity, and other ingenious creations of M. Villemain's brain were swept into the void. The control of the Université over the staff, if not over the curriculum and general conduct, of voluntary schools was largely diminished. But, on the other hand, the *projet Salvandy* was decidedly exacting in regard to the degrees to be possessed by teachers : and, above all, the ban on unauthorized congregations was not removed.

The Catholics were bitterly disappointed. Even Dupanloup declared the measure unacceptable. Montalembert at once gave the signal for the agitation to be renewed, and parental petitions again flowed in. He refused to be discouraged by the attitude of the bishops, hardly one of whom, for all his supplications, ventured to lift up his voice in protest. As against this silence he could set the distinctly more friendly tone of public opinion.

A new Pope, too, Pius IX, had assumed the tiara in 1846 : and all parties in France combined to sing the praise of one who (strange irony) was regarded as a ' liberal ' pontiff. Guizot himself declared that the future author of the *Syllabus* of 1864 would ' effect the reconciliation of the Church and modern society ' !

When Montalembert, speaking in the House of Peers, reproached him with his unwillingness to give full freedom to the Catholics, the Prime Minister excused himself on the ground that he had been forced to allow for prejudices which would disappear some day. As a further sop to Catholic feeling, the lectures of Michelet incurred the same fate as had befallen Quinet's. Events seemed to be moving in the direction of a peaceful settlement of the education question when the sudden outbreak of the Revolution of 1848 put an end to the Orleanist dynasty and sent Louis Philippe and Guizot in hurried flight to England.

The fortunes of Catholicism under the Second Republic lie outside the scope of this book. It must suffice to say that in the *loi Falloux* of 1850 (so called after the name of the minister who introduced it, the friend and biographer of Mme Swetchine) the protracted struggle for freedom of education for Catholics was at last crowned with victory.

The monopoly of the Université was swept away. The old *Conseil Général de l'Université* gave place to a *Conseil Général de l'Instruction Publique*, in which the eight representatives of the Université formed a minority in face of the other fourteen members, who included four bishops and two ministers of Protestant denominations. The same situation was reproduced, but still more disadvantageously to the Université, in the eighty-six *conseils académiques* (one for each department) which were henceforth to take the place of the twenty *académies* formerly existing for the local control of education. Schools were to be of two kinds : (1) public, i.e. supported by the State, the department, or the commune ; (2) private, i.e. conducted by individuals or associations. There was no mention of religious congregations : but it was understood that members of these shared in the permission to open schools accorded to every Frenchman of twenty-five years of age and over.

The only conditions required of teachers were certain tests of character and capacity. The latter were not exacting. The inspection of secondary schools was entrusted to *inspecteurs d'académies*, that of primary schools to *inspecteurs primaires* in collaboration with local representatives, including the *maire* and curé. In the case of voluntary schools, the functions of inspectors were to relate only to ' morality, hygiene, and health,' and were to have nothing to do with the teaching given except to certify that it was not contrary to morality, the constitution, or the laws. The teaching given in the primary schools was to be ' moral and religious.' The *petits séminaires* were maintained in possession of all their privileges, subject only to inspection by the State. Nothing was said as to any limitation in the number of their pupils.

It is true that even these terms did not satisfy the *Univers*. Veuillot called the measure ' detestable, a false and dangerous mitigation of slavery,' and declared that he would fight it with all his might. On the other hand, Victor Hugo denounced it as creating ' a monopoly in the hands of those who desire to make education proceed from the sacristy and government from the confessional.' Perhaps, conscious, and possibly weary, as we are by this time of the lengths to which ' religious ' controversy can go in France, we shall strike a balance between these two views and pronounce the work of M. Falloux to be, if not an ideal arrangement, at least wise and equitable on the whole.

EPILOGUE

IT would be pleasant to end on the note of triumph. But truth compels the admission that the two signal successes of the *parti catholique* under the Second Republic—the Roman expedition in support of the fugitive Pius IX in 1849 and the *loi Falloux* of 1850—were purchased at the price of a third achievement by which the party at once betrayed its past and perverted its future. Hitherto it had relied on its own native strength, claiming for itself no more than freedom to do so. Of this freedom the Republic seemed to promise a wide extension : and for this reason its coming was acclaimed with enthusiasm—at first. The clergy blessed the new order and won in return a popularity they had never known before.

But the bloody tragedy of the ' days of June ' brought a rude awakening to the Catholics. Their belief in liberty for its own sake had never been complete : and if they had welcomed the Republic, it was less from the desire to serve it than to use it. Terrified at the uncertain future, the *parti catholique* under Montalembert entered into an unhallowed alliance with the *bourgeois* Liberals, led by Thiers, to support the candidature of the future Napoleon III for the republican presidency. That unscrupulous self-seeker was ready to promise anything ; the Catholics were strongly organized (though for how different an end originally!) ; and the ' Saviour of Society ' successfully traversed the first stage towards the throne of his dreams.

Three years later the plébiscite of December 26, 1851, achieved the second and decisive stage—once more with Montalembert's support, though Lacordaire, Dupanloup, and others counselled opposition or at least a studied neutrality. Later on, the Catholic leader repented bitterly of what he described as a 'capital error,' 'my grief' for which (he wrote) 'will only end with my life.' But the bulk of his party had no such regrets. The willingness to rely on 'the arm of the flesh' was not yet eradicated. The bishops were lyrical in their praise of the Prince-President ; Dom Guéranger declared that 'our unhappy country can only enjoy repose under a despotic régime ' ; Veuillot spat again and again in the face of Liberty. Liberal Catholicism sank by the wayside, to die by inches : while the main body of the Church marched steadily down the road of reaction that led to the Syllabus of 1864 and the Vatican Decrees of 1870.

BIBLIOGRAPHY

THIS bibliography makes no claim to be complete, but merely indicates the most important books in French and (as far as possible) all those in English.

A. BOOKS ON THE WHOLE PERIOD

DEBIDOUR. *Histoire des rapports de l'Église et de l'État en France de 1789 à 1870.* 2nd edition, 1911. (Accurate and comprehensive, but strongly anti-clerical.)

NIELSEN. *History of the Papacy in the XIXth Century* (Danish). English translation. 2 vols. John Murray, 1906.

MOURRET. *L'Église et la Révolution : L'Église contemporaine.* Vols. vii and viii of *Histoire Générale de l'Église.* (Very Ultramontane.)

BAUNARD. *Un siècle de l'Église de France, 1800–1900.* 1919. (Full of information.)

TAINE. *Origines de la France contemporaine.* 6 vols., 1876–94.

BODLEY. *The Church in France.* 2 lectures. Constable, 1906.

SPARROW-SIMPSON. *French Catholics in the XIXth Century.* S.P.C.K., 1918.

GALTON. *Church and State in France, 1300–1907.* Arnold, 1907.

B. BOOKS ON SPECIAL PERIODS AND SUBJECTS

I. THE CHURCH BEFORE 1789

E. DE PRESSENSÉ. *L'Église et la Révolution française.* 1864. English translation, 1869.

MÉRIC. *Histoire de M. Émery et de l'Église de France pendant la Révolution.* 1885.

JERVIS. *The Gallican Church and the Revolution.* 1882.

WALLON. *Le clergé de quatre-vingt-neuf.* 1876.

DE TOCQUEVILLE. *L'ancien régime et la Révolution* (1856). English translation, Oxford, 1904.

TALLEYRAND. *Mémoires.* Vol. i, 1891. English translation, 1891.

2. THE CHURCH AND THE REVOLUTION

PRESSENSÉ, MÉRIC, JERVIS, as above.

SCIOUT. *Histoire de la constitution civile du clergé*, 1790–1801. 4 vols., 1872–81.

P. DE LA GORCE. *Histoire réligieuse de la Révolution française.* 5 vols., 1909–23.

BARRUEL. *Histoire du clergé pendant la Révolution française.* 1794.

DE PRADT. *Les quatre Concordats.* 4 vols., 1818–20.

THEINER. *Documents inédits rélatifs aux affaires réligieuses de la France*, 1790–1800. 2 vols., 1857–8.

3. CHATEAUBRIAND

CHATEAUBRIAND. *Mémoires d'Outre-Tombe.* 12 vols., 1849–50. English translation, 6 vols., 1902.

SAINTE BEUVE. *Chateaubriand et son groupe littéraire sous l'Empire.* 2 vols., 1850.

SAINTE BEUVE. *Portraits Contemporains.* Vol. i.

BERTIN. *La sincérité réligieuse de Chateaubriand.*

VINET. *Études sur la littérature française au XIXme siècle.* Vol. i, 1849.

4. THE CONCORDAT OF 1801

PRESSENSÉ, MÉRIC, JERVIS, DE PRADT, as above.

Cambridge Modern History. Vol. ix.

CARDINAL MATHIEU. *Le Concordat de 1801.* 1903.

CONSTANT. *L'Église de France sous le Consulat et l'Empire* (1800–14). 1928.

D'HAUSSONVILLE. *L'Église romaine et le premier Empire.* 5 vols., 1868–9. (Contains many documents.)

CONSALVI. *Mémoires.* 2 vols., 1864.

BOULAY DE LA MEURTHE. *Documents sur la négotiation du Concordat et sur les autres rapports de la France avec le Saint Siège*, 1800–1. 5 vols., 1891–7.

THEINER. *Histoire des deux Concordats.* 2 vols., 1869.

5. THE CHURCH AND NAPOLEON

D'HAUSSONVILLE, CONSTANT, JERVIS, MÉRIC, DE PRADT, CONSALVI, as above.

WELSCHINGER. *Le pape et l'empéreur*, 1804–15. 1905. (Carefully based on documents.)

PACCA. *Memorie.* 2nd edition, 1830.

Bibliography 307

TALLEYRAND. *Mémoires.* Vol. ii, 1891. English translation, 1891.
ARTAUD. *Histoire du pape Pie VII.* 2 vols., 1824.
CHOTARD. *Le pape Pie VII à Savona.* 1887.

6. THE RESTORATION

VIEL-CASTEL. *Histoire de la Restauration.* 20 vols., 1860–78.
GEOFFROY DE GRANDMAISON. *La Congrégation,* 1800–30. 1889. (Strongly Clerical.)

7. DE MAISTRE : BONALD : LAMENNAIS

SAINTE BEUVE. 'Joseph de Maistre' in *Portraits littéraires.* Vol. ii, 1844.
LORD MORLEY. 'Joseph de Maistre' in *Critical Miscellanies.* Vol. ii, 1871.
VIDALOT. *L'autorité d'après Joseph de Maistre.* 1898.
MAUDIT. *Les conceptions politiques et sociales de Bonald.* 1913.
BOUTARD. *Vie de Lamennais.* 3 vols., 1913. (Excellent : very fair and balanced.)
MARÉCHAL. *La jeunesse de Lamennais.* 1913.
HON. W. GIBSON. *The Abbé de Lamennais and the Liberal Catholic Movement in France.* 1896.

8. THE CHURCH UNDER LOUIS PHILIPPE

THUREAU-DANGIN. *L'Église et l'État sous la monarchie de Juillet.* 1880.
FOISSET. *Vie du R. P. Lacordaire.* 2 vols., 1870.
CHOCARNE. *Lacordaire, sa vie intime et réligieuse.* 1866. English translation, *The Inner Life of Père Lacordaire.* 1867–8. 8th edition. Washbourne, 1901.
D'HAUSSONVILLE. *Lacordaire.* English translation, 1913. (A charming sketch.)
H. L. SIDNEY LEAR. *Lacordaire.* 1882.
LECANUET. *Vie de Montalembert.* 3 vols., 1895–1901. (Excellent.)
MRS. OLIPHANT. *The Comte de Montalembert.* 2 vols., 1872.
FALLOUX. *Mme Swetchine, sa vie et ses oeuvres.* 2 vols., 1860.
LAGRANGE. *Vie de Mgr Dupanloup.* 3 vols., 1883.
H. L. SIDNEY LEAR. *A Dominican Artist* (Jean Baptiste Besson), 1870.
O'MEARA. *Frederick Ozanam, his life and works.* 1878.
GUILLEMANT. *Pierre Louis Parisis.* 3 vols., 1916–25.

INDEX

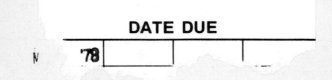

DATE DUE

'78